THE VALOIS

The Valois

Kings of France 1328–1589

Robert J. Knecht

**hambledon
continuum**

Hambledon Continuum

The Tower Building,
11 York Road,
London, SE1 7NX

80 Maiden Lane,
Suite 704,
New York, NY 10038

First Published 2004 in hardback
This edition published 2007 in paperback

Reprinted 2008

ISBN 978-1-85285-420-1 (hardback)
ISBN 978-1-85285-522-2 (paperback)

A description of this book is available from the
British Library and from the Library of Congress.

Typeset by Carnegie Publishing, Lancaster,
and printed in Great Britain by Biddles Ltd, King's Lynn, Norfolk

Contents

Illustrations

Introduction

Among the beautiful miniatures painted by Jean Fouquet for the book of hours known as *Les Heures d'Etienne Chevalier* there is one that depicts St Michael fighting a seven-headed dragon.[1] It is a reminder of the close relationship that existed between that saint and the French royal house of Valois. The earlier Capetian dynasty had been devoted to St Denis. It was under the Valois monarchs that St Michael was chosen as protector of their persons and kingdom. According to Scripture, the Archangel Michael was the leader of the heavenly host that cast Lucifer into Hell. His other roles were to protect the dying from temptation and to weigh souls at the Day of Judgment.

The Valois kings liked to think that St Michael assisted them in various ways. Charles VI noted an improvement in his health after a pilgrimage to the Mont Saint-Michel in 1393, and he called his daughter, Michèle, the first time this name had been used in the royal family. But it was Charles VII who made St Michael the patron saint of France. He ordered his image defeating the dragon to be embroidered on the standard which escorted him at his entries into Rouen and Paris. It replaced the old oriflamme of St Denis, which Charles refused to use. The king believed that the saint had saved his life in 1422 when a floor had collapsed beneath him. In 1425 a vision of the saint was seen over the Mont Saint-Michel as the garrison beat off three successive English assaults. Such was Michael's reputation that all his sanctuaries came to be seen as impregnable. In the course of the Hundred Years War, he became the archangel not merely of resistance but of reconquest. The dragon was identified with the English. In 1451, as an English garrison in Poitou surrendered to the French king, the sign of St Michael – a white cross set against a dark cloud – was seen in the sky. It was taken to mean that God wanted France to be given back to its rightful king. Not surprisingly, St Michael looms large in the story of Joan of Arc. He was among her 'voices' and his image adorned her standard at the siege of Orléans. Even when peace was restored, St Michael continued to be venerated by the Valois kings. Louis XI believed that the saint had saved his life when he had been attacked by a wild boar. In 1469 the king founded the chivalric order of St Michael. Its members wore a collar of sea-shells from which hung a medallion containing a picture of St Michael slaying the dragon. In 1476 Louis XI founded a college of canons who were to pray to the saint 'who continually without a break conducts our affairs and those of our kingdom'.[2] The cult of St Michael continued into the Renaissance. In 1518 Francis I received from the pope a painting by Raphael of St Michael that eventually adorned the royal chapel at Fontainebleau. The magnificent tent pitched by Francis I at the Field of Cloth of Gold in 1520 was topped by a life-size statue in gold of St Michael killing the dragon.

If ever there was a time when France needed divine protection it was in the fourteenth century, when the Valois first gained the throne. The kings of England had a claim to the French crown which the tenure of the Valois frustrated. For more than a century the two kingdoms were locked in conflict during which the English occupied or destroyed large areas of France. The French armies suffered terrible defeats. In 1356 King John the Good was not only defeated, but captured and imprisoned in England. Yet the monarchy survived. For much of the late middle ages, the Valois rulers had to face challenges to their authority from powerful vassals, notably the dukes of Burgundy and Brittany. The struggle between two factions – the Armagnacs and the Burgundians – was to a large extent occasioned by the insanity of Charles VI. His son, Charles VII, was for a time reduced to ruling only a portion of France south of the River Loire – hence his nickname of 'King of Bourges'. Yet, aided by Joan of Arc, he managed to be crowned at Reims and to regain control of Paris. Meanwhile, the English were driven out of Guyenne and Normandy; in the end, Calais remained their only possession in France. A major problem for the French monarchy throughout the period covered by this book was how to raise enough money for its needs, particularly in wartime. It was Charles VII who first managed to tax his subjects without obtaining their consent. He also created a standing army. But it was left to Louis XI significantly to enlarge the kingdom by absorbing Provence and Burgundy. Soon afterwards

Brittany was also annexed as a result of a marriage between its duchess and Charles VIII of France. By degrees France became the most powerful monarchy in western Europe, one which even dared to oppose the sweeping international pretensions of the Holy See.

By the late fifteenth century the king of France dared to venture beyond the Alps on the first stage of a crusade aimed at the reconquest of Jerusalem. Invoking claims inherited from Charles of Anjou and Valentina Visconti, Charles VIII, Louis XII and Francis I led a series of invasions of Italy aimed at acquiring the duchy of Milan and the kingdom of Naples. This drew the house of Valois into conflict with the house of Habsburg in the person of the Holy Roman Emperor Charles V, whose dominions virtually encircled France. The Italian Wars produced another disaster, when Francis I was defeated and captured at Pavia in 1525. Once again the French throne stood empty. Yet Francis was able to regain his freedom in return for a huge ransom and without ceding territory. By this time, however, a new foe had come into being in the form of the Protestant Reformation. This threatened to destroy the religious unity of the kingdom which was deemed inseparable from its political unity. After hesitating for a time, the Valois threw in their lot with the papacy. A savage campaign of religious persecution in France led directly to the Wars of Religion between Catholics and Protestants (or Huguenots). A leading figure at this time was Catherine de' Medici, the widow of Henry II, who tried to keep the kingdom together for the sake of her young sons, Francis II, Charles IX and Henry III, who succeeded each other on the throne. The monarchy survived, but not the Valois dynasty. It ended as Jacques Clément, a fanatical Catholic friar, plunged a knife into Henry III's abdomen. The last of the Valois, and probably the most intellectually gifted, was also the first king of France to be assassinated by one of his subjects. Curiously enough, Henry had deserted St Michael by creating a new order of chivalry dedicated to the Holy Ghost.

My story then is one of survival, achievement and catastrophe. How far the monarchs themselves contributed to that process is what I have tried to indicate within the narrow constraints of this book. It is not intended as a general survey of French history over more than three centuries, for I am only too aware of the cursory treatment I have had to dispense to such momentous events as the Black Death, which

exterminated a large part of France's population. This evidently had a
profound effect on the life of all French people, but to do it justice
would have drawn me away from my task of focusing on the dynasty.
The social and economic background is sketched in only in so far as it
explains the political developments. I have tried, as far as possible, to
compromise between narrative and analysis. This has inevitably entailed
a measure of overlapping, but I hope to have indicated the distinctive
contributions to the development of the French state made to a greater
or lesser degree by each of the Valois monarchs.

I am grateful to Professor Nigel Saul for kindly inviting me to contribute
to his series of dynastic histories, and also for exercising his authority
as General Editor with so much tact and diligence. His advice and the
corrections which he has brought to the text are much appreciated;
any surviving errors are entirely my responsibility. I also wish to record
my gratitude to my wife, Maureen, without whose generous support
no writing would be possible. The author and publisher are grateful
to the National Trust for permission to reproduce plate 1 and to the
Bridgeman Art Library for permission to reproduce plates 2–8. The
names of French kings are given in French before their accession and
English thereafter.

1

A New Dynasty

Charles IV, the third and youngest son of Philip the Fair, died on 1 February 1328. His third wife, Jeanne d'Evreux, had given him only daughters, but she was pregnant when he died. If she produced a son, the kingdom only needed a regent pending his birth; if, on the other hand, she gave birth to a daughter, a different procedure would come into play for which a precedent had been set in 1316. On the death of Louis X's posthumous son, the late king's brother, Philip, had first assumed the regency, then taken the crown, setting aside the rights of the late king's daughter. The notion that 'no woman can succeed to the throne of France' may have been invoked at this stage, but as yet it had no legal basis. Likewise, in 1322, on the death of Philip V, Charles IV had succeeded him without discussion regardless of the daughters of the last two kings. Given these precedents, it seemed likely that a woman's right to occupy the French throne would again be ignored in 1328. But if a woman could not take the crown herself, might she not pass on her right to her male heirs? If this were admitted, then Charles IV's heir was the king of England, Edward III, who was the grandson of King Philip the Fair by his mother, Isabella of France, and the nephew of the last three kings of France; but if a woman could not pass on her right to the throne, then Charles IV's heir was Philip of Valois, the son of Philip the Fair's brother, Charles of Valois. He was the first cousin of the last kings as well as being count of Valois, Anjou, Maine, Chartres and Alençon.

Soon after Charles IV's death a large number of peers and barons met in Paris to appoint a regent. They seem to have ruled out the daughters of earlier kings without discussion. Edward III was represented at the meeting and several doctors of civil and canon law supported his claim to the regency, but a majority ruled him out on the ground that custom allowed neither a woman nor her son to succeed to the throne of France.

Philip of Valois was accordingly chosen as regent. French historians have discerned a certain nascent nationalism in Philip's appointment, but that is debatable. He was almost certainly picked for political reasons, as he was more likely to prove malleable than Edward III. He also had the advantage of being an adult who lived in France. The decision of the notables was not based on the Salic law, as tradition would have it, for this was unknown at the time. It lay forgotten in the library at St-Denis until its rediscovery by a monk in the 1350s. The Salic law was not cited in any royal ordinance regulating the royal succession between 1375 and 1407. It was only in 1464 that an anonymous writer stated that the law had been invoked in the debate over the succession in 1328.[1] When Charles IV's widow gave birth to a daughter on 1 April, Philip of Valois was acknowledged as king by the barons. He was crowned at Reims on 29 May. By way of consolation, Jeanne d'Evreux was given the kingdom of Navarre as well as the counties of Angoulême and Mortain and some lucrative *rentes* in lieu of Champagne.

Early in 1329 the new king, Philip VI, sent the abbot of Fécamp to England to call on Edward III to do him homage for his French territories of Guyenne and Ponthieu. When Edward failed to respond, Philip called a meeting of barons who decided to hand over to him the revenues of Guyenne. Subsidies were levied in Languedoc and the feudal levy was ordered to muster at Bergerac. Four ambassadors travelled to England in a final bid to secure the king's homage. This time Edward replied positively. He met Philip VI at Amiens in June 1329 and did verbal homage for his fiefs of Guyenne and Ponthieu. Two years later, letters patent issued under his great seal declared that the homage given at Amiens had to be taken as 'liege'. Philip sent the letters to his chancery for safekeeping, but they proved worthless as Edward eventually repudiated his homage.

The Kingdom's Limits

In 1350 the kingdom of France covered a smaller area than France does today. In the north, Calais was English and was to remain so for two centuries. The county of Flanders was part of the French kingdom, but the count's loyalty to his suzerain was severely tested by his subjects, who were for the most part pro-English for economic reasons. Their cloth industry depended on imports of English wool. The Bretons were subjects of the king of France, as were the inhabitants of English Guyenne. Further south, in the Midi, the border with Castile and Aragon did not follow the crest of the Pyrenees exactly. At the western end, the small kingdom of Navarre was independent, although its king belonged to the French royal line. At the eastern end, Roussillon lay outside the French kingdom. France's eastern border remained essentially the same as that laid down in the treaty of Verdun of 843, more or less following the rivers Scheldt, Meuse, Saône and Rhône. From north to south most of what is now eastern France lay outside the kingdom, including Hainault, Lorraine, the county of Burgundy (now called Franche-Comté), Savoy, Dauphiné and Provence. France thus only had a relatively short stretch of the Mediterranean coast.[2]

Linguistically, France was divided horizontally across the middle. The north was the *pays de langue d'oïl*, and the south the *pays de langue d'oc*. Southerners who needed to do business outside their own area had to learn French as it was spoken by the king and his entourage, but their strong accent provoked derision. Major economic differences also existed between north and south. Northern France had rich cornfields, large villages, textile manufacturing towns, the fairs of Champagne, and the busy River Seine, linking Paris and Rouen. But, in 1350, the north was in crisis. Harvests were bad, cloth-making depressed and the fairs of Champagne in decline. By contrast, the south was booming. The countryside was less fertile, and there were fewer large towns, but the cloth industry in the Languedoc prospered. The Midi's economy only began to suffer when English raids began in 1355.[3]

Another division existed in France between east and west. Communications in the west from Flanders to Gascony by way of Normandy and Brittany were relatively easy. Nobles had ties and merchants had customers in many parts of the west. In Burgundy or Champagne, the people looked east. The inhabitants of territories situated on either side of the frontier, dividing France from the Holy Roman Empire, had much in common, including roads which, following the Saône and Rhône, linked the Mediterranean to the North Sea. Activity along these roads increased in the early fourteenth century as a consequence of the papacy settling in Avignon. Within a few years the city grew rapidly in size. It had a population of 30,000 in 1376. As trade in the area responded to Avignon's needs, the fair at Chalon revived in 1320–60. Trade routes also shifted. Traffic, which had once served the fairs of Champagne, now passed through Bresse, Bugey and Maurienne. Merchants in Burgundy and Savoy developed common interests and princes followed suit. The house of Burgundy formed diplomatic and family alliances with the house of Savoy. Thus France was split into two large zones where the economic pulse beat at a different rate. Both, however, looked to Paris. The royal court, though peripatetic, often stayed in Paris and parts of it had become fixed there. The Parlement, the highest court of justice under the king, received appeals from all over the kingdom. The university of Paris was influential throughout Christendom.[4]

Population

The Florentine chronicler Villani described France as 'a very large, very rich and very powerful kingdom'. This is confirmed by the *État des paroisses et des feux*, of 1328 which listed the number of hearths subject to taxation, grouping them into parishes, *bailliages* and *sénéchaussées*. Leaving out of all the appanages, eight major lordships and the fiefs of Brittany, Burgundy, Flanders and Guyenne, the survey lists 23,671 parishes and 2,469,987 hearths. On the basis of this evidence, it seems that the kingdom contained 32,500 parishes and 3,363,000 hearths, pointing to a population of between seventeen and eighteen million, a far cry from the population of England, estimated at around five to six million before the Black Death. The *État des paroisses et des feux* is also interesting for the light it sheds on the the king's administrative effectiveness. The fact that his agents were able to compile such a survey shows a large measure of control over an extensive territory.[5]

The population of France suffered a catastrophic decline around the middle of the fourteenth century following the Black Death, a terrible plague brought to Marseille by merchant ships coming from the Black Sea. Attempts were made to drive them off when their cargo was found to be lethal, but the plague soon spread along trade routes reaching out to the Atlantic coast and ultimately to Normandy and England, as well as to Paris, northern France and beyond. The plague was of two kinds: a bubonic version, carried by fleas, and an airborne pulmonary version.

The first was most virulent in the summer and the second in winter. Froissart tells us that a third of France's population was wiped out, a figure no one has disputed. Paris registers tell a grim story. At Givry in Burgundy the annual death toll before the plague was around twenty to twenty-five; in 1348 the number was 649. Marriages were likewise affected. As against a norm of twenty per year, none took place in 1348. It seems that the plague raged for three or four months, then subsided and slumbered before flaring up again. The impact of the Black Death on local communities was terrible. A doctor summed it up as follows: 'People died without a servant and were buried without a priest. The father did not visit his son, nor the son his father.'[6] Victims were abandoned and cemeteries had to be enlarged or new ones created to meet the increased demand for tombs. Grave-diggers became hard to find as many succumbed to the disease themselves.[7]

Destructive as it was, the Black Death was not the only cause of demographic decline in fourteenth-century France. Regional studies have revealed a dip in the years leading up to the Black Death. This can be blamed on poor harvests in Flanders and northern France in 1315 to 1317. The population of Normandy also declined at this time, and in southern France a series of dearths in the first half of the fourteenth century preceded a large-scale famine in 1346–47. It seems that the Black Death therefore worsened an existing demographic decline. Even so, its effects should not be minimised. It continued to rampage for many years, notably in 1360–63 and again in 1373–74. The psychology of the age, as reflected in contemporary religious art, was profoundly affected by it. The *Dance of Death* was painted on the walls of churches, and the tombs of nobles and churchmen assumed a two-tier form with a fully clothed living effigy of the deceased at prayer above, and a naked, emaciated and maggot-ridden corpse below. Frenchmen may have feared death less than its immediate aftermath. They were afraid of having to appear before their Maker uncleansed of sin. The century witnessed a growth of religious mysticism. The invocation of healing saints, like St Sebastian or St Roch, enjoyed a great vogue. Pilgrimages increased in popularity and there was a significant rise in the number of religious confraternities, providing mutual aid to their members, and of charities dispensing poor relief. The performance of good works took on a new lease of life as the Grim Reaper wielded his scythe.[8]

The Early Valois

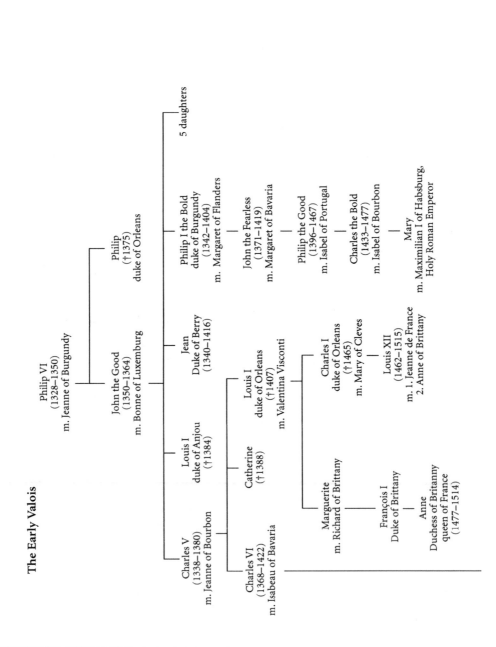

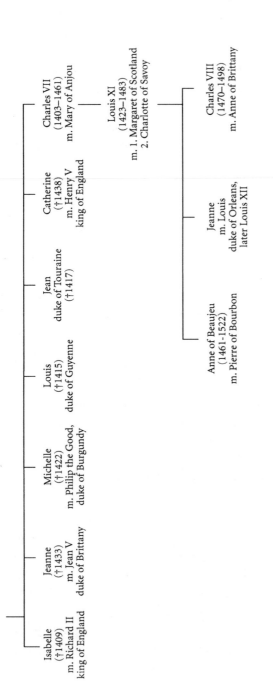

Isabelle (†1409) m. Richard II king of England

Jeanne (†1433) m. Jean V duke of Brittany

Michelle (†1422) m. Philip the Good, duke of Burgundy

Louis (†1415) duke of Guyenne

Jean duke of Touraine (†1417)

Catherine (†1438) m. Henry V king of England

Charles VII (1403–1461) m. Mary of Anjou

Louis XI (1423–1483) m. 1. Margaret of Scotland 2. Charlotte of Savoy

Anne of Beaujeu (1461-1522) m. Pierre of Bourbon

Jeanne m. Louis duke of Orleans, later Louis XII

Charles VIII (1470–1498) m. Anne of Brittany

Social Structure

Christine de Pisan divided French society into several estates, each
defined by its mode of living. They were the princes, nobles, clergy,
bourgeois, artisans and 'common folk', but society was more usually
divided into three social categories: the people who prayed (the clergy),
those who fought (the nobles) and those who toiled. The last group,
which included merchants and artisans, was sometimes described as the
non-nobles (*ignobles*). It was only in the fifteenth century that it became
known as the 'third estate'. An analogy was commonly drawn between
the social estates and parts of the human body: the prince was the head,
the nobles and knights were the arms and hands, and the common
people were the stomach, legs and feet.

Jean Gerson, the famous Parisian theologian, believed that unity and
hierarchy were essential to a well-ordered society. He took his cue from
Dionysius the Areopagite, who held that the world was organised as a
divinely ordained hierarchy. Gerson attached a particular virtue to each
estate: power to the nobility, wisdom to the clergy and obedience to the
non-noble laity. The place occupied by each person in the hierarchy was
deemed to be a gift of nature: in other words, each person was given his
or her social slot at birth. The king, who topped the hierarchy, was given
three lives by Gerson: bodily, spiritual and public. Whereas the bodily
and spiritual lives were temporary, the public one was permanent: 'it
lasts in this kingdom by lawful succession in the royal line without fixed
term and as though permanently'. Endowed with 'sovereignty', the king
was emperor in his kingdom. He was accountable to no one but God.
He also had 'majesty'. Roman law acknowleged the king's sacredness by
viewing the crime of *lèse-majesté* as tantamount to sacrilege. From the
reign of Charles V onwards kings of France bore the title of 'the Most
Christian King'.[9] This was taken to mean that the king of France not
only held his power of God but was also especially favoured by Him.
Despite frequent quarrels between royal officials and churchmen, relations between church and state were inextricably close. To respect the
king was to honour God.[10]

The king did not stand alone. He was part of the royal lineage
through which flowed a special blood which he shared with his kinsmen.
After his eldest son, known as the dauphin, the closest were his younger

sons, then his brothers, then his paternal uncles and their sons. Altogether Charles VI had some fifty first cousins of both sexes. The circle of people claiming a share of royal blood was actually much larger, but some thirty lords, who were the king's closest kinsmen, dominated France's political society. Their authority resulted from a policy of combining noble lineage with landed wealth and social dignity. Thus in 1360, under John the Good, the *comté* of Anjou was upgraded to the rank of *duché-pairie* for the benefit of Louis, the king's second son, and, in the same year, his third son became duke of Berry and Auvergne. In 1363 Philip, the king's fourth son, became duke of Burgundy. In short, the king exercised his patronage in the interest of his closest kinsmen. Their privileges, however, were balanced by duties. In addition to being loyal to the king, they were expected to advance the welfare of his kingdom and subjects. They might be used as leaders of diplomatic missions, as military commanders or as chairmen of public bodies. In 1401–2 the king turned to them when tax collectors encountered popular resistance in northern France. Advice was what the king mainly wanted from princes of the blood. Official documents repeatedly state that a decision was taken by Charles VI with the advice of 'those closest to his blood and lineage and of his great council'.[11]

The king relied heavily on the nobility to carry out his wishes. Nobility was either inherited or given by him. The number of nobles varied from province to province, but, as a general rule, there was one noble hearth per parish. There were 32,500 parishes in France and about 40,000 noble families. In other words, the nobility represented a little more than 1 per cent of the population, but its political significance far outweighed its minority status. The proportion of nobles remained fairly stable during the fourteenth and fifteenth centuries, yet many lineages which existed in 1300 had disappeared by 1500. They were replaced by other families ennobled by the king. But all nobles liked to claim that their lineages reached far back in time, for a nobleman by birth was regarded as more honourable than one of recent creation. Not all nobles, of course, were equally wealthy. The noble estate was a social pyramid. At the bottom was an anonymous crowd of esquires (*écuyers*), too young to be dubbed as knights or too poor ever to be considered for such elevation. Above them were the knights (*chevaliers*), whose nobility was made more explicit by dubbing. In earlier times all or nearly all noblemen had been knights, but their number was declining by the fourteenth century. Under Charles VI there was probably one knight for nine esquires. The knights constituted an elite, but they were insignificant alongside the 'big fish' – the counts, dukes and peers – at the top of the pyramid.

Historians once imagined that in the fourteenth and fifteenth centuries the old feudal nobility, while retaining the trappings of power, handed over its reality to bourgeois, rich merchants and relatively humble civil servants. Nothing could be further from the truth. Even if the landed revenues of the nobles declined, they could make up for any loss by serving the crown. Fighting for the king was their privileged vocation, and his armies were filled with them. But war was dangerous and costly. If some families benefited from royal wages and the profits of war, others were ruined by ransoms they had to pay or by losses suffered in battle. Nor was fighting the only activity open to nobles. Many, better educated than is often assumed, found employment in the church or the royal administration. At the start of Charles VI's reign, half the councillors of the Parlement of Paris belonged to noble families.

The Early Valois

Philip VI of Valois (1328–50) has not endeared himself to French historians on account of his defeats at the hands of the English: Crécy in 1346 and the loss of Calais in the following year. Yet he was not unpopular among his subjects. A Parisian chronicler described him as a 'wise man, gracious and courteous'. Physically big, he took part in jousts and tournaments and was praised by Froissart for his swordsmanship, yet he was no philistine. About 1326 he commissioned a history manual in order to find out more about his future kingdom. He took the trouble to read over letters which he had dictated without relying on his chancery, and laid down certain guiding principles on which to act: 'It is reasonable to change one's mind'; 'In all things it is better to prevent than to be prevented'; and 'It is always best to be in the right with regard to one's enemies and to let them be in the wrong'. Caution was his watchword. An early expedition to Italy in aid of Pope John XXII deterred him from ever going on other Mediterranean adventures. Before his accession he concentrated his efforts on establishing his authority in his counties of

Maine and Anjou; as king, he strove to do likewise in the rest of France. A letter written by Philip to his son, John, reveals him as a family man. He advises John, who is campaigning in Brittany, to write to his young wife, who is fretting over his safety, and to reassure her as to his safety. Philip VI's queen, Jeanne, was the sister of the duke of Burgundy and headed a faction at court. A contemporary chronicler wrote about her: 'the lame Queen Jeanne de Bourgogne ... was like a king and caused the destruction of those who opposed her will'.[12]

King John the Good (1350–64), born in April 1319, has been judged severely by French historians. Under the Third Republic they liked to mock the chivalric virtues of the man who had been defeated and captured by the English at Poitiers. In his own day, however, John was praised for the courage he had shown in that terrible battle. Yet, he was no warrior. Always in poor health, he lived surrounded by physicians and surgeons. Nor was he a sportsman. He jousted little, but enjoyed hunting, if only because of his love of nature. Literature and art appealed to him most. Petrarch, who visited his court in 1361, noted his intellectual interests. John purchased manuscripts, employed artists to illuminate them and commissioned translations of Latin works. His collection of books formed the nucleus of the famous library created later by Charles V. Several of John's books formed part of the booty captured by the English at Poitiers. Painters and musicians also benefited from his patronage. During his imprisonment in England, he asked one of his musicians to find him new instruments. But John had a notoriously foul temper. Froissart described him as 'hot-tempered and passionate' (*chaud et soudain*). His temperament was not suited to the delicate task of upholding the brittle nexus of friendships at court. The murder of his constable, Charles of Spain, upset him so much that he would not speak to anyone for four days.[13]

Charles V (1364–80), who became the dauphin in 1349, was born at Vincennes on 21 January 1338. His father, the future King John the Good, was only eighteen at the time, which may explain the rivalry that later developed between the two men. For the contemporary writer, Christine de Pisan, Charles was a model prince. Physically, he was anything but warlike. He was slim with a large head bent slightly forward and resting on bony shoulders. Since adolescence he suffered from a mysterious complaint which often kept him in bed and eventually carried him off when he was only forty. He thus preferred the study to the battlefield. Though far from cowardly, he never commanded his army, preferring to leave this task to a military expert. Army life did not suit him. He liked lavish festivities at court, collected works of art and also books, not simply for their bindings and illuminations but because he liked to read them. He commissioned French translations of Aristotle's political writings and of histories by Latin authors. No French king since Philip the Fair was so conscious of his royal majesty. As Christine de Pisan wrote, Charles V's love of elaborate progresses 'was not simply indulgence, but in order to keep, maintain and give example to his successors in time to come that in solemn order should be held and conducted the most worthy status of the high crown of France, to which all sovereign magnificence is due, pertains and must be paid'.

It was during the reign of Charles V that histories and legends were used to enhance the image of the king of France. If the coronation or *sacre* no longer made the king, it nevertheless retained a unique prestige which the Valois monarchs exploited in defence of their authority. The *sacre* conferred on the king a semi-priestly dignity; it made him, according to Jean Golein, 'the vicar of Christ in his temporality'. About 1364, Charles V commissioned a new set of rules or *ordo* which may have been used for his own coronation. The ceremony, which took place at Reims, linked the anointing to the crowning. The king was anointed with a chrism, a mixture of a balm and of sacred oil from the Holy Ampula, which had been carefully saved after the baptism of Clovis. For Golein, the king of France was not like other kings. He was anointed not with 'an oil or balm concocted by some bishop or apothecary, but with the holy and celestial liquor contained in the Holy Ampula'.

No king of France since St Louis was more dutiful than Charles V. Scrupulous almost to excess, he was ever anxious to have right on his side. He looked for assurance that taxes were for the good of the kingdom, that his wars were just and that all his actions were lawful. But this led him into casuistry. Two difficult regencies, from 1356 to 1360 and in 1364, had taught Charles to distrust men and to overcome difficulties by flexibility and patience. Along with an exalted sense of his own righteousness, he could be petty and devious in pursuing his objectives. Christine de Pisan's assertion that he was loved by everyone and never harmed anyone was disproved two years after his death when one of his subjects expressed the wish that Charles had died ten years sooner so that taxes might have been remitted that much sooner.[14]

Charles V was a notable builder. He gave Paris a new curtain wall enclosing a large number of buildings erected beyond the wall built by Philip Augustus in the twelfth century. The new wall, which Charles VI completed around 1420, was 4875 metres long and formed a semi-circle on the right bank of the Seine, enclosing the Louvre. Though not high, it was effective against a military attack as it was protected by a water-filled moat, an earth rampart and a dry moat to an overall depth of ninety metres, that is to say, beyond the range of a medieval catapult. The six gateways were covered by forts, known as *bastides*. The most famous was the Bastille, built between 1356 and 1383. It controlled access to the royal palace of Saint-Pol within the city and to the castle of Vincennes a few miles outside. The Bastille's flat roof was designed to carry artillery, and arrow-slits at the base of each of its eight round towers allowed for raking fire at ground level. Charles V's wall marked the boundary dividing the city of Paris from its suburbs or *faubourgs*.

The King and his Court

The word 'state' was never used on its own in fifteenth-century France, only in conjunction with the king and the kingdom, as in 'the state of the king and his kingdom', but the thing itself existed. Its hub was the king, who was seen as possessing two bodies: his own person, which was mortal; and his royal function which was eternal. His sovereignty was exercised within the territorial limits of his kingdom; beyond it, as in Dauphiné, which belonged to the heir to the throne, he had only rights. No one was allowed, not even the Holy Roman Emperor, to trespass on the king's sovereignty. There was therefore an outcry when the Emperor Sigismund, on a visit to Paris, dared to create a knight in the Parlement. The conferment of nobility was held to be one of the king's essential attributes; others included the legitimising of bastards, the creation of notarial offices and the setting up of fairs. Only he could use the phrase 'by the grace of God', and only he could raise troops within the kingdom. When the duke of Brittany did homage to Louis XI in 1461, the king told him bluntly that a vassal, even a prince, was the king's 'subject'. By the close of the fifteenth century, no one in France dared to challenge the king's sovereignty or his legitimacy. Neither the madness of Charles VI nor the innovations of the treaty of Troyes succeeded in upsetting a tradition established in 1374. Following his coronation in 1429, Charles VII ordered a kingdom-wide search for manuscripts of the Salic law in order that its text should be definitely established. It soon became universally accepted, so that when Charles VIII died without issue in 1498, he was automatically succeeded on the throne by his uncle, Louis of Orléans, his nearest kinsman in the male line.

If the king's sovereignty pointed towards the future development of the French monarchy, he himself remained in several respects distinctively medieval. He was a knight surrounded by vassals and expected to have warlike virtues. John the Good was loved and admired on account of his courage and impetuous nature, whereas his father was despised for having fled from the field of Crécy. His son, Charles V, was dismissed as a mere bureaucrat. Charles VI, as a young man, much enjoyed army life. He was placed in command of armies during the civil war, but he was wisely prevented from fighting at Agincourt. Charles VII was not particularly bellicose, yet he did command in the decisive campaigns that ended the Hundred Years War without exposing himself to danger. Louis XI, as dauphin, commanded troops but, after his accession, avoided fighting as far as possible.

Whether as soldier or bureaucrat, the king remained accessible to all of his subjects. Councillors who dared to obstruct this process were roundly denounced by contemporary chroniclers and other writers; and they were not successful. Countless instances exist of ordinary people speaking to the king. Thus an old hermit from Corbières complained to Charles VI about burdensome taxation, and numerous popular preachers penetrated royal residences to denounce the ills afflicting the kingdom. But for ease of access to the monarch, Joan of Arc might never have met her 'gentil dauphin'. The free and easy relationship between king and subject is also exemplified by Louis XI's habit of calling unannounced on some bourgeois of Tours to share a flagon of wine.

The court was inseparable from the king's person. Wherever he was, there was the court. It was not a formal institution, but a gathering of his relatives and friends, officials and councillors, visitors from far and near – and of all social ranks – who came to deal with affairs of state or private matters. Under Charles VII they numbered around eight hundred. The heart of the court was the king's household (*hôtel du roi*) which comprised various departments serving his domestic needs. It was on two levels: above and below stairs. Above stairs was the *chambre* with a staff numbering 150 to 200 persons, including *chambellans*, *valets tranchants* and *écuyers d'écurie*, who, despite their titles, were senior members of the court. It was from their ranks that the king recruited his confidential advisers, councillors, local government officials and captains. Below stairs there were six departments: *paneterie, cuisine, fruiterie, écurie, échansonnerie* and *fourrière*. In addition, there was the almonry, the chapel, a physician, an apothecary and an astrologer. A military establishment was created by Charles VII in the form of a Scottish guard of a hundred men. The household's expenses were controlled by a central treasury that distributed funds to the various departments. The *chambre aux deniers* dealt with day-to-day expenses and the *argenterie* paid for clothes and furnishings. The king also had coffers in which he kept his jewels and pocket money. The household was managed by up to thirteen stewards or *maîtres d'hôtel* under a superior, who eventually acquired the title of Grand Master (*Grand maître*).

The king, as fount of all justice, continued, in theory at least, to administer it in person to his subjects. This was known as *justice retenue* as distinct from *justice déléguée* which was left to the so-called 'sovereign courts' like the Parlement, which had 'gone out of court' and become fixed in Paris. The king was now too busy to sit in judgment, as St Louis had done under an oak tree in the park at Vincennes, but he remained free to do so if he wished. Normally he delegated the task to six or so *maîtres des requêtes de l'hôtel*, who acted as intermediaries between the defendant and the king's chancery.

The queen, the royal children, and princes of the blood had households of their own which need to be taken into account when estimating the overall size of the court. Housing so many people inevitably posed problems. In Paris, the court could no longer reside at the *palais* on the Île-de-la-Cité, which was occupied by the Parlement. As a replacement Charles V built the Hôtel Saint-Pol, which could accommodate his household and that of the queen. It included spacious rooms, inner courtyards, galleries, gardens, orchards and a menagery containing a lion. The palace was evidently intended for relaxation and pleasure, unlike the Louvre, a stern fortress dating back to the reign of Philip

Augustus. Here too, Charles carried out improvements aimed at creating a more congenial setting for the court. He did not substantially alter the existing plan, but added two wings and an external spiral staircase (*grand vis*) leading directly to his lodging on the second floor. It was open so that he could be seen; and, as he crossed from one side of the Louvre courtyard to the other, he received petitions handed to him by his subjects. New furniture was also acquired and the library reorganised. In several parts of the Louvre the king installed lifelike statues of himself, his queen and children. There were also gardens and another menagery, again with lions.

At Vincennes, a few miles east of Paris, in the midst of a walled park where the Capetian monarchs had once hunted, Charles V built a powerful fortress to which he and his court might retire in the event of some political upheaval in the capital. Work on the keep, which began in 1361, lasted eight years. The entrance gateway was adorned with symbols of royalty, including more statues of the king and queen. In 1373 work began on a vast outer-ward, protected by deep moats, a high curtain wall, three fortified gates and six towers. Charles V died before his great scheme could be completed. According to Christine de Pisan, he 'planned to turn it [Vincennes] into a walled town and he set up two manors there as residences for several of his favourite lords, knights and others, intending to give each one a life tenancy. He wanted the place to be free of all services and to carry no tax or duty in the future'.[15]

Charles V resided at the Louvre and at the Hôtel Saint-Pol, which Charles VI also used. Outside Paris, both kings liked to stay at Vincennes or Beauté-sur-Marne. Charles VII seldom visited Paris; nor did Louis XI, both kings preferring to spend most of their time in the Loire valley, at Chinon, Mehun-sur-Yèvre, Montils-lès-Tours, Plessis and Amboise.

Government

A period of relative peace enjoyed by France since the mid-thirteenth century facilitated a gradual strengthening of royal authority. The royal court or *curia regis* of early medieval times, consisting of the king and his circle of relatives, friends and vassals, had long since broken up into a number of specialised departments and the process was still going on.

The king's household (the *hôtel du roi*) now served only the domestic needs of the monarch. It was subdivided into six departments under the overall control of the *Chambre aux deniers* (first mentioned in 1303), which provided the necessary funds, and the *Argenterie* (created in 1315), which looked after the king's furniture and jewels. The household staff, numbering about 500 in the mid-fourteenth century, was fast growing in size.

Outside the household were a number of departments dealing with affairs of state. The most important was the king's council, an essentially fluid body which defies precise description. At times it was large, comprising all the officers of the court and leading nobles and churchmen, but it usually consisted simply of the king and a few close friends and vassals. There were also councillors, who were appointed, received fixed wages and sworn to keep their proceedings secret. The king's council was not purely consultative; it also had executive powers and dispatched orders arising from its decisions to other departments. The council also had judicial powers, reserving to itself the right to judge lawsuits which the king, as sovereign, could alone decide. He received petitions brought to him by the masters of requests (*maîtres des requêtes de l'hôtel*).

Four or five other departments at the centre of the administration focused on certain specific tasks. The *Trésor*, run by two or three treasurers and a *changeur*, cashed revenues from the domain, made payments or warrants as ordered by the council, kept complex accounts and judged domainial disputes. The *Monnaie*, under a master, and the *Forêts*, with a staff of masters and measurers, each had its own administration with judicial powers. The notaries and secretaries of the chancery sent out all royal acts under the great seal or privy seal (*sceau du secret*), hence the name of 'secretaries' reserved to those clerks who dealt with the sovereign's private correspondence.

By 1328 two essential institutions, soon to acquire a great importance, had only just become independent. The Parlement, unlike its English namesake, was a law court, not a representative body. The highest court of law under the king, it owed its organisation to King Philip V, but only acquired the name of *Cour de Parlement* in 1345. Its permanent staff of presidents, lay or clerical councillors, and masters of requests was divided into four tribunals: the *Grand' chambre*, *Chambre criminelle*, *Chambre des enquêtes* and *Chambre des requêtes*. The judges were not only keen defenders of customary law but also of the king's authority. They received appeals from the *bailliages* and *sénéchaussées* and also from the courts of the greatest vassals. An appeal to the Parlement was the most powerful tool used by the king to meddle in the great fiefs. When the Parlement was in recess, certain provinces received delegations of councillors, known as *Échiquier* in Normandy and *Grands Jours* in Champagne, who judged local appeals on the spot.

The *Chambre des comptes* had achieved autonomy in 1304, but only received its constitution in January 1320. It has been called 'the keystone of the monarchical administration'. All royal officials handling cash, from the treasurers down to the humblest *prévôt*, were accountable to it. As guardian of the domain, the court looked out for usurpations and corrupt alienations. It also received surveys of fiefs, and monitored all the services. It resisted royal prodigality and prosecuted corrupt or negligent officials.

Although the central government was becoming more specialized, it still employed only a small staff that was easily kept under control. The Parlement had more than a hundred judges, but all the other departments combined only employed eighty or eighty-five officials excluding inferior staff. All in all, the government did not have more than two hundred officials. Local government required a much larger personnel. It was distributed among the *bailliages* and *sénéchaussées* whose boundaries were often ill-defined, allowing much scope for royal agents to enforce the king's authority at the expense, not only of residents of the domain, but also of vassals, great and small. The *baillis* and *sénéchaux* were usually recruited among the lesser nobility. In financial matters, they farmed out the domain to the *prévôts*, *bayles* or *viguiers*, and kept a close watch on the activities of the *receveur du bailliage*, the forest officials, and fiscal commissioners. They chaired the court of the *bailliage* and received lawsuits on appeal from seigneurial courts without prejudice to the Parlement's jurisdiction. Beneath them were a chancellor or keeper of the seal and an ever-growing number of sergeants, ushers and bedels. Despite their modest wages, these officials were generally honest.

All governments need money. Probably the biggest single problem faced by the Valois kings was how to fund their various activities without alienating their subjects. Unlike modern governments, they were not concerned with social welfare or public health, but they had to pay for their court, buildings, officials and servants. They needed to buy the loyalty of their nobles and the friendship or neutrality of their foreign neighbours. War, however, was by far their largest expense, and all the more difficult to cope with on account of its unpredictability. Military technology was developing fast. By the early sixteenth century, artillery was coming into its own. Bronze cannon and portable firearms were very expensive. Fortifications had to be refurbished, even redesigned, to meet the new challenge. Sieges became more frequent and the composition of armies changed. Cavalry alone could no longer win wars on its own; infantry was also required in ever larger numbers. As well-trained native troops were not available in sufficient numbers, the Valois had to employ foreign mercenaries, who were notoriously grasping.

It was in the fifteenth century that France acquired a fiscal system which survived more or less unchanged until the close of the Ancien Régime. It was not perfect, being riddled with anomalies and beset by corruption. There were two broad categories of royal revenue, described as 'ordinary' and 'extraordinary'. The 'ordinary' was the revenue which the king drew traditionally from his domain. It consisted of a variety of feudal payments and profits of justice. The king had the right to call out the feudal levy (*ban et arrière-ban*), but often preferred to take money instead of actual military service from his less warlike vassals. Income also reached him from the church. Thus he enjoyed the right of *régale*, whereby he could take the revenues of a vacant bishopric or abbey.

If the king ran short of money he could fleece certain groups of people, including the Jews (before their expulsion in 1394) and the so-called 'Lombards', money-lenders who left Paris en masse in 1420. The king could also speculate on the currency. By modifying the coinage, he could instigate a new minting and pocket the difference between the price of the precious metal used and the face-value of the coin. This was known as 'seigneurage' and the profit could be as much as 40 per cent. But in the long term currency speculation could harm the kingdom's economy, as indeed happened before 1360. Stability was restored by the creation of the franc in 1360, but after 1385 the currency declined slowly until a new wave of speculation began in 1417. Good money was restored in 1436, but overall the currency weakened during the century.

An alternative to currency manipulation was taxation. Taxes became known as '*finances extraordinaires*' because originally they were intended to be temporary and for a specific purpose. They were direct and indirect. The main direct tax was the hearth-tax or *fouage*, created by Philip the Fair, which acquired the more familiar name of *taille* after 1384. Between 1384 and 1450 each *taille* was levied for a specific military purpose, but, from 1451, it was levied annually under the name of 'the soldiers' tax' (*taille des gens de guerre*) and used to meet any of the crown's expenses. The *taille* was a distributive tax. A global amount was decided upon by the king's council, then distributed among taxpayers, starting with dioceses and working down to parishes. Surveys were carried out to quantify the number of eligible taxpayers, but the surveys needed to be kept up to date so as to allow for demographic change. There were two sorts of *taille*: '*personnelle*' in northern France and '*réelle*' in the Midi. The one was assessed on the social status of the taxpayer; the other on his land. In northern France, the *taille* was collected by officials called *élus*, who, in spite of their name, were appointed by the king. They were responsible for fiscal districts, called *élections*, numbering eighty-five under Louis XI. In the south, the *taille* was levied by commissioners with the assistance of the local representative estates.

The collection of indirect taxes, known as *aides*, was farmed out. They were levied on the sale of goods: one *sou* per *livre* or 5 per cent, except for wine which was taxed at a thirteenth wholesale and a quarter retail. The *gabelle*, a tax on salt, became firmly established in 1383, but it did not apply to the whole kingdom, large areas being completely exempt from it. Elsewhere, it was collected in two different ways. In northern France, the salt was taken from the place of production to warehouses (*greniers*) where it was left to dry for two years before being weighed, taxed and sold. In the south it was taxed where it was produced.

The king got much less from his domain than from taxation. In 1470 the royal treasury received 100,000 *livres* (or 2.5 per cent of its total revenue) from the domain, but not all receipts went to the treasury. Many royal gifts, alms and payments to officials were made locally. Even so, the yield from taxation was relatively much greater: it amounted to nearly two million *livres* under Charles V: 17 per cent from the *gabelle* and 30–40 per cent from the *taille*. The rest came from indirect taxes. These figures remained stable under Charles VII before rising to more than four million at the end of Louis XI's reign. The burden, however, stayed roughly the same for the taxpayer as the currency weakened and the economy and population grew.

In theory, the king could not tax his subjects without their consent. In order to obtain this, he needed to call the Estates-General representing the clergy, nobility and towns of the kingdom. These estates, however, seldom met. More usually the estates of the north (Languedoïl) and south (Languedoc) met separately. In return for their consent, they aired grievances and tried to gain a measure of control over the royal administration. For this reason, the king avoided calling them if at all possible. After 1451, as we shall see, he managed to do without them, though he continued to consult the local estates. The fiscal authority of the king of France became the envy of his royal neighbours, but it was largely illusory. The Valois kings were always beset by money problems.[16]

2

The Hundred Years War

From 1337 until 1453 the kingdom of France was involved in a series of wars with England which became known as the Hundred Years War. It may be said to have begun following the decision taken on 24 May 1337 by King Philip V of France to confiscate the duchy of Aquitaine, which belonged to the English king, Edward III, but the origins of the war can be traced back much further in time.[1] In 1137 King Louis VII of France married Eleanor, the only daughter of William X, duke of Aquitaine. The Capetian domain, which had so far been limited to the Paris region, trebled or quadrupled in size after acquiring the whole of south-west France. But the marriage did not last. In 1152 Louis repudiated his wife, who soon afterwards married Henry Plantagenet. Henry thus acquired Aquitaine in addition to the county of Anjou, which he had inherited from his father. In 1154 Henry succeeded to the English throne as King Henry II. He now ruled England, Aquitaine, Anjou and also Normandy. Later in the century the French king, Philip Augustus, managed to seize a large part of the Plantagenet fiefs in France, an achievement consolidated by his successors, Louis VIII and St Louis. By the mid-thirteenth century the English possessions in France had been reduced to a relatively small territory in the south west. The English kings claimed that they had been unfairly dispossessed, whereupon St Louis signed the treaty of Paris in 1259. This restored to Henry III Plantagenet a number of territories in return for which Henry agreed to do 'liege' homage for his French fiefs to the king of France. The difference between simple and liege homage was of considerable importance to both sides. Simple homage was merely an acknowledgement of lordship: it scarcely, if at all, limited the vassal's freedom. Liege homage, on the other hand, implied acceptance of sovereignty and *ressort*. Sovereignty expressed the French king's claim to be 'emperor in his own kingdom'; *ressort* was his right to be the supreme judge in respect of appeals from lower courts.

Henry III's agreement to do liege homage implied his subordination to the French king and restricted the exercise of his authority as duke of Guyenne. It opened up the possibility of his vassals appealing against him to Paris. He might also be required by the king of France to perform obligations, including military service, which would clash with his interests as king of England.[2]

The compromise was too one-sided to last. As the French monarchy began to intervene more often in the affairs of Guyenne during the early fourteenth century, disputes over jurisdiction led to wars between Edward I and Philip the Fair, and again between Edward II and Charles IV. In 1328 a new source of friction arose in the form of a dispute over the succession to the French throne between Philip of Valois and the English king, Edward III. In 1329 Edward did 'simple' homage at Amiens, and followed it up with 'liege' homage in 1331, but Anglo-French discussions in 1332 revealed deep differences between the two sides. Edward III broke his oath of fealty by offering protection to Robert of Artois, who had fled to England after being condemned as a traitor in France, but the French king played a similar game by offering his protection to the King of Scots, David II. On 24 May 1337 Philip VI of Valois proclaimed the confiscation of the duchy of Guyenne. Edward III promptly retaliated by withdrawing his homage, claiming the crown of France and declaring war on Philip 'who calls himself king of France'. For several years military operations in the south of France took the form of a stand off. Strong garrisons faced each other on either side of the border, but it was in the Low Countries that England and France first came to blows. Edward decided to use Flanders as his base for an attack on France. He sought the alliance of the Flemings by means of economic pressure and by exploiting their traditional dislike of the French monarchy. In September 1340 he carried out a destructive raid in northern France. Philip VI called out his nobility and communes but failed to engage the enemy. On 24 June he suffered a crippling naval defeat at Sluys, in Flanders.[3] Some two hundred ships on either side were involved and many thousands of men. The battle gave England command of the narrow seas so that Edward could now land troops on the Continent without risk of interception. During the summer both belligerents raised forces – possibly the largest of the Hundred Years War – in preparation for a battle that never took place. The English returned home after trying unsuccessfully to capture St-Omer and Tournai. Financially both sides were exhausted and needed a respite. They signed a truce at Esplechin on 25 September.

The next stage of the war was fought in Brittany. In April 1341 the duke, John III, died, leaving two rival heirs, John de Montfort and Charles of Blois. Each looked for support abroad. While Montfort was promised an English earldom, Blois gained the support of Philip VI. Brittany was important to England and France. While Philip VI was anxious to control the duchy and its ports, Edward III saw it as a gateway to France's interior. It also commanded England's maritime traffic with Guyenne. In the autumn of 1342 Edward conquered parts of Brittany and planted English garrisons in a number of towns and fortresses. A truce signed in January 1343 interrupted hostilities.[4]

In July 1346 Edward III landed in Normandy with an army some 15,000 strong. Encountering little resistance, he overran the province, collecting a huge amount of booty. Marching eastward, the king pillaged and burnt his way to the outskirts of Paris. On 16 August he marched north in order to join an English army based in Flanders. After much dithering, Philip VI set off in pursuit. He caught up with Edward near Crécy-en-Ponthieu, but Edward had time to pick a favourable position. His army consisted of some 2000 men-at-arms, mostly recruited from the nobility or gentry, 2000 or 3000 mounted archers (who dismounted to fight), 3000 to 4000 foot archers and 3000 to 4000 Welsh infantry. Edward III distributed his cavalry in three blocks and instructed them to fight on foot, a tactic calculated to give confidence to the archers who were posted on the wings. Battle with the French was joined on 26 August. As the French men-at-arms charged, they came under a shower of arrows from the English archers and broke up in confusion. The survivors regrouped and charged again, but were unable to break through the enemy line. As night fell, the French defeat was complete. Philip VI, though slightly wounded, managed to escape from the field. Flushed with their success, the English marched on Calais and besieged it for eleven months. Calais fell on 4 August 1347, giving the English a precious foothold in northern France which they were to retain until 1557.[5]

The French Army

The defence of France rested on a network of fortifications that included not only castles and walled towns but also houses, free-standing towers, churches, forts and fortresses. In the early stages of the Hundred Years War, local communities and individual nobles undertook to maintain such defences at their own expense. Towns were often allowed to use the proceeds of royal taxes for the upkeep of their walls and garrisons.[6]

However, fortifications alone could not keep out an invader. An adequate supply of armed men was also required. In England the feudal levy was almost a thing of the past. A system of military indentures had come into being, enabling the English monarch to know how many troops he disposed of and how much money he needed to pay them. Nothing comparable existed across the Channel. Early fourteenth-century France lacked a standing army. The crown had to raise troops for each military campaign. In an emergency, the king could call on all noblemen between the ages of eighteen and sixty to come to a given place on a certain day, fully equipped for war. Anyone, who failed to turn up for a valid reason, was expected to pay a fine. This mobilisation, known as the *arrière-ban*, could only be required in times of dire necessity and only applied to those parts of France under effective royal control. Guyenne, Brittany or Flanders were excluded. Commoners could secure exemption by paying a fine. In fact, the *arrière-ban*, which was summoned seven times between 1338 and 1356, was primarily a fund-raising exercise. In addition to such troops, the army included militiamen supplied by towns and volunteers recruited under contract.

With a much larger population than England – twenty million as against five million – France might have been expected to have a much larger army, but this did not follow. Philip VI was, it seems, able to raise very large forces in the early stages of the conflict. In September 1340, for example, his armies in northern and south-west France consisted of 30,000 men-at-arms and 30,000 foot soldiers. As each man-at-arms was accompanied by one or two auxiliaries and as many horses, the army would have comprised some 60,000 horses and 100,000 men, including non-combatants. But the English king also raised substantial forces. During the siege of Calais in 1347 he paid 22,000 combatants, representing a total force of 60,000 men. At Crécy the forces on either side were roughly equal. The English had between 13,000 and 15,000 men, and the French had 2000 *communiers*, less than 10,000 men-at-arms and some 7000 Genoese crossbowmen.

The French army consisted mainly of cavalry and infantry. About 1340 the men-at-arms were all mounted. Their chief weapons were the sword and the wooden lance, while their defensive equipment consisted of a small triangular shield, a helmet or bassinet, and a protective garment, often a coat of chain mail padded with leather or cloth. As from the start of the fourteenth century, the richest men-at-arms wore suits of armour made of iron or steel plates. These became heavier and more expensive in time. Not every man-at-arms had the same number of horses. Two per man-at-arms were the norm. The infantry consisted of crossbowmen and archers. The crossbow was less effective than the English longbow: its range was shorter and its rate of fire much slower. A crossbowman needed to be accompanied by a *pavesier*, who protected him with a shield as he loaded his weapon.

Aristocratic Discontent

Not all the French nobles were satisfied with the Valois succession of 1328. A few powerful nobles in north-west France swore allegiance to Edward III, but the majority did not turn to England. While pressing for government reform, they looked to the house of Evreux for leadership. This line derived its prestige mainly from Jeanne, queen of Navarre, the daughter of Louis X. Her husband, Philip possessed the Norman county of Évreux. Their son, Charles II of Navarre (1332–87), commonly known as Charles the Bad, inherited a large clientele of aristocratic malcontents. They professed loyalty to the French crown, but were regarded as traitors by Philip VI. The Hundred Years War was marked by a sharp increase in the number of treason trials in France leading to executions of prominent nobles. In the wake of Crécy and other French defeats the call for a reform of the royal administration grew so loud that Philip VI had to take placatory measures. He admitted several members of the Evreux clientele to his council.

In August 1350 Philip VI died. He was succeeded on the throne by his son, John II 'the Good', who angered the nobility of north-west France by executing one of their number, Raoul de Brienne, constable of

France. By now Charles the Bad had come of age and had become king of Navarre. He subsequently married John's daughter. Ties of clientage carefully nurtured over several years enabled Charles to lead a formidable opposition party. This gained strength when John replaced the executed constable with his own favourite, Charles of Spain, an enemy of the Évreux clan. Early in 1354 Navarre instigated the murder of Charles of Spain, inaugurating a decade of Valois-Évreux hostility that complicated the larger Anglo-French conflict. John tried to defuse the situation by adding Navarrese lords to his council. He also undertook peace negotiations with England. But Edward III insisted on holding his French lands in full sovereignty. This was unacceptable to Charles the Bad, who would have been isolated by such a deal. Parisians and many reformers also opposed the dismemberment of the realm. When the Estates-General met in December 1355 opponents of the government pushed through a number of reforms, but a substantial tax levy was needed to give them effect. This was now opposed by Charles the Bad, whose commitment to reform was not as strong as his hostility to the king. In April 1356 John imprisoned Charles and executed some of his followers. This plunged Normandy into civil war.[7]

Meanwhile the Anglo-French war flared up again. One of the heroes of Crécy had been Edward III's eldest son, Edward, Prince of Wales, the so-called 'Black Prince'. In the autumn of 1355 he carried out a raid or *chevauchée*, lasting two months, from Bordeaux across Languedoc. Similar raids were to be repeated several times elsewhere in France during the next few years. Their purpose was threefold: to oblige the French to remain on the defensive everywhere; to sap the confidence of King John's subjects in his ability to protect them; and to undermine the enemy's economic potential while yielding booty and prisoners for ransom. At first, John chose to ignore the Black Prince in order to have a free hand in dealing with Charles of Navarre, but in 1356 he launched a counter-attack against an English army in Normandy. He seized Évreux and Breteuil. In the meantime, the Black Prince, at the head of an Anglo-Gascon army, marched north from Bordeaux. After advancing to Romorantin, Edward veered towards Tours and crossed the Loire before falling back to avoid King John's forces. The latter, however, forced a battle at Maupertuis near Poitiers on 19 September 1356. In the hope of averting disorder, John ordered his men-at-arms to imitate the English by dismounting and fighting on foot, but this change of tactics proved a failure. Once again, as at Crécy, the French heavy cavalry succumbed to the deadly fire of the English archers. The king's own 'battle' was overwhelmed and he was forced to surrender along with his youngest son, Philip. John was taken to England, where he remained as a prisoner until October 1360.

He was not the first king of France to be taken prisoner. St Louis had been captured by the Mameluks, but this had happened in Egypt. John was the first to be captured on French soil. His subjects had witnessed his humiliation as he had been escorted to Bordeaux by the Black Prince.

Two Revolts

Following John's capture the government of France passed into the hands of the Dauphin Charles, who was only eighteen and politically inexperienced. Faced with an empty treasury, he summoned the Estates-General only to run into opposition from the Parisian bourgeoisie. King John's ransom was not the issue: vassals expected to pay their lord's ransom. It was the competence of the administration that was being questioned. The leader of the opposition was Etienne Marcel, the *prévôt des marchands*. He was a rich merchant and in effect the mayor of Paris, and spoke for the leading citizens at the Estates-General of October 1356. He won the support of followers of Charles the Bad, king of Navarre, who was still in prison. The estates demanded a complete overhaul of the administration. They wanted the king's council to be elected and its members to include four prelates, twelve nobles and twelve bourgeois. In short, they wanted to place the crown under tutelage. Early in November the dauphin adjourned the estates before meeting the Emperor Charles IV in Metz. During his absence, the crisis in Paris deepened, as Marcel resisted a proposal by the government to launch a new, stronger, coinage. Parisians were ordered by Marcel to stop work and to arm themselves. Hoping to defuse the situation, the Dauphin Charles recalled the estates and sacked nine of his councillors. When they met, on 5 February, 1357 the estates voted a subsidy but insisted on controlling its use. A commission of nine 'reformers-general' was set up to clean up the administration and to punish its allegedly guilty members.

The tax revenue was to be regularly monitored by the estates, and six deputies were to join the king's council. This reform programme had grave implications for the monarchy, but provincial France showed little enthusiasm. Defence was its main concern. A visit to Normandy encouraged the dauphin to stand up to the estates. At the same time, King John dashed the reformers' hopes by announcing a truce with England and forbidding the levy of the tax recently voted by the estates. When they tried to press on regardless, the kingdom refused to follow. In August 1357 the dauphin hit back. He recalled the sacked councillors, suspended the work of the 'reformers-general', and restored the officials who had been recently cashiered. Charles also warned Marcel in future to attend only to municipal matters.

Early in November 1357 a new challenge confronted the dauphin when Charles of Navarre escaped from prison. He came to Paris with the dauphin's permission, but soon returned to Normandy, intent on reasserting his position there. Marcel, meanwhile, distributed red and blue hoods to his followers and took as his slogan: 'A bonne fin'. On 22 February 1358 he provoked a riot in Paris. Three thousand armed men gathered in the city centre. As Renaut d'Acy, a member of the Parlement, crossed their path, they lynched him. They then marched on the Palais, burst into the dauphin's chamber and before his very eyes slaughtered two of his closest friends, marshals Robert de Clermont and Jean de Conflans. Marcel insolently asked the dauphin 'when will you begin to govern?' He then addressed a large crowd outside the town hall: the bad men, he announced, were dead, but the dauphin was safe.

Charles now seemed to be Marcel's puppet, but he was playing a skilful game. At the first opportunity, he left Paris and, while pretending to support the Parisian reformers, gained the support of the estates of Champagne. He also occupied Meaux whence he could cut a major supply route to Paris. He asked Marcel to send him artillery that was kept at the Louvre, but the mayor moved it to the town hall for his own use. He sent an ultimatum to Charles: 'Your people of Paris grumble much about you and your government'. In May the dauphin wrote to Marcel from Compiègne. He said that he did not blame the whole of Paris for recent events, but that he could not forgive certain crimes. Sensing danger, Marcel set about strengthening the capital's defences.

At this juncture a new revolt broke out quite independently of the

Parisian one. This was the Jacquerie, an explosion of anger among peasants of the Beauvaisis. It began in a village on 28 May 1358 and soon spread like wildfire across large parts of northern France. The peasants involved were not the poorest. They were mostly small peasant proprietors who had been hard hit by higher taxes, a stagnant grain market, declining profits on the sale of their produce, a rise in the cost of agricultural implements, an increase of feudal dues, and the ravages of freebooters and other miscreants. Unlike landless day-workers, they could not take advantage of the rise in wages caused by demographic decline. They were rich enough to be taxed and subject to requisitioning orders. The Jacquerie was not a cohesive movement and had no real leaders, no organization and no programme; it was an uncontrolled torrent of hatred unleashed against all nobles. A contemporary, Jean de Venette, wrote of the rebels: 'They killed, massacred and exterminated all the nobles they could find, even their own lords. Not content with this, they destroyed their houses and fortresses. Even more lamentable was their killing of noblewomen and small children.'

The Jacquerie offered Charles of Navarre a chance to take up a politically advantageous cause. He became the defender of the nobility. Marcel, on the other hand, courted the support of Parisian artisans and small tradesmen. He dispatched an armed force to assist the rebellious peasants. The result was a terrible massacre of the rebels at Meaux by Navarre's cavalry. 'Then men-at-arms of every kind burst out of the gates and ran into the square to attack those evil men', writes Froissart. 'They mowed them down in heaps and slaughtered them like cattle; and they drove all the rest out of the town, for none of the villeins attempted to take up any sort of fighting order. They went on killing until they were stiff and weary and they flung many into the River Marne.'[8] Jean de Venette wrote: 'Our mortal foes, the English, would not have done what the nobles then did in our homeland'.

As Navarre seemed to be winning support in Paris, the dauphin lifted the blockade of Paris and prepared to leave Meaux for Dauphiné, but an unexpected event caused him to change his mind. An affray in Paris by English troops employed by Navarre triggered an explosion of anger among the citizens. Marcel ordered the expulsion of all Englishmen from the capital, but continued to look to Navarre for armed assistance. Parisians, however, were becoming tired of them both. A draper, called

Maillart, suddenly rode down the rue St-Antoine shouting the dauphin's war-cry: 'Montjoie au roi de France et au duc!' A crowd of Parisians followed him to the Halles where Marcel was holed up. He tried to reason with them, but they would not listen. Instead, they felled him to the ground. On 2 August, the dauphin, knowing that Marcel was dead, returned to Paris. He forgave the *menu peuple* for the revolt but punished the ringleaders: eight were beheaded in four days. Writing from London, King John thanked the Parisians for their show of loyalty.[9]

Anglo-French talks which took place under the aegis of papal legates focused on two questions: John's ransom and the handover of new territories. In January 1358 the first treaty of London fixed the ransom at four million gold *écus* and handed over to Edward III 'greater Aquitaine', along with Poitou, the Limousin, Quercy, Rouergue, Bigorre, Calais and Ponthieu. But Edward was not satisfied and threatened a new invasion of France. Under the second treaty of London, of 24 March 1359, John gave up the entire Atlantic coast from Calais to Bayonne along with Brittany's homage. In May, however, the Dauphin Charles prevailed on the Estates-General to reject this treaty. Edward retaliated on 28 October 1359 with a new armed raid into France from Calais. Charles withdrew, creating a vacuum in front of the advancing English, who, after a feeble attempt to besiege Reims, marched south into Burgundy, threatened Paris and ended up in Beauce. Meanwhile, French ships based in Normandy carried out raids on the south coast of England.

A further round of Anglo-French talks led on 8 May 1360 to the draft treaty of Brétigny. Two months later King John was taken to Calais where Edward III joined him after the first instalment of John's ransom had been paid. On 24 October the treaty was signed and John set free. Keen as ever to lead a crusade, he called on Pope Urban V at Avignon, but John had first to implement the treaty of Brétigny. His ransom had been reduced to three million *écus* payable in annual instalments of 400,000 *écus*. As security for the payment, a number of French hostages, including princes of the blood, were sent to London. 'Greater Aquitaine', including Périgord, was ceded in full sovereignty to Edward III. Under a separate convention, John was supposed to renounce the sovereignty of Aquitaine and Edward his claim to the crown of France, but the exchange never took place. This omission was to have grave consequences.

Implementing the treaty proved to be a tedious business. In Poitou, the handover of lands to the English lasted from September 1361 until March 1362. Yet the process was more easily achieved than the collection of John's ransom. A royal ordinance of 3 December 1360, imposing a tax on salt and wine, yielded a substantial sum, but even after three years less than one million *écus* had been collected. Meanwhile, the French hostages, including the dukes of Anjou and of Berry, were moved to Calais. In the hope of hastening their release, they signed an agreement with the English, known as 'the treaty of the hostages', on 21 November 1362. This committed King John to surrender certain disputed territories while the hostages themselves undertook to surrender a number of castles in Berry, but the French estates, meeting at Amiens in October 1363 rejected the treaty. Fearing for his honour, John, who was a man of his word, returned voluntarily to London early in 1364. He was about to negotiate a new treaty when he fell ill and died on 8 April, aged only forty-five. Edward III gave him a splendid funeral at St Paul's cathedral. His body was then carried in great pomp across the Channel and on to Saint-Denis for burial.

In the spring of 1364 an English spy reported the intentions of the new French king, Charles V. His plan, he said, was to lull the English with fair words until he had recovered the hostages. Meanwhile, he would make war on Charles of Navarre and build up his army. Once the hostages had been returned, he would reconquer the parts of France occupied by the English. Events were to confirm this prophecy, yet Charles had too many urgent problems at home to envisage an early resumption of the Anglo-French conflict. He needed above all to deal with the large number of unpaid troops rampaging through France. These included Englishmen. At Brétigny Edward III had promised to evacuate his troops from French soil, but he merely stopped their wages. Forced to live off the French countryside, they formed *compagnies* or bands of about one hundred men, known as *routiers*, each under a captain. Not all were English. Some were German and many came from Brittany or Gascony. Among them were many petty nobles and bastards whose patrimonial lands were insufficient to sustain them. The *compagnies* operated under no authority and existed simply to pillage.[10] They would seize a castle from which they would terrorise a district, hold the inhabitants to ransom and seize supplies. In June 1360 several thousand *routiers* appeared in Burgundy. They were drawn south for various reasons. Philippe de Rouvres, the young duke of Burgundy, who had recently paid 200,000 *écus* rather than defend his territory, seemed unlikely to resist. The riches ascribed to the papacy may also have drawn them. Numerous Gascons may have wanted to draw closer to their native region. Lacking the necessary resources, Charles V left the responsibility of dealing with the *compagnies* to local communities, which often preferred to buy them off rather than fight them. In January 1361 Pope Innocent VI proclaimed a crusade against them after they had seized Pont-Saint-Esprit, but the result was a feeble settlement: the *compagnies* were paid 14,500 florins to evacuate the town. While some of them went to Italy to fight the Visconti, others poured into Languedoc where they seized towns and pillaged monasteries. In 1363 a royal army was cut to pieces by the *compagnies* at Brignais near Lyon. It seemed that the only way of getting rid of them was to offer them a bait outside the kingdom. They showed no interest in going to Hungary to fight the Turks, but some agreed to serve under the Black Prince in Castile, where civil war had broken out. When the prince returned to Bordeaux in September 1367, the compagnies once again found themselves unemployed. Charles V took part of them into his army. They were promised absolution from papal excommunication and engaged for three months. Thereafter, their captains were invited to remain in royal service in return for 12,000 francs per month.[11]

Between 1364 and 1368 Charles V did his utmost to fulfil the terms of the treaty of Brétigny. He paid at least half of the ransom of the French hostages, but an unforeseen development upset the peace. The Black Prince, needing money urgently to pay for his military campaign in Castile, obtained a subsidy from the estates of Aquitaine. Two Gascon noblemen refused to levy the tax on their lands. They appealed first to Edward III, then to Charles V. Legal experts assured the latter that he could receive the appeals, as he had not formally renounced his suzerainty. The appellants were soon joined by nine hundred others. On 3 December 1368 Charles V justified his reception of the appeals in a proclamation, and in January 1369 the Black Prince was ordered to appear before the Parlement of Paris. He agreed to do so but only with a basinet on his head and escorted by an army 60,000 strong. On 8 June Charles V declared war on him and, on 30 November, he declared Aquitaine confiscated to the French crown.[12]

Charles V's Army

Charles V continued to levy the tax which had been set up to help pay
for his father's ransom. It was not uniformly levied throughout the
kingdom. All kinds of local circumstances had to be taken into account.
Flanders, Burgundy and Brittany did not contribute, but the tax enabled
the king to set up and maintain a more disciplined, albeit smaller, army
than in the past. It was made up essentially of men-at-arms recruited in
various parts of France and of native and foreign crossbowmen. To
these were added a small number of archers as well as *sergents* and
pavesiers provided by towns. Altogether the army comprised 2400 men-
at-arms and a thousand crossbowmen. During the fighting season it
received additional troops in the form of men-at-arms recruited on a
contractual basis. Between 1369 and 1380 Charles V's army numbered
5200 troops during one third of the year and 3400 during the other two
thirds. Athough artillery was still at an early stage of its development, it
played a significant part at the siege of Saint-Sauveur-le-Vicomte, in
1375. The cannon came from Paris, Saint-Lô and Caen. Of thirty pieces
manufactured at Caen, the biggest weighed more than 2000 pounds and
fired cannon balls weighing 100 pounds. The amount of gunpowder
used increased tenfold between 1350 and 1380, but cannon-balls made of
stone were not hard enough to breach town walls. The best way of capturing a town was still to mine the walls or to mount a surprise attack
using scaling ladders.

Charles V never called the *arrière-ban*, but on at least four occasions
he resorted to a *semonce générale* aimed at all sorts of men-at-arms and
crossbowmen. He looked to all the nobility and the 'good towns' for
support. He encouraged the creation of companies of archers in the
towns, who might serve elsewhere in time of need. In 1380 the countryside was asked to supply missile men (*gens de trait*). Nobles who
responded to the *semonces* were paid out of taxation, while crossbowmen were usually paid by the towns. In the main, Charles V's army
consisted of volunteers whose leaders had signed indentures. Recruitment became more centralised than in the past. Though Charles V
rarely strayed outside Paris or its region, he alone directed military operations. A continual traffic of messengers kept him fully informed of
developments and he kept a close watch on subordinates.

When operational, the royal army was divided into units, called *routes* or *compagnies*. The normal strength of a *route* was defined in 1374 as one hundred men-at-arms. Its captain was allowed to recruit his own men, to dismiss them if they proved unsatisfactory, and to grant them leave on valid grounds. He was expected to maintain his company at full strength, to notify the war treasurers of any absentees, and to impose an oath on his men. They had to promise not to leave the company without leave or to damage the property of the king's subjects. The captain was to become the backbone of the army. As from 1368 the word *chambre* entered the military vocabulary. A company or *route* was divided into a number of *chambres*. The ideal number was defined in 1374 as ten per company, each containing ten men. Crossbowmen were divided into units of forty or fifty men known as *connétablies* under captains or constables. Companies were distributed into garrisons during the winter months and would regroup at the start of the fighting season. The system of monthly inspections or musters was regularised under Charles V. Only twelve people were authorised to hold musters. To facilitate the task of the war treasurers, the duration of military service was defined in months rather than days. It seems that under Charles V the troops were paid more regularly than in the past. A stronger currency made it possible for wages to be fixed at a more remunerative level.[13]

A large-scale campaign was undertaken under Charles V to repair the walls of towns and castles. Moats were cleared of rubbish and buildings obstructing ramparts demolished. A survey of the *bailliage* of Melun in 1367 listed twenty-seven forts, thirty-nine fortified churches, three fortified towns and ten castles capable of offering shelter to the inhabitants. The watch and guard (*le guet et le retrait*) were organised by the towns and by lords. These measures evidently proved effective as very few towns were captured during the next stage of the Hundred Years War.[14]

The Great Schism

The Hundred Years War was not the only conflict helping to divide Christendom in the fourteenth century; another was taking place at the very centre of the church. Having settled at Avignon at the start of the century, the popes hoped sooner or later to return to Rome. Urban V tried to do so in 1367 but failed. His successor, Gregory XI, was more successful. On 17 January 1377 he returned to Rome, but a quarter of the college of cardinals remained in Avignon. Following Gregory's death in 1378 the cardinals in Rome were mobbed by Roman crowds, who were afraid that if another French pope were elected, he would take the papacy back to Avignon. The cardinals elected an Italian who took the name of Urban VI. He soon alienated so many people by his violent and overbearing ways that the cardinals declared his election invalid on the ground that it had been carried out under duress. They chose in his place a Frenchman, Robert of Geneva. As Pope Clement VII he took the Curia back to Avignon, while Urban appointed twenty-seven new cardinals from all over Europe.[15]

European governments were left to choose between two popes and two sacred colleges. The king of France had an interest in retaining the papacy at Avignon. A French pope residing close to him could be a valuable asset. He might give the king diplomatic support against England, allow him to tax the French clergy and grant him effective control of nominations to benefices. On 16 November, therefore, Charles V recognised Clement VII, and his decision was endorsed in May 1379 by an assembly of the French clergy, but the king's decision did not meet with universal approval. In the Midi the clergy and universities tended to support Urban VI. The university of Paris also disapproved of the king's policy. Some theologians, who argued that a General Council of the church should be called to end the schism, had to leave Paris. Once purged of Urbanists, the university formally backed Clement VII. Other countries did likewise, but England and the Empire opted for Urban. The great religious orders were similarly divided.[16]

The Reconquest

The war between England and France in the 1370s was different from that of earlier decades. Charles V tried as far as possible to avoid a pitched battle: he aimed to harass the English *chevauchées* and to capture as many strongholds and castles as possible. His commander-in-chief was Bertrand Du Guesclin, a petty nobleman from Brittany, who had gained military experience fighting the *routiers* along the Breton border and in Castile. He was appointed Constable of France on 22 October 1370, and his fame became such that, in the eyes of contemporaries, he joined

Charlemagne, King Arthur and Godefroi de Bouillon as the fourth *preux*. Long after his death, old soldiers boasted of having served under 'the good Constable'. Ill health forced the Black Prince to abandon the government of Aquitaine in 1371 as it came under attack from the French. The English high command failed to offer any effective response. *Chevauchées*, led by Sir Robert Knolles in 1370 and John of Gaunt, Edward III's son, in 1373, achieved little. In the summer of 1372 Castilian galleys destroyed an English fleet off La Rochelle thereby depriving the English in Guyenne of much-needed supplies and reinforcements. Gradually, the French reoccupied much of the province. Meanwhile, having rebuilt a fleet since the battle of Sluys, they carried out raids against the south coast of England. In July 1380 another English *chevauchée*, this time led by Thomas, earl of Buckingham, set out from Calais, hoping to mop up French troops in Brittany. After skirting Paris, the duke moved south to the Loire valley, then west to Brittany. Following the death of Du Guesclin, the task of shadowing and containing the English was entrusted to Philip, duke of Burgundy. Buckingham reached Nantes on 4 November, but failed to take the town. He moved on to Rennes, then to Brest, and finally returned to England in the spring of 1381.

Charles V, known as 'The Wise', died on 16 September 1380, knowing that he had reconquered most of the territories lost as a result of the peace of Brétigny. Solid as this achievement was, it left much to be done. Calais, Cherbourg, Brest, Bordeaux and Bayonne remained in English hands. The enemy also controlled, directly or indirectly, a large number of fortresses, mainly in Quercy, Rouergue, Auvergne, Velay and Gévaudan, from which they carried out destructive raids in the neighbouring countryside. For example, the English, who occupied Lusignan until 1374–75, destroyed fifty-two parishes and ten monasteries. John of Gaunt, duke of Lancaster, stripped the countryside far and wide outside Montpont in 1370 in order to feed his men. Peasants watched helplessly as their crops were destroyed, their homes burnt down, and their trees and vines uprooted. Many abandoned their holdings and looked for safety in towns which became consequently overcrowded.

Plague followed in the wake of the armies. An epidemic in 1360–62 spread slowly from east to west, killing off the generation born since the Black Death. The plague struck again in 1373–74, and in August 1379 when a heavy death toll in Paris forced the king to flee to Montargis. In the following year, his two sons were sent to Melun to escape from another epidemic in and around the capital. Famines also occurred, increasing the death toll. A particularly serious one hit the Midi in the winter of 1374–75, causing a sharp rise of grain prices.

As if war, plague and famine were not enough, France in September 1380 had to face another hazard. The new king, Charles VI, was only eleven years old. Since he was too young to rule, the government needed to be directed by one of his senior relatives. A royal minority was usually accompanied by a struggle for power among leading courtiers, something France could ill afford as it was still trying to fend off a powerful foreign enemy.

3

The Marmousets

Standing next to the throne of the young Charles VI stood four uncles, keen to exert influence during his minority. The oldest of them, Louis of Anjou, was designated regent, but his fiscal exactions as Charles V's lieutenant in Languedoc had made him unpopular. It was also feared that he would use tax revenues to promote his own ambitions in Italy. The youngest brother, Philip the Bold, duke of Burgundy, stood to acquire the lands of his father-in-law, Louis de Mâle, count of Flanders. Like Anjou, he hoped to use French resources to advance his own interests in that region. He enlisted the support of the other two royal uncles, Jean of Berry and Louis of Bourbon, as he sought to reduce Anjou's authority.

Soon after Charles VI's coronation, his uncles called a meeting of the Estates-General at which Louis of Anjou requested new taxes. This provoked such disturbances in Paris and elsewhere that the uncles were forced to back down. They cancelled all extraordinary taxes levied since the reign of Philip IV. They then tried unsuccessfully to obtain grants from regional assemblies. In January 1382 more opposition was provoked by the government's reimposition of indirect taxes. Risings occurred in towns across France, notably in Paris and Rouen, which were put down by a mixture of force and conciliation. Heavy fines were imposed and municipal privileges curtailed. A major rebellion led by Ghent had erupted in Flanders in 1379. Louis de Mâle appealed to the French king for military assistance, and on 27 November 1382 a royal army crushed the rebels at Roosebeke.[1] The victory did not end the revolt, but it strengthened the hand of the French government as it set about extinguishing the last embers of the uprisings in French towns. Indirect taxes were now restored, but not the hearth tax.[2] In Languedoc, popular unrest was exacerbated by a long-standing feud between the successive counts of Armagnac and Gaston Phoebus, count of Foix.

Jean of Berry was appointed as the king's lieutenant in the province in
November freeing Louis of Anjou, who had previously occupied that
position, to pursue his interests in Italy. He went there in March 1382
never to return. With two of his brothers otherwise engaged, Philip,
duke of Burgundy was able to gain control of the government in Paris.

The Flemish rebellion had a bearing on Anglo-French relations, for
the English government responded positively to an appeal for help from
the rebels. Henry Despenser, bishop of Norwich, led an expedition
under guise of a crusade in support of Urban VI, one of the two popes
competing for the headship of the church. Charles VI and Louis de Mâle
supported his rival, Clement VII. The bishop crossed the Channel in
May 1383 and after wresting Gravelines and Dunkirk from the French
laid siege to Ypres. However, when the bishop learnt that a large French
army had been mobilised, he took fright and returned home. The col-
lapse of his so-called crusade helped to discredit the 'war party' at the
English court where influential opinion swung in favour of an accommodation with France.

The deaths of the countess dowager of Flanders in 1382 and of Count
Louis de Mâle in 1384 brought to Philip the Bold, duke of Burgundy, an
inheritance that was to make him one of the most powerful princes in
Europe. He and his wife moved quickly to establish a strong position
in the Low Countries. They arranged for two of their children to marry
into the Wittelsbach family, the rulers of the neighbouring counties of
Hainault, Holland and Zeeland, and they were instrumental in arrang-
ing the marriage of Charles VI to Isabeau, a member of the senior
branch of the same family. The relative speed with which Duke Philip
attained his ends in the Low Countries enabled him and the French
government to plan an attack upon England aimed at ending the Anglo-
French conflict. In 1385 two expeditionary forces were assembled at
Sluys: one under the constable, Olivier de Clisson, was to land near the
Thames estuary and march on London; the other, under the Admiral of
France, Jean de Vienne, was to go to Scotland and attack Durham. Clisson, however, was detained in Flanders by continuing popular unrest,
and de Vienne met with a cool reception in Scotland and carried out
only a timid raid across England's northern border. Yet Charles VI was
not discouraged. In 1386 he tried again. A large fleet was assembled at
Sluys as well as an army, but bad weather caused the project to be

shelved. Revived in 1387, it was again called off. Bad weather alone was not to blame for these successive failures. The dukes of Berry and Brittany showed little enthusiasm for projects organised by the constable, Olivier de Clisson. There may have been other reasons too: the government ran out of money, the troops began to pillage and it was feared that the Flemings would revolt again once the troops had left.

Long and tortuous Anglo-French talks at Leulinghen culminated in a truce on 18 June 1389. Initially for three years, it was subsequently extended several times. Not all Frenchmen wanted war. Disenchantment with it, on moral as well as practical grounds, was expressed by such writers as Philippe de Mézières and Christine de Pisan. The former praised the English king, Richard II, for wishing to end fighting among Christians. On the English side, even John of Gaunt became less aggressive towards France. Having received Aquitaine from Richard II as a personal apanage, he needed peace to establish himself there. Yet the duchy's status remained a problem. The French agreed to cede most of old Aquitaine but stood firm on the question of sovereignty.

In June 1387 John IV, duke of Brittany, hoping to please the English and to satisfy a personal hatred, had Clisson arrested and clapped in irons. According to Froissart, the duke planned to kill him, but was persuaded that such an act would have grave consequences for himself. He was, therefore, content to set Clisson free in return for a huge ransom and the surrender of more than a dozen strongholds. The event had the effect of wrecking France's military preparations. It also shocked Charles VI and his brother, Louis of Touraine, who had become deeply attached to the constable. The royal uncles, Berry and Burgundy, tried to mediate between John IV and the king of France, but the duke failed to meet Charles VI at Orléans as arranged. The king angrily ordered the duke to hand back the ransom and all but one of the strongholds he had taken from Clisson.

Meanwhile William, duke of Guelders, an ally of England, issued a public defiance of Charles VI. He threatened Brabant, a territory which Philip of Burgundy hoped one day to absorb through inheritance. A punitive expedition led by Charles, Philip of Burgundy and Clisson set off in September 1387 and within six weeks the duke of Guelders submitted. On its return march, however, the royal army encountered bad weather, harassment from 'Germans' and suffered severe losses while fording a swollen river. At Reims, the king held a meeting of his council at which the bishop of Laon, Pierre Aycelin de Montaigu, made a speech. The king, he said, was now old enough to take charge of affairs. Charles VI, who was now almost twenty years old, thanked the dukes of Berry and Burgundy for their services. They tried to get the king to change his mind on the road back to Paris, but he refused. The dukes accordingly retired from the council which now became dominated by a group of men, led by Clisson, who have come to be known as the 'Marmousets'.[3]

Charles VI's new councillors were first called 'marmousets' by Froissart and the name was picked up in the nineteenth century by Michelet who assumed that it meant *petites gens* – people of low social status. Yet the Marmousets were nothing of the kind. They were not princes 'born to govern', and may, therefore, have been seen as 'upstarts', but, except for Olivier de Clisson, who belonged to the old nobility, men, like Bureau de La Rivière, Jean le Mercier and Jean de Montaigu were from the middling nobility or had bourgeois origins. Some had served Charles V while he was still dauphin or Charles the Bad. They held various positions in church and state, but were mostly attached to the royal household or military leadership. According to the contemporary chronicler, Michel Pintoin, the Marmousets took an oath to sustain each other and to act as one. Their solidarity, however, should not be exaggerated: in 1392 it proved less important to some than survival.[4]

The government of the Marmousets has been described as a time of total change when peace, economy and persuasion replaced war, heavy taxes and coercion. Concerned as they were about the oppressive burden of taxation which the French people had recently had to carry, the Marmousets inaugurated a period of frugal administration and careful management of resources. In May 1389 they concluded a three year truce with England, the first of a series of agreements which replaced twenty years of conflict with more than fifteen years of peace. Military costs were reduced accordingly. In December 1388 the crown reduced indirect taxes. As from February 1389 a series of ordinances were aimed at reforming the Parlement, the king's household, the administration of waters and forests, the management of the *aides* and the *Chambre des comptes*. A general reform of the kingdom by a team of *réformateurs* was also ordered. As a goodwill gesture towards the Parisians, the

Marmousets created an official to replace the *prévôt des marchands* whose post had been abolished after the uprising of 1382.[5]

The Marmousets' intellectual godfather was Philippe de Mézières, Charles VI's former tutor, whose *Songe du vieil pèlerin* outlined a programme of political action stressing the need to reduce taxes and public expenditure, to restore the royal domain and to make competence the criterion for choosing government officials.[6] Departing from medieval tradition, the Marmousets developed a concept of the state in which crown officials were to see themselves as public servants rather than as the creatures of princes. Many of the new measures, of course, threatened vested interests and the Marmousets made a dangerous enemy by trying to curtail the privileges of the university of Paris. They tried to regulate appointments to the Parlement and made the royal council responsible for choosing *baillis* and *sénéchaux*.[7]

The Marmousets' desire to reform the government was demonstrated most spectacularly in Languedoc where the duke of Berry's administration had become very unpopular. He had taxed the region heavily and seemed not to have used the funds for the region's benefit. In 1389 Charles VI decided to make a personal tour of the province. His progress was a carefully planned ritual of sovereignty. While its ultimate objective was Toulouse, the king took a circuitous route making ceremonial entries at Lyon, Montpellier and Béziers. In Languedoc, the king sent an official to pay for *routiers* to evacuate certain fortresses. He himself reached an accord with Gaston de Foix which ended his age-old quarrel with the Armagnacs. As for the duke of Berry, he was persuaded to resign from his lieutenancy on the ground that the king's presence in Languedoc made it redundant. After providing for the reform of financial abuses in Languedoc, Charles VI returned to Paris. In March he was received magnificently in Dijon by the duke of Burgundy.[8]

The rise of the Marmousets led to increased royal support for the house of Anjou and to a growth of the political influence of the king's younger brother, Louis, duke of Touraine.[9] The Marmousets, it seems, approved of Louis because unlike the king's uncles, he did not have vast lands and was dependent on the king. But Louis soon set about building up his landed possessions and in time gained a reputation for cupidity rivalling that of his uncles. Though he was not yet sufficiently mature politically to challenge them, he was old enough to attract clients and favourites. Among them were people associated with the Marmousets. In 1389 Louis married Valentina Visconti, daughter of the duke of Milan, and used some of her dowry to buy the counties of Blois and Dunois. In 1392 he exchanged Touraine for the larger and richer apanage of Orléans. He was known henceforth as Louis, duke of Orléans. In foreign policy the regime of the Marmousets was characterised by a surprising consensus. They and the king's uncles all wanted peace with England. Philip of Burgundy, hoping to consolidate his position in the Low Countries, played an active role in seeking a lasting settlement. The nobility, it seems, wanted an end to a war which had damaged their seigneurial incomes while saddling their tenants with an intolerable fiscal burden. Peace usually led to troops being disbanded which would then form bands and terrorise the countryside. One way of avoiding this danger was to send them abroad. The Marmousets sponsored two such expeditions in 1390: one, a crusade, led by the duke of Bourbon, against the Saracens of Tunisia; and the other, an invasion of Italy, led by Louis II of Anjou, in pursuit of his father's claim to the kingdom of Naples. The first ended in fiasco, and the second ran into trouble. Besides the Angevin branch of the Valois family, Louis of Orléans had strong Italian ambitions. Having married into the ducal house of Milan, he now dreamt of carving for himself a kingdom in the north of the papal states. An invasion of Italy appealed to Charles VI, who had military ambitions, and also to all those Frenchmen who wanted to end the papal schism by installing Clement VII in Rome in place of Urban VI. A large army was scheduled to assemble in Lyon in March 1391, but the death of Urban VI followed by the election of Boniface IX radically altered the situation. The new pope appealed to Richard II of England not to make peace with Charles VI unless the French promised to stay out of Italy. Richard agreed and engaged in a flurry of diplomatic activity aimed at frustrating the French design. When Charles VI was warned by English ambassadors in February 1391 that an attack on the Roman pope would violate the Anglo-French truce, he promptly abandoned his invasion plan.[10]

The King's Madness

In 1392 Charles VI tried to settle finally a long-standing quarrel with John IV, duke of Brittany. Among the main differences between them were the nature of ducal homage for Brittany, the appellate jurisdiction of the Parlement of Paris over Breton cases, and the question of rights over the church in Brittany. The dukes of Berry and Burgundy busily acted as intermediaries and in January an agreement was reached, although the duke stated ominously that concessions made under duress did not need to be honoured. A deep personal enmity also existed between John IV and the French constable, Olivier de Clisson. This now flared up again and the duke found a willing instrument in Pierre de Craon, an unsavoury character, who had recently been banished from the French court. One night in June 1392 he and his man attacked Clisson as he was returning home after dining with the king. The event caused outrage at court where it was seen as a direct assault on the king's majesty. Charles VI ordered Craon's arrest, but he managed to escape, whereupon the king ordered the seizure of his propery and the destruction of some of his houses. Eventually, he was sentenced to perpetual banishment, but the French government, influenced by Clisson, blamed John IV for what had happened, and decided to attack Brittany. The king's uncles felt insulted at not having been consulted before the decision was taken.

On 5 August 1392, as Charles VI led his forces out of Le Mans en route for John IV's fortress of Sablé, he suffered a serious mental breakdown. He suddenly attacked his brother, Louis of Orléans, who was riding beside him and killed four men before his chamberlain was able to restrain him. Charles was taken back to Le Mans where he recovered after lying motionless for two days. People said that he had been poisoned or bewitched, but his doctors diagnosed a long-standing 'weakness of intellect'. Ten months later, in June 1393, Charles caused concern by making 'undignified gestures'. More such episodes were to occur in the future. The king's bouts of madness or 'absences', as they were called, have been diagnosed as paranoid schizophrenia. As he often appeared sane, he was allowed to continue to rule, but his illness inevitably affected the conduct of his greater vassals.[11]

Philip of Burgundy quickly took charge of the government and called off the Breton campaign. He easily brushed aside the king's brother, Louis of Orléans, and in so doing may have inaugurated the famous hostility between uncle and nephew. Louis's failure to stand up for himself has been ascribed to his 'frivolity and impetuosity'. The king's

uncles now began the overthrow of the Marmousets. Le Mercier, La Rivière and Villaines were arrested. They and others also had their salaries
and pensions stopped. In December the Parlement stripped Clisson of
the office of constable, fined him 100,000 francs and declared him banished. But many of the reforms of the Marmousets were allowed to
remain in effect. When Charles VI returned to Paris in October he
showed no eagerness to dismiss the uncles or to recall his old advisers.
Leaving politics to others, he preferred to enjoy himself in a series of
celebrations and balls.[12]

The Elusive Peace

French foreign policy in the 1390s had three principal objectives: to
make peace with England; to end the papal schism; and to launch a crusade against the Infidel. The Anglo-French peace talks at Leulinghen
encouraged people to hope that peace was in the offing, but Charles VI's
nervous breakdown and Richard II's journey to Ireland caused a
planned meeting of the two kings to be postponed. Despite a deteriora-
tion of relations between the two countries in 1394–95, the meeting did
eventually take place in 1396 when Richard II, a widower of thirty-seven
years of age, married Charles VI's eldest daughter, Isabelle, who was
only six. The marriage contract, drawn up on 9 March, was followed by
a twenty-eight year truce. The meeting of the two kings and their escorts
took place in a meadow outside Ardres and was almost like a dress-
rehearsal of the more famous Field of Cloth of Gold of 1520. On both
occasions great care was taken to avoid any provocation by either side.
The two kings agreed to combine their efforts to end the schism in the
church and to lead a crusade, but their alliance was essentially personal;
it did nothing to remove the obstacles in the path of a lasting peace
between England and France, it even made the situation worse by arousing the suspicions among Richard II's subjects, who feared that his
faternising across the Channel might be part of a search for French aid
against his own rebels.[13] Richard's alliance with France certainly played
into the hands of the aristocratic opposition led by Henry of Lancaster
and to the king's deposition at Michaelmas 1399. The accession of
Henry IV to the English throne made it less likely that a lasting peace
with France would soon be achieved.[14]

The death of the Avignon pope, Clement VII, on 16 September 1394 appeared to the French government a heaven-sent opportunity to end the schism. Of the various options available, it favoured 'the way of cession'; that is, it wanted the two rival popes to stand down in order to make way for a new pope acceptable to everyone. A message was sent from Paris to the cardinals in Avignon begging them not to elect a new pope, but it arrived too late; they had already elected Pedro de Luna, who took the name of Benedict XIII. Early in 1395 a high-powered embassy, including the dukes of Burgundy, Berry and Orléans, travelled to Avignon, hoping to persuade the new pope to stand down, but he resisted their entreaties. Charles VI responded by withdrawing his kingdom's obedience from Benedict, but other European princes, while signifying their approval in principle, failed to follow the king's lead. Benedict was supported in Castile, Navarre and Béarn. Meanwhile, French efforts to secure the resignation of the Roman pope encountered strong resistance from the clergy and universities in England and the Empire.[15]

Two years were spent preparing a new crusade. While information regarding the Turks and their armies was being gathered, embassies were sent out from France to various countries to mobilise participants. Princes levied taxes and nobles mortgaged their estates in the hope of returning home laden with eastern riches. Command of the expedition was to be entrusted to seasoned military leaders, like John of Gaunt and Philip the Bold, but the latter delegated his role to his son, John, count of Nevers, who was too young to restrain the mad impulses of the French men-at-arms. On reaching Hungary, the crusaders, outmatched by the army of Sultan Bayezid I, were routed at Nicopolis. John of Nevers and Henry of Bar were taken prisoner and huge ransoms were paid for their release.[16] It was at this time that John acquired the nickname of 'the Fearless'.

4

Armagnacs versus Burgundians

Until 1404 the government of France was effectively in the hands of Philip the Bold, duke of Burgundy, who had the support of his brother, John, duke of Berry, and of other princes. Philip's death in 1404 gave Louis, duke of Orléans, and brother of Charles VI, an opportunity to seize power, which he did with the help of Queen Isabeau, whom many suspected of being his mistress. Orléans soon dominated the government. On 5 June he married off his son to Charles VI's daughter, Isabelle, the widow of King Richard II of England, and, next day, became captain-general and lieutenant in Picardy and Normandy. According to the Monk of Saint-Denis, Louis had become the virtual ruler of France. He was also unpopular, hence a royal ordinance of 27 July ordering 'the most rigorous punishment of those who write, distribute or fix defamatory pamphlets on gates, doors or houses'.[1]

When Philip the Bold lay dying in 1404, he asked his sons, John and Anthony, to swear loyalty and obedience to Charles VI. John, known as 'the Fearless', who now became duke of Burgundy, did not enter the French political arena until February 1405, when, at a meeting of the king's council, he opposed a tax proposed by Louis of Orléans. His anti-tax stance won him popular support, as did also his lavish distribution of Burgundian wine among influential Parisians. John began to be seen by many as a desirable alternative to Louis of Orléans as unofficial regent of France.

In July 1405, in a rare moment of sanity, Charles VI brought more princes into his council. Among them was John the Fearless, who came to Paris escorted by a thousand knights and squires. Anticipating a coup, Orléans withdrew from Paris to Melun, taking Queen Isabeau with him, and began assembling troops. He arranged for the ten-year-old dauphin, Louis, duke of Guyenne, to join him, but he was intercepted by John and brought back to Paris. 'The next day', writes the

chronicler Monstrelet, 'the rector and a large part of the University of
Paris came to pay their repects to the duke of Burgundy, and to thank
him publicly, with all humility, for his great love and affection towards
the king, the royal family, and the whole realm.'[2] John the Fearless and
Louis of Orléans seemed prepared to fight for control of the government, but they merely exchanged accusations before disbanding their
troops. In January 1406 John replaced his late father in the council of
regency that had been set up to rule France during Charles VI's
'absences'.[3]

A period of uneasy truce followed during which Duke John and Louis
of Orléans seemed to collaborate. In the summer, they were given parts
to play in a military campaign against the English: John was to attack
Calais and Louis to besiege Bordeaux, but neither achieved anything.
In September 1406 John was ordered by Charles VI to attack the English in Picardy, but he complained that funds promised to him by the
king had been sent instead to Louis. A royal decision to cancel the
Picardy campaign compounded John's frustration. He also had other
grievances. Whereas his father had drawn nearly half his revenues from
the French royal treasury, he himself received from it neither pension
nor gifts. Louis, on the other hand, was receiving funds which Philip
had once enjoyed. John also resented Louis's control of Luxemburg,
which blocked a possible expansion of Burgundian territory into the
Netherlands.[4]

In short, John had many reasons for wanting Louis of Orléans out of
the way. Contemporaries believed that a personal grudge also underlay
their enmity. Louis was a notorious womaniser who had allegedly tried
to rape John's wife, Margaret of Bavaria. It was also said that John had
accidentally stumbled on her portrait in a gallery where Louis displayed
portraits of his female conquests. Be that as it may, John now plotted
Louis's assassination. On 23 November 1407, as Louis was returning
from the queen's residence, he was set upon by a group of armed men.
They cleaved his skull, scattering his brains on the pavement, and cut
off a hand. 'Thus', wrote Nicolas de Baye, clerk of the Parlement 'he,
who was such a great and powerful lord, and to whom naturally, whenever there was no effective ruler, the government of this realm belonged,
in so brief a moment ended his days, hideously and shamefully.'[5]

An official enquiry established that the assassins had taken refuge in the Hôtel d'Artois, the Parisian residence of the duke of Burgundy. Though he attended Duke Louis's funeral, he soon afterwards admitted that he had instigated his murder. Many contemporaries were horrified. Not only had he broken an oath given to Louis only four days before, he had also not given him time to be shriven. Not everyone, however, was upset. Parisians hated Louis whom they blamed for heavy taxation. Duke John, on the other hand, was popular and powerful. From the historical standpoint, the assassination of the duke of Orléans has been described as one of the most important events in French history on a par with the Dreyfus affair. It inaugurated twelve years of internal strife, conflict and calamity which only ended on 10 September 1419, when John the Fearless was himself murdered on the bridge at Montereau.[6]

John the Fearless

After Louis of Orléans's funeral in 1407, John the Fearless retired to Bapaume, on the borders of Artois. He rewarded Raoul d'Anquetonville, the duke's principal assassin, with an annuity 'in consideration of notable services which ... [he] had rendered to the king and [the duke of Burgundy]'. But the murder was condemned by Charles VI. While John was formally excluded from the government, the dauphin Louis was handed over to the queen's custody. Duke John, however, was not ready to efface himself. In January 1408 he moved to Amiens while his brothers, Anthony and Philip, took up his cause with the dukes of Berry and Anjou. In February, John returned to Paris with an armed escort. He issued a manifesto, claiming that the assassination of Louis of Orléans had been an act of altruism. A lengthy proclamation read out in his name to the French court on 8 March justified the crime.[7] It accused Louis of high treason and of resorting 'to black magic in an effort to kill the king by some slow disorder which would not rouse suspicion of murder'. Next day, John the Fearless was formally pardoned by the king; but Louis's widow, children and many supporters continued to demand justice.

In July 1408 John the Fearless left Paris to put down a rebellion at Liège. It seemed at first that the dukes of Berry and Bourbon and other French princes would use his absence to topple him, but they did not do so. 'The government of France, divided between the royal dukes, a

vacillating and pleasure-loving queen, an insane king, the youthful
dauphin and various councillors, was irresolute, decrepit, half-hearted.'[8]
Apart from revoking John's pardon, they did nothing, and on 2 November the court fled secretly to Tours, clearing the way for the duke's
return to Paris on 28 November. This time he did not bring an army;
instead, he engaged a personal bodyguard of seven hundred men-at-
arms. He tried at the same time to lure the court back to Paris, a move
facilitated by the death on 4 December of Valentina Visconti, Louis of
Orléans's widow. Following a reconciliation of the parties early in
March 1409, the court returned to Paris. Duke John could feel reasonably secure, but Berry and Bourbon, egged on by the Grand Master, Jean
de Montaigu, continued to oppose him. In July, however, John formed
an alliance with Charles of Navarre. In September they arrested, supposedly for the good of the king and the kingdom, certain 'malefactors
and false traitors', including Montaigu, who had opposed the duke of
Burgundy over several years. On 17 October he was summarily beheaded
in front of a large crowd in Paris, an event soon followed by a purge of
royal officials.

In November 1409 John the Fearless gained effective control of Queen
Isabeau, the titular ruler of France, and, in December, he received the
dauphin's guardianship. A royal ordinance of 31 December, formally
authorising the dauphin to rule the kingdom during his father's
'absences', effectively gave the duke control of the government. As the
chronicler Monstrelet puts it: 'At that time the duke of Burgundy, being
in Paris, had more power than all the other princes, and affairs were carried on by him and his partisans. There is no doubt that this made
several people envious of him'.[9] Some princes of the blood, in fact, were
more than envious; they wanted John's removal. Among the duke's
enemies was Bernard VII, count of Armagnac, who gave his name to a
party formed at Gien on 15 April 1410. This provided for the mobilisation of an army 5,000 strong. In a manifesto, issued on 2 September, the
Armagnac princes announced their intention of rescuing the king and
dauphin from Burgundy's tyranny and of restoring them to power.

Both sides now mustered troops in and around Paris, but no fighting
ensued. In November peace was signed at Bicêtre, and a supposedly
non-party, non-princely government was set up, but it was doomed
from the start. Yet the royal council continued to be dominated by

Burgundians. John the Fearless drew support from the artisans of Paris. Having won them over by opposing taxation, he now presented himself as the champion of administrative reform. They apparently accepted the murder of Louis of Orléans and the execution of Jean de Montaigu as part of the fight against corruption. Although highly praised by the anonymous Bourgeois of Paris, John the Fearless took no chances. He retained his personal bodyguard and shut himself up in a strong tower that he had built in Paris.[10]

Opposition to John the Fearless was translated into military action during the summer of 1411. In May Charles, duke of Orléans, wrote to Charles VI, demanding the dismissal of certain Burgundian councillors. John, for his part, sought military aid from his Flemish subjects as well as from Lorraine, Brabant and Savoy. On 14 July, Charles of Orléans, Philippe count of Vertus and Jean count of Angoulême, issued a declaration at Jargeau in which they demanded that John be punished for his crimes. They accused him of breaking the peace of Chartres by his murder of Jean de Montaigu, of usurping the government, of holding the king and the dauphin in subjection, and of breaking the peace of Bicêtre by keeping his men in power. Denouncing him as a 'false disloyal traitor', the Armagnacs challenged him: 'we cause you to know', they said, 'that from this time on we shall harm you with all our power and in all the ways we can'.[11] Civil war now erupted in Picardy, Paris and Burgundy. The Armagnacs, after occupying Vermandois, raided towns close to territories belonging to John the Fearless or his brother, but they failed to follow up these attacks. John laid siege to Ham and, on 22 September, drew up his army at Montdidier while Charles of Orléans advanced to within a few miles of the town. For some days the rival armies faced each other without coming to blows. John then withdrew to Arras and the Armagnacs closed in on Paris, capturing Saint-Denis and Saint-Cloud.

The English government willingly took advantage of the civil war in France. In September 1411, an English embassy was sent to John the Fearless in order to arrange a marriage alliance between his daughter and Henry IV's eldest son. Meanwhile, a sizeable English force enabled the duke to join the king in Paris. On 3 October, Charles VI outlawed the dukes of Orléans and Bourbon, the count of Alençon and other Armagnac princes, and two days later he ordered all French towns to give free passage to John the Fearless and his troops. On 6 October the nobles of Artois and Picardy were ordered to take up arms for the duke, and, on 14 October, all royal vassals were summoned to fight the Armagnacs. Their banishment from the realm was proclaimed in Paris, and their excommunication pronounced at Notre-Dame. In early November, John the Fearless drove the Armagnacs out of Saint-Cloud and Saint-Denis and captured nearly all their strongholds in Picardy and around Paris. The year 1412 saw him at the height of his power. The king and queen, her brother Louis of Bavaria, and the king of Navarre all accepted him as the effective regent of France.

During the winter of 1411 the dukes of Berry and Orléans managed to repair their relations with England. In return for the offer of an enlarged Aquitaine, Henry IV agreed under a treaty, signed in May 1412, to send them 1000 men-at-arms and 3000 archers. The roles were now reversed. Assuming that of defender of the crown, John the Fearless, with the king and dauphin in tow, prepared a large-scale offensive against the 'enemies of the kingdom'. On 11 June a royal army laid siege to Bourges, but failed to capture it. The Armagnacs waited in vain for the English assistance they had been promised. As the bourgeoisie grumbled about the cost of these princely games, both sides came to terms. At Auxerre, on 12 August 1412, they renounced all foreign alliances. But no sooner had this agreement been signed than the English appeared. After landing in Normandy, they crossed the province, destroying apple orchards on the way, and reached Anjou. This was the first major *chevauchée* seen in France for thirty-two years. Suddenly realising the folly of invoking English aid, Charles of Orléans decided to send them home, but their leader, the duke of Clarence, only retired to Bordeaux in return for a substantial payment.

A new English invasion of France seemed imminent and Charles VI needed to prepare for it. Above all, he needed money to fund an army. John the Fearless persuaded him to call a meeting of the Estates-General of Languedoïl. They met at the Hôtel Saint-Pol in Paris in January 1413. The procedure was controlled by John the Fearless: each province and each estate within each province debated separately. The duke, meanwhile, posed as a great reformer. His spokesman, Simon de Saulx, made a speech in which he urged the need to tax the princes, to force officers of the crown to disgorge their ill-gotten wealth, and to weed out

incompetent government servants. A lengthy list of grievances submitted by the university of Paris accused the *gens de finance* – the king's
financial officers – of robbing the king. The reformists, in addition to
short-term measures, advocated a slimming down of government personnel, a reorganisation of justice and a closer monitoring of royal
accounts. Pending the findings of a commission set up by the dauphin,
all existing royal officials were suspended.

The meeting of the Estates-General generated a wave of unrest among
small Parisian tradesmen, artisans and journeymen. The most vocal
were the butchers, led by a slaughterman, Simon Le Coutelier, alias
Caboche. A riot, which broke out on 27 April, soon developed into a
mass movement. Thousands of armed Parisians marched on the Bastille
where the hated *prévôt des marchands*, Pierre des Essarts, had taken
refuge. The rioters, known as Cabochiens, gathered outside the
dauphin's residence and asked him to hand over fifty 'traitors'. Certain
leading figures of the court and government were arrested and imprisoned. The revolt proved embarrassing to John the Fearless, as
the leaders were his protégés and he alone, among the French princes,
was popular with the mob. His role in the uprising was at best
equivocal: he tried to curb the mob's worst excesses. A second revolt
on 22 May led to the arrest and imprisonment of the queen's brother,
Louis of Bavaria, and of several of her attendants and ladies-in-waiting.
Soon afterwards the *Ordonnance Cabochienne* was published. Despite
its name, this was not a revolutionary document but a detailed
programme of government reform containing 258 clauses. It was designed to make government cheaper and more efficient, but was never
implemented.[12]

One effect of the Parisian uprising was to turn the dauphin into a
staunch Armagnac, at least for the time being.[13] Charles VI, too, who
had regained his sanity for a time, offered his backing to the Armagnacs. They also gained the support of a growing number of moderates
in Paris. After coming to terms with the Armagnacs at Pontoise in
July, John the Fearless fled to the safety of Flanders. His enemies
issued a barrage of edicts and proclamations in the king's name. All
past edicts against the Armagnac princes were revoked. On 14 November Charles VI accused John of disobedience. The captains and
inhabitants of towns were ordered to deny him and his men access

and transit. By the end of 1413 he had been completely excluded from the government.

Duke John, however, was not yet beaten. Decisive as ever, he published letters, which he had allegedly received from the dauphin in December 1413, requesting his help against the Armagnacs, who were accused of holding him prisoner in the Louvre. On 23 January 1414, John left Lille for Paris. He collected an army 2000 strong which was joined at Compiègne by another led by his brother, Philip of Nevers. Soon afterwards they were reinforced by Burgundian cavalry. For a week in February the duke of Burgundy threatened Paris, but, as the government would neither fight nor talk, he had to withdraw. In April the government fought back. John resisted effectively as the king's army besieged Arras. On 4 September a new peace treaty was signed which has been described as 'a triumph of John the Fearless's duplicity', for it failed to settle any of the major differences. By using proctors, John kept open the possibility of disowning promises made in his name.[14]

Agincourt

In 1413 Henry V mounted the English throne. Young, warlike, ruthless and self-righteous, he tried to exact more concessions from the French government. As he received no satisfaction, he prepared for war. An army of 2000 men-at-arms and 6000 archers was transported across the Channel in fifteen hundred ships. On 14 August 1415 Henry laid siege to the port of Harfleur. Though well fortified and stoutly defended, it surrendered on 22 September. During the siege, dysentery swept through the English camp, killing off about a thousand men. Henry V also had to detach troops to garrison Harfleur. This left him with only 1000 men-at-arms and 5000 archers. He could have returned directly to England, but preferred to march north instead. After crossing the Somme near Amiens, he reached Péronne. Charles VI, meanwhile, raised an army of 6000 men-at-arms and 4500 archers. Remembering Crécy and Poitiers, the French had misgivings about engaging the English in battle, yet the king's council decided to do so. The decision was not unanimous. While the dukes of Alençon, Bourbon and Orléans wanted to fight, the constable, Charles d'Albret, and Marshal Boucicaut wanted to let Henry V go on his way so as to concentrate on recapturing Harfleur. In the absence of Charles VI, who was unfit to lead his army, and of John the Fearless, who had been refused a command, a form of collective leadership took charge. 'It was at this moment that France missed the presence and personal leadership of an inspiring king. The English on the other hand, had both.'[15]

Early on 25 October the French and English faced each other at Agincourt. Heavy rain had fallen the night before, making the ground muddy and slippery, hardly ideal fighting conditions for heavily armoured men-at-arms. Both sides stood still until 10 a.m., when the English advanced, stopping some 200 yards from the French. The English archers drove stakes into the ground to protect themselves from an enemy cavalry charge. Fighting began when the English archers began shooting. Under a deadly shower of arrows, the French men-at-arms charged, only to run into the English stakes. As some horses were impaled, others galloped away in fright, spreading panic among the French troops coming up behind. As the English line was narrower than theirs, the French men-at-arms had to close ranks as they attacked. Jostling each other, some slipped in the mud and fell. At this juncture, the English men-at-arms counter-attacked, soon to be joined by the archers, who, having used up their arrows, emerged from behind their stakes and finished off the French men-at-arms who lay on the ground with swords, axes, knives, daggers and the mallets they had used to drive in their stakes.[16]

The victorious English did not try to pursue the enemy after the battle. They had only a few horses left and were hampered by the large crowd of prisoners they had taken. After a brief pause to celebrate his victory, Henry V resumed his march on Calais. On 23 November, he returned to London. In the meantime, Bernard d'Armagnac, who had replaced Charles d'Albret (killed at Agincourt) as constable of France, tried unsuccessfully to retake Harfleur.[17] It was partly to relieve French naval pressure on the port that Henry V organised a new expedition to France. He landed in Normandy in August 1417 with an army 10,000 strong and began systematically to conquer the province: Caen, Alençon, Cherbourg, Evreux fell, as did Rouen after putting up a stout resistance. Pontoise followed on 31 July 1419. Paris next came under threat.[18]

The End of John the Fearless

The battle of Agincourt took a heavy toll of the Armagnac leadership yet made little impact on the domestic situation in France. The struggle for power between Burgundians and Armagnacs continued regardless. In November 1415 a large army under the duke of Burgundy threatened Paris from Lagny, but the Armagnac government stood firm. Its hand was strengthened by the death on 18 December of the Dauphin Louis, who had pursued a moderate policy of his own. Bernard, count of Armagnac, now became constable of France, dashing John the Fearless's hopes of regaining power. He accordingly withdrew from Lagny, hoping to profit from the marriage of his niece, Jacqueline of Bavaria, to the new dauphin, Jean, duke of Touraine. In November 1416 he formed an alliance with William, duke of Bavaria. They aimed to install the dauphin in Paris with the help of Queen Isabeau, but Bernard died on 4 April 1417, and was soon followed to the grave by Duke William. Duke John now turned to Henry V of England, whom he met at Calais in October 1416. Henry V, it seems, hoped to convert the duke into his ally and possibly his vassal. But even with English support, John's bid to regain power in France made little headway.

In 1417 the tide turned once more. In April John the Fearless issued a manifesto, charging the Armagnacs with all sorts of crime, including the murder of the two successive dauphins and the violation of past treaties. They were even accused of allowing Henry V's invasion of France and of helping to bring about the English victory at Agincourt. Promising to abolish or reduce taxes, John called on the king's subjects to join him against the Armagnacs. This marked, in effect, a return to civil war. Several important towns now fell to the duke, some without a blow. Others, like Lyon, remained firmly Armagnac. The Burgundian and Armagnac parties had supporters in almost every town so that the success of either party was usually the result of a struggle within the walls. Actual fighting in the summer of 1417 was confused, sporadic and indecisive.

In November 1417 John the Fearless pulled off another coup. He joined Queen Isabeau at Tours after luring her away from her Armagnac custodians. During the winter of 1417–18 she and the duke set up a government at Chartres, then at Troyes, in opposition to that of the dauphin Charles and Armagnacs in Paris. On 11 November the queen, writing to the towns, urged them to obey her and the duke, and on 10 January 1418 she authorised John to govern France in the king's name. On 16 February she abolished the Parlement and *Chambre des comptes* in Paris, replacing them by equivalent bodies in Troyes. The new government, staffed entirely by Burgundians, seized the king's revenues. By the spring of 1418 much of France had recognised the new Burgundian administration in Troyes.

On 28 May, under cover of specious peace talks, John the Fearless gained control of Paris. The dauphin fled to the Bastille in his nightshirt and was later carried off to Melun by Armagnac nobles. A reign of terror ensued in the capital. The count of Armagnac, the Chancellor of France and any Armagnacs who could be found were slaughtered in cold blood. On 14 July, once the turmoil had subsided, John the Fearless and Queen Isabeau returned to the capital in triumph. The duke controlled the king and the government. He disposed of ample funds and could issue letters and ordinances in Charles VI's name, yet his authority did not go unchallenged. He had to reckon with the fifteen-year-old dauphin, who assumed the title of regent, and also with Henry V, who claimed the crown of France and aimed to conquer the kingdom. A rival administration was created for the dauphin in parts of France that were loyal to him. It consisted of a Parlement at Poitiers, a *chambre des comptes* at Bourges and a second sovereign court at Toulouse. Thus in 1417–18 three powers competed for the political control of France: John, duke of Burgundy, the Dauphin Charles and Henry V of England.

The Bridge at Montereau

On 10 September 1419 John the Fearless was murdered by a group of Armagnacs on the bridge of Montereau. The Dauphin Charles was heavily implicated in the crime, which seems to have been committed by servants of the late Louis of Orléans. In July 1426 Jean de Poitiers, bishop of Valence, recalled a conversation with a friend, Robert le Maçon, shortly before the crime was committed. After speaking to the dauphin, le Maçon had fallen on his bed saying: 'Please God, my lord of Valence, that I were at Jerusalem without a penny or a stitch, and that

I had never seen this lord here, for I am very much afraid that he's badly advised, and that he'll do something today by which his kingdom and he himself will be lost.'[19] The consequences of the murder at Montereau did indeed prove disastrous for Charles. When King Francis I visited Dijon in 1521 a Carthusian friar showed him the skull of John the Fearless. Pointing to a gash made by the assassins, he explained: 'it was through this hole that the English entered France'.[20]

As news of the murder spread, a wave of anger swept through Paris. The university conveyed its sympathy to the duke's widow and offered to help her by means of 'sermons and letters missive'. The new duke of Burgundy, Philip the Good, allied with Henry V, who was about to marry Charles VI's daughter, Catherine. In May 1420 the two kings met at Troyes and signed a treaty that was sealed by the marriage. Charles VI recognised Henry as his son and heir, thereby repudiating his real son; the Dauphin Charles. Charles VI was allowed by the treaty to retain his crown for his lifetime, but Henry V was given charge of the government. He kept Normandy and his other French conquests as a kind of apanage. Following his marriage to Catherine on 2 June 1420, Henry V captured Sens, Montereau and Melun. On 1 December, he and Charles VI entered Paris. They were joyfully received by the inhabitants and, after attending a *Te Deum* at Notre-Dame, took up residence in the city, Henry at the Louvre and Charles VI at the Hôtel Saint-Pol. On 23 December the murderers of John the Fearless were condemned as traitors. The dauphin was banished from the kingdom and deprived of his right to the throne. Four days later, Henry V returned to England with his bride. The defence of Paris was entrusted to English captains. According to the chronicler, Chastellain, the city had become 'another London'.

France was now divided into three zones. The first was English, consisting mainly of Normandy and governed from Rouen. The administration remained more or less the same as before, retaining its French personnel. Only the defence of the province was entrusted exclusively to English garrisons posted in a scattering of castles. The people of Rouen accepted English rule if only because it suited their economic interests, but a majority of Norman noblemen left their estates to join the dauphin. The peasantry in general were hostile to the English. The second zone, a band of territory between the River Somme and the middle Loire, was ruled jointly by the English and Burgundians and governed from Paris, where the most important administrative institutions, including the Parlement, were based. The duke of Burgundy, however, was allowed exclusive control of his own patrimony, including Flanders, Artois and the duchy of Burgundy itself. The third zone was central and southern France, excluding English Guyenne, which remained loyal to the Dauphin Charles. He was soon to be derisively called 'the king of Bourges', for it was mainly in that city that he set up his administration. But Poitiers was the seat of his judicial administration, a Parlement being created there in September 1418. Many officials, who had been dismissed from their posts in the north by the Anglo-Burgundians, joined the dauphin's service. In theory at least, the 'kingdom of Bourges' was much wealthier than Lancastrian France and should have been able to mobilise and support a proportionately larger army, but the tax revenues did not always reach the dauphin's coffers. His years of exile were marred by poverty. A court gathered around him as he wandered from château to château. Being always short of money, he resorted to frequent devaluations of the currency. His greatest weakness, however, was his own fecklessness.

Early in 1420 the Dauphin Charles spent nearly five months securing his authority in Languedoc. On 22 March he defeated the English at Baugé, and on 8 May he reached an accord with the duke of Brittany. The estates of Languedoïl, meeting at Clermont on 18 May, voted Charles an *aide* of 800,000 *livres*. In June, he laid siege to Chartres and threatened Paris. Until the summer of 1421 he seemed active. He appeared at the head of his troops wearing full armour and was often seen by his subjects as he travelled across parts of France that were loyal to him. His entourage, decked in his colours of white, red and blue, projected an image of authority, while his device of an armoured hand clasping a sword and a banner, depicting St Michael slaying the dragon, showed resolve to fight the kingdom's enemies.

In June 1420 Henry V suddenly reappeared in France at the head of a powerful army. After meeting Philip the Good, the new duke of Burgundy, he entered Paris on 4 July. He then seized Dreux and other towns. In September he laid siege to Meaux and, in June 1422, he entered Compiègne and Senlis. As the Armagnacs were driven out of northern France, the dauphin seemed to lose interest in the war. He retired to the

Loire valley and ceased to appear among his troops. He seemed only interested in his marriage to Marie d'Anjou and in the day-to-day activities of his court. According to Pierre de Fenin, Charles's advisers 'kept him always away from his enemies as much as they could'.[21] They could not afford to lose their uncrowned king. Charles 'did not willingly arm himself and did not love war at all if he could avoid it', yet it does not follow that he was ineffective. If we are to believe Chastellain, he was subtle and quite inscrutable. As Vale points out, a fifteenth-century monarch did not have to fight to be effective. Fighting could be left to others.[22]

In the spring of 1422 Henry V fell seriously ill as he was marching on the Nivernais. He was carried in a litter to Vincennes, where he prepared to meet his Maker. He entrusted his infant son, the future Henry VI, to his brother, the duke of Bedford, and instructed him never to make peace with the dauphin without obtaining from him at least Normandy. Henry V wanted the duke of Burgundy to serve as his son's regent in France if he so wished; if not, Bedford was to do so. He advised the princes of his entourage never to forsake their alliance with Burgundy. Following Henry's death on 31 August, Philip the Good confirmed the treaty of Troyes, but declined the regency offered to him by Bedford, who consequently assumed it himself. On 19 September the mad and decrepit Charles VI returned to Paris from Senlis. He died on 21 October and was buried on 11 November at Saint-Denis. As his body was lowered into its grave, a herald called out: 'Long live Henry by the grace of God king of France and England!'[23]

5

From Bourges to Paris

Charles VII has had a generally bad press from historians. Always frail, he was a poor specimen of humanity with short legs, knobbly knees and an ungainly walk. He had a big head, a long nose, thick, sensual lips, a strong jaw and small furtive eyes. According to Chastellain, he was a 'loner', ever prone to worry, distrust and envy. Paranoid about assassination, he became distrustful of floors and bridges. In October 1422 the floor collapsed as he was holding court in a room at La Rochelle. Some of his companions were killed while Charles himself was bruised. Towards the end of his life he was plagued by ulcers, yet he was not devoid of qualities. Chastellain tells us that 'what he lacked in courage ... he gained in judgment'. Though timid and cautious, he was flexible and astute. He learnt to use faction as a means of serving his own ends. Without a standing army until 1445, he made skilful use of patronage to attain his objectives: he arranged marriages, offered positions at court, granted pensions and annuities and bribed shamelessly. He had charm, was well-read and a good latinist. Above all, he was devout. His pious gifts and religious observances were lavish. He heard two or three masses each day and state business was never allowed to interrupt his devotions. He trusted God, but also astrologers.[1]

At the start of his reign Charles VII was surrounded by favourites, all of them Armagnacs who had an interest in preventing a reconciliation between the king and the duke of Burgundy, but they were soon supplanted by the king's formidable mother-in-law, Yolanda of Aragon, who had set herself the task of defending Maine and Anjou – her son's inheritance – against the duke of Bedford. She wanted to promote a rapprochement between Charles VII and the duke of Burgundy, but, to achieve that, she needed to push aside the king's Armagnac councillors. With the backing of John V, duke of Brittany, Yolanda managed to get his brother, Arthur, count of Richemont, who was the brother-in-law of

Philip the Good, appointed as constable of France on 8 March 1425. The Armagnac faction tried to get rid of him, but Richemont gained the support of many towns and nobles at an assembly held in Bourges in June 1425. Charles VII announced that he intended henceforth to act on Richemont's advice, but he soon fell under the influence of Pierre de Giac, a former councillor of John the Fearless, who set about obstructing Richemont's efforts to reform the army, whereupon the constable allied with a group of nobles including Georges de La Trémoille. On 8 February 1427 Giac was kidnapped by a gang led by Richemont, summarily tried and drowned. Soon afterwards La Trémoille married Giac's widow. Richemont's triumph, however, was short-lived. La Trémoille took advantage of his frequent absences from court to win the king's favour. He consolidated his position by distributing largesse to courtiers. In August 1427 Richemont and other nobles planned to get rid of La Trémoille, but in September 1427 the duke of Brittany upset Charles VII by signing a treaty with Henry VI of England. Charles blamed Richemont for the duke's action and banished him from court.[2] According to Vale, Charles exploited faction to ensure his own survival: 'the ability to turn what might be considered a defeat to a profitable end could serve a prince in Charles's position well. He was ... permanently bound to no man'.[3]

If the king's policy of manipulating faction kept him in power, it was of little benefit to his kingdom. Richemont's banishment triggered a private war between him and La Trémoille that lasted five years and devastated Poitou. Elsewhere in France, the king's lieutenants pursued only their own private interests. Jean de Grailly, the lieutenant-general in Languedoc, used the province as a source of revenue which he kept largely to himself. His lieutenant, Guillaume de Champeaux, was equally corrupt. In Poitou and neighbouring provinces, the king's own captains behaved no better than robber barons. They imposed illegal tolls, minted false coin, murdered rivals, kidnapped heiresses, held peasants to ransom and raped their wives, and robbed travellers. The highest nobles were equally lawless. The count of Clermont, for example, caused Martin Gouge, bishop of Clermont and chancellor of France, to be imprisoned for months in spite of protests from king, pope and Parlement. In the end, the king had to pay his ransom.[4]

The 'kingdom of Bourges' was, in short, anarchical. Subsidies voted by the provincial estates were difficult to collect and often earmarked to settle debts. Unable to afford a standing army, Charles VII had to hire foreign mercenaries, but only for short campaigns.[5] He looked to diplomacy rather than force to drive the English out of France, sending out countless embassies, but his efforts to break up the Anglo-Burgundian alliance failed. The English, meanwhile, tightened their hold on northern France. Such forces as Charles VII was able to mobilise suffered two catastrophic defeats. On 31 July 1423 an army sent to open up communications between the 'kingdom of Bourges' and Champagne was cut to pieces by an Anglo-Burgundian force at Cravant, and in December the Burgundians got perilously close to Bourges by seizing La Charité-sur-Loire. An army 14,000 strong mobilised by Charles VII in May 1424 was almost wiped out at Verneuil on 17 August 1424 by a smaller, more effective, English army under Bedford.[6] Many French nobles were killed or captured. Charles VII reverted to his former state of apathy. Yet Bedford was unable to follow up his victory as he had to return to England to deal with a domestic crisis. Military operations languished until 1428 when the English resumed fighting in earnest. Pushing southwards, they laid siege to Orléans on 7 October.[7]

Joan of Arc

The story of Joan of Arc has acquired legendary status. One can easily take it for granted and overlook its extraordinary character. That a young peasant girl should assume the responsibility of driving the enemy out of France and ensure that her king is duly crowned at Reims beggars belief, yet that was Joan's achievement, and all that she got in return was a terrible death. The details of her story are too well known to need repeating here. We shall focus on the seemingly inglorious role of King Charles VII.

One day in 1425, the year in which the Burgundians attacked Domrémy, her native village in Lorraine, Joan heard voices of saints ordering her to go to the king and save the kingdom. She approached Robert de Baudricourt, the captain of the neighbouring town of Vaucouleurs, but it was only in 1429, after it had been besieged, that he took her seriously and provided her with an armed escort. She reached Chinon on 4 March where she was received by Charles VII, who had been forewarned of her coming. Not everyone at court was well disposed towards her. The chancellor, Regnaut de Chartres, archbishop of Reims, was suspicious of visionaries and prophets, especially if they were women. The church at the time was wary of mystics who claimed that they had a direct line to the Almighty. Joan was not alone of her kind. So Joan's presence at Chinon caused little surprise. She was examined by matrons who pronounced her to be a virgin (and therefore not in league with the devil) and by theologians who vouched for her orthodoxy. The Maid (or *La Pucelle*) was then given a suit of armour, horses, an armed escort and a white banner bearing the device 'Jesus Maria'. In addition to 'fans' who had followed her from Lorraine, she won the support of various captains and young noblemen, including the duc d'Alençon.[8]

On 29 April Joan managed to enter Orléans under the noses of the English who were besieging the city. This raised the morale of the garrison and of the inhabitants. Following a series of military actions, the English lifted the siege. News of this success spread like wildfire across France, eliciting praise from such luminaries as Jean Gerson and Christine de Pisan. More successes soon followed. Several towns in the Loire valley were recaptured, and on 18 June the English were defeated at Patay, some of their best captains being either killed or taken prisoner.[9] The morale of the English drooped and their hold on Normandy began to look precarious. The time seemed ripe for a royal offensive in that direction, but Joan wanted her '*gentil dauphin*', as she called Charles VII, to take the road to Reims so that he might become a fully-fledged monarch. Not everyone at court shared her ambition, for under French law Charles was already king, but Joan clung to the popular belief that a king needed to be anointed. Charles, it seems, shared this opinion. By commissioning the artist, Jean Fouquet, to adorn his copy of the *Grandes Chroniques* with several illuminations depicting the coronation of a king of France, he showed the importance he attached to that ceremony. Joan got her way. An army was assembled to escort the king to Reims, which lay inside Burgundian territory. The town of Auxerre refused to open its gates to the royal party and Troyes only did so after it had been threatened with a siege. Eventually, Charles entered Reims and on 17 July was anointed by Regnaut de Chartres, who was officiating for the first time in his own cathedral. The coronation service had to be improvised, for the royal insignia and crown were in English hands at Saint-Denis. Nor did Reims have a copy of Charles V's *Ordo*. A substitute crown and the last Capetian *Ordo* had to be used instead.[10] Several peers were also missing. The only absentee prelate was Pierre Cauchon, bishop of Beauvais, who was an English sympathiser. Alençon, the only lay peer present, represented the duke of Burgundy. Other peers were likewise represented by lesser fry. Joan of Arc, who stood beside the altar during the service, now took to calling Charles VII *'gentil roy'*. Once anointed, he could perform priestly functions. Four days after his coronation, he went to the shrine of Saint Marcoul at Corbeny and exercised his miraculous power of healing the sick. As his envoys to Pope Pius II later asserted, their master's healing power proved the sanctity of the royal house of France as well as his sovereignty over the church.[11]

In the meantime, fortune continued to smile on the king's arms. A number of towns within Burgundian territory fell into his hands, but Paris held firm and Charles decided to leave it alone after signing a truce with Philip the Good. The war now became a series of minor engagements aimed at defending or conquering various towns. On 24 May 1430 Joan of Arc was captured at Compiègne. Her captor, Jean de Luxembourg, a follower of the duke of Burgundy, sold her to the English. The university of Paris accused Joan of heresy and asked that she should be tried by the Inquisition. The court's president was bishop Pierre Cauchon in whose diocese Joan had been captured. As Beauvais was in royal hands, the court sat at Rouen where Cauchon was living under English protection. The trial began on 20 February 1431. The judges, made up of theologians and academics, regarded Joan as a witch who had used evil spells and communed with the devil. She was also regarded as a rebel because she claimed that God's commands had reached her directly without priestly intercession. The judges, however, followed correct procedures, as they did not wish to provoke complaints. Joan was questioned from 20 February until 15 March and an indictment containing seventy charges was extracted from her statements, but this was revised and the number of charges reduced to twelve. These were submitted to the university, and, in the meantime, an attempt was made to demolish Joan's pride. Torture was considered but ruled out, in order not to compromise the trial. On 23 May the university of Paris declared Joan guilty of idolatry, superstition, schism and heresy. Next day, she was taken to the cemetery of Saint-Ouen and her sentence read out to her. Faced by the spectre of being burnt alive, Joan abjured. She was sentenced to life imprisonment, but the English wanted her death, and Joan played into their hands by retracting her abjuration. Overjoyed, Cauchon could now pass sentence on Joan as a relapsed heretic. On 31 May she was handed over to the secular arm and burnt in Rouen's market square.[12]

Why did Charles VII fail to save Joan's life? It has been suggested that she was sacrificed for the sake of reconciliation with the duke of Burgundy, but she was not opposed to such a policy. She drew a clear distinction between England and Burgundy. Whenever she spoke of the English, she told them to quit France, but when she addressed the duke of Burgundy, she urged him to submit to his king. So how are we to explain Charles VII's inaction? Should he not have offered payment for Joan's release? This may not have crossed his mind, for her social status did not command a ransom: she was only a peasant, not a noblewoman. The king may also have suspected that the English would not release the Maid on any terms. An attempt to rescue her by force was also out of the question, for Rouen was too well defended.[13]

The Congress of Arras

The trial and execution of Joan of Arc were played out against a background of desultory warfare along the borders of Normandy, in Ile-de-France, Champagne and Nivernais. The English, under the duke of Bedford, were short of troops, and Philip the Good, duke of Burgundy, was reluctant to compromise his future by fighting an all out war. If Charles VII had made the effort, he might have succeeded in sweeping the enemy out of France, but he was indolent and his councillors were more interested in pursuing their own selfish ends. France was also exhausted and the prospect of raising and supporting an army of several thousand men was altogether too daunting for the king. He contented himself for the time being with holding on to the gains he had made during his march on Reims. From Troyes, Lagny and Compiègne his captains carried out forays as far as the walls of Paris.

Now that Charles VII had been crowned at Reims, he only needed to conquer Paris to think of himself as truly king of France, but the Parisians still supported the duke of Burgundy. The only option available to Charles, since he lacked the funds needed to build up an army, was to seek a reconciliation with Philip the Good. He had never completely severed relations with the duke. Philip was too much of a pragmatist to close the door on a reconciliation with the Valois monarch, but his alliance with England stood in the way. He had hoped that the treaty of Troyes would give him a hold on Henry VI similar to that which his father had exercised in respect of Charles VI, but this had not happened. Philip now calculated that he might stand a better chance of dominating Charles VII by ceding Paris to him. He feared that Charles might make a separate treaty with England, but did not want to ditch his English ally without good cause. The death in November 1432 of Philip's sister, Anne of Burgundy, who was the duke of Bedford's wife, helped to loosen his ties with England, for she had acted as peacemaker whenever Philip had quarrelled with Bedford. The duke's chancellor, Nicolas Rolin, also conveniently discovered that Henry VI had no right to the French throne. Charles VI had recognised Henry V as his heir presumptive following his marriage to Catherine of France, but, as Henry had predeceased his father-in-law, he had never acquired the French crown and therefore could not bequeath it. This argument conveniently released Philip from the oaths he had sworn at Troyes.[14]

At the court of Bourges the main opponent of a reconciliation with Burgundy was Georges de La Trémoille, but in June 1433 he fell into a trap laid by his enemies and only saved his life by promising to quit the court for good. This enabled Yolanda of Aragon, the king's mother-in-law, and the constable, Richemont, to recover their political influence, but talks between France and Burgundy yielded no positive results until early in 1435. Philip the Good had several meetings at Nevers with the French chancellor and constable which resulted in a preliminary accord. This was left to be finalised at an international congress to be held in Arras.

Philip the Good was more likely to acquire international prestige by restoring peace to Christendom than merely by patching up his quarrel with the king of France. He was backed by Pope Eugenius IV, who needed to stand up to the conciliarists meeting at Basle. The English delegation to the congress of Arras was led by Henry VI's elderly uncle, Henry, Cardinal Beaufort. Also present were a large number of prelates, princes of the blood, soldiers and ministers, each with a sizeable escort. French towns were represented, as was the university of Paris which had become used to throwing its weight politically. Anglo-French relations occupied the delegates during August 1435, but Bedford was unwilling to abandon the 'dual monarchy' which he had so resolutely defended for thirteen years. He offered to cede to Charles VII the provinces which he already held, but insisted on Henry VI remaining king of France and retaining Paris. What is more, he insisted on 'Charles of Valois', as he called him, doing homage to Henry for his half of the French kingdom. The French response was to demand the total evacuation of France by the English and their renunciation of the French crown. On 1 September Cardinal Beaufort broke off the talks and left Arras with his retinue.[15]

The uncompromising attitude of the English at Arras gave Philip the Good the pretext he needed to abandon his erstwhile ally. Peace with France was concluded on 20 September. On the surface it seemed wholly favourable to Burgundy. Philip was to keep the Mâconnais, the county of Auxerre, Ponthieu, and the county of Boulogne. He was also given several towns along the Somme. Finally, a special clause freed him during Charles VII's lifetime from the obligation of doing him homage for his French fiefs. This did not mean that Philip wished to be permanently independent of the French monarchy; only that he did not want to be the vassal of the man he blamed for his father's murder. As for Charles, he humiliated himself on the altar of reconciliation. While denying his own complicity in the murder, he promised to punish those responsible, to erect an expiatory monument and to set up masses for the victim's soul One of his councillors did public penance in Charles's name before the duke, but the king did gain some advantage from the deal. By effectively renouncing the leadership of the Armagnac faction, he completed his transformation into the king of France which his coronation at Reims had initiated.[16]

The peace of Arras encouraged the French to redouble their efforts against the English in Normandy. They recaptured Dieppe on 28 October 1435 and urged the peasants of the Pays de Caux to rise. They responded in large numbers and helped the king's troops to capture Harfleur, but they were defeated outside Caudebec, whereupon the English unleashed a devastating campaign of terror across the Pays de

Caux. The peace of Arras also made possible the reconquest of the Ile-de-France. In February 1436 the French under Richemont blockaded Paris by controlling the rivers that carried its supplies. On 13 April the constable entered the capital with the help of Burgundians within the city. Fearing an English counter-offensive, he planted garrisons in various fortresses of the Ile-de-France. The recovery of Paris sealed the triumph of the house of Valois and Charles VII lost no time in informing his subjects by a wide distribution of official bulletins. The Lancastrian dream was over, yet the English still occupied Normandy, part of Maine and of Guyenne.[17]

In 1437 a twofold offensive by the French in Normandy and Guyenne led to the recapture of various towns, including Pontoise. Charles VII's forces concentrated their efforts on capturing Montereau and Meaux, but as yet the king failed to curb the depredations of bands of freebooters who terrorised large areas of northern France. They were known as *écorcheurs* (flayers) because they would strip peasants down to the shirts on their backs. Jean Jouvenel des Ursins, bishop of Beauvais, in his epistle *Loquar in tribulatione*, compared the kingdom to a cadaver. He urged Charles VII to leave his châteaux in the Loire valley and reaffirm his authority by moving to Paris. The king, it seems, heard this appeal. On 12 November 1437 he made his entry into Paris wearing a full suit of armour and mounted on a fine steed covered with blue velvet strewn with gold fleur-de-lys. Beside him rode the first esquire of the stable carrying the king's crowned helm. Another carried his sword. An escort of archers surrounded the king, who was followed by the dauphin and other princes and nobles. At the rear of the procession came the army. At the gate to the city, Charles VII was offered its keys by the mayor as a token of its obedience. He then processed through the streets under a blue canopy adorned with fleur-de-lys. As usual a number of *tableaux vivants*, mostly depicting religious subjects, were performed along the processional route leading to the cathedral of Notre-Dame, where a service of thanksgiving was celebrated.

In 1441 John Talbot, the best English captain of the day, was driven out of Pontoise. A campaign by the duke of Somerset in Normandy in 1443 yielded few results. On 28 May 1444 truces signed at Tours brought the Anglo-French conflict to a temporary halt.[18]

Charles VII's Private Life

The peace of Arras and the recovery of Paris appear to have given Charles VII a new sense of purpose. He regulated his timetable and worked punctually with his councillors. He also took part in some military campaigns. Yet he continued to spend much of his time in the Loire valley amidst his favourites. The queen, Marie d'Anjou, was a feeble creature by comparison with her mother, Yolanda, who died in 1442. She appears to have lost control of Charles who suddenly turned to a life of pleasure and debauchery. A Milanese ambassador reported that 'the king of France is entirely ruled by women'. In 1444 he spent several months at Nancy taking part in sumptuous festivities among a brilliant display of chivalry. It was here that he fell in love with Agnes Sorel, the beautiful daughter of the sire de Coudun, who soon became his mistress. She was showered with gifts, pensions and lands. Agnes gave the king four daughters before she died on 9 February 1450. She was then replaced in the king's affections by her cousin, Antoinette de Maignelais, who remained his *maîtresse en titre* till the end of the reign. Both Agnes and Antoinette were politically influential. It was thanks to Agnes that a lesser nobleman, Pierre de Brézé, became Charles VII's favourite. Along with the counts of Foix and Tancarville, he managed more or less to drive the Angevins from court. René d'Anjou retired to his domains, his son, the duke of Calabria, left to govern Lorraine, and Charles d'Anjou, who had been the king's favourite for a decade, ceased to attend the council regularly. The palace revolution, however, did not have unfortunate consequences, for the majority of royal councillors were men of ability and loyalty who staunchly defended the king's prerogatives.[19]

The Pragmatic Sanction of Bourges

The church was a dominant component of French society in the Middle Ages and its relationship to the crown was a matter of great political importance. 'You are not only a lay person but a prelate, the first in your kingdom after the pope, the right hand of the church.' Thus did Jean Jouvenel des Ursins address Charles VII and with reason, for the king played a major role in the affairs of the French church. One of his main contributions was the ordinance known as the Pragmatic Sanction of

Bourges, which sought to regulate the church's allegiance to king and pope. It marked an important shift away from submission to the papacy towards a more independent or 'Gallican' position.

In the fifteenth century the Holy See levied taxes from the French church and claimed the right to appoint to its more important benefices. In order to maintain a level of subsistence consistent with its dignity, the French clergy clamoured for a reduction of papal taxation. It also asked for the suppression of abuses such as *commendams* and pluralism, the restoration of canonical elections and the appointment to benefices of worthy men. The onus of bringing about such reforms rested initially on the general council of the church, which the papacy consistently opposed as threatening its own authority. Pope Eugenius IV tried to dissolve the council which met at Basle in 1431, but eventually he had to accept it, only to be deposed by the council in 1438.[20] Claiming superiority over the pope in matters of faith and discipline, the fathers at Basle enacted a number of reforms and asked Charles VII to implement them in his kingdom. An assembly of the French clergy, meeting in his presence in Bourges in June, endorsed the Basle decrees with certain modifications tailored to French needs. The outcome was the Pragmatic Sanction.

After denouncing abuses committed or tolerated by the Holy See, the ordinance affirmed the council's supremacy in matters of faith and discipline, and endorsed the obligation for a council to meet every ten years. In the wake of several disciplinary clauses, the Sanction set about reducing to a minimum the pope's rights regarding ecclesiastical benefices and trials. Bishops and abbots were henceforth to be elected by chapters and convents. The pope was no longer to reserve the collation to benefices or to impose his own candidates by means of 'reservations'. He was forbidden to create canonries where the number had been fixed; nor was he to consecrate a bishop unless he was in Rome at the time of his election. In this event, the bishop was required to swear obedience thereafter to his immediate superior. Annates – a papal tax on the first year's revenues of a benefice – were abolished in principle. The pope was denied the right to judge lawsuits on appeal unless all intermediate jurisdictions had been exhausted, but the Sanction did make some concessions to Eugenius IV whom Charles VII did not wish to alienate completely. He was allowed to retain one fifth of the taxes previously levied, but only for his lifetime; he also retained a personal entitlement to the usual reservations.[21]

The papacy did not like the Pragmatic Sanction and tried consistently from 1438 onwards to have it rescinded. This suited the king well. He could use the Sanction to put pressure on the pope by either suspending it or reviving it. The Sanction, moreover, did not rule out royal interference in the day-to-day affairs of the French church. The king was allowed to put forward 'benign and well-intentioned solicitations' in support of candidates for benefices, provided they were deemed worthy. Charles VII, in fact, flouted the Sanction repeatedly. In 1445 Jouvenel des Ursins accused him of allowing Eugenius IV to abuse 'reservations' and 'provisions'. For his part, the pope acceded to requests from the king in favour of his protégés. Thus he conferred the see of Carcassonne on the king's councillor, Jean d'Etampes whose election had been opposed by the chapter. In 1439 Charles VII upheld a bishop elected by the chapter of Angers, yet in 1447 he persuaded the pope to nominate a bishop who had been rejected by the chapter of Meaux.[22]

From 1438 until 1516 the church in France was governed in theory by the Pragmatic Sanction, but it could not be strictly applied because the church lacked the cohesion needed to withstand external pressure. Within a short time electoral freedom succumbed to force and bribery. Frequent disputes arose and lawsuits flooded into the Parlement of Paris. The church displayed 'an overflow of personal or collective selfishness, a state of universal and permanent war'.[23] In these circumstances it was easy for the monarchy to determine the outcome of episcopal elections. From 1438 the royal attitude seems to have been to invoke the Pragmatic Sanction if it was profitable; to ignore it if it was not.[24]

Jacques Coeur

Charles VII was short of money for much of his reign. It has been claimed that in 1439 the Estates-General, realising his need for a standing army, allowed him to raise a *taille* on his own authority alone. This, however, is a misconception. The vote of a *taille* in 1439 was no different from any previous grant by the estates. There is no evidence that the estates requested the military reforms subsequently carried out by the king. He planned to call another meeting in 1440, but had to put it off following the outbreak of a revolt, called the 'Praguerie', yet he continued to levy the tax. Towards the end of the reign it was bringing to the crown 1.2 million *livres* per annum, a sum far in excess of the revenue from the domain, which did not rise above 50,000 *livres*. This reflected a serious crisis in the rural economy. The idea has also been advanced that Charles VII still needed consent to taxation from estates which continued to meet in certain provinces. This is true, but after 1450 more than half the provinces had no estates at all. The crown allowed them to vanish simply by not calling them. By the end of the reign only Normandy, Languedoc, Dauphiné and a few counties in the south and centre had more or less regular estates. They became known as *pays d'états*.

In addition to taxation, kings of France in the late Middle Ages resorted to loans. Charles VII borrowed from Jacques Coeur, the son of a furrier of Bourges.[25] After working in the local mint in the 1420s, Coeur had travelled to the Levant only to be shipwrecked in Corsica on the return leg and ransomed. He then thought of developing trade between France and the Levant and set up goods depots in various parts of Europe. With an interest in cloth, wool, leather, grain and arms, Coeur commissioned a number of armed ships, and after operating from Montpellier, switched his maritime activities to Marseille. Spices, cotton and silks imported from Alexandria were carried up the Rhône or overland to Bourges, Paris and Bruges. The royal court was a great outlet for Coeur's goods. As the king's *argentier*, an office which he acquired in 1440, he ran a vast bazaar providing the court with all its needs from ostrich feathers to suits of armour. His 'pawnshop' was permanently in Tours, while he himself accompanied the king on his travels. He also carried out financial and diplomatic missions for Charles VII.

Jacques Coeur was also a banker. He raised capital by investing in the silver mines of the Lyonnais and by currency speculation. In 1447 he was appointed visitor-general of the *gabelles*, thereby gaining control of the salt trade in the Midi and Lyonnais. He increased the tax yield, but probably took the largest share for himself. He certainly used part of the proceeds to build up his fleet of galleys. Like other rich commoners, Coeur dreamt of enhancing his social status by investing in land. His house in Bourges bears witness to his luxurious life-style. But Coeur attracted envy and enmity, particularly among his debtors. Jean

Jouvenel des Ursins accused him of driving a thousand honest merchants out of business and judged him no better than a thief. Courtiers felt humiliated when Coeur purchased their lands or lent them money.[26]

In 1451 Coeur was accused of poisoning Agnes Sorel, the king's mistress. Arrested on 31 July, he was thrown into prison and remained there untried for three years. Charles VII showed him neither gratitude nor justice. On 29 May 1453 he was found guilty of *lèse-majesté* and other crimes, but the charge of poisoning Agnes Sorel was dropped. Coeur's goods were confiscated. Thanks to the intercession of Pope Nicholas V, he was not sentenced to death, but ordered to do penance instead, to pay the ransom of a Christian slave held by the Saracens and to restore 100,000 *écus* to the king. Banished from the kingdom for good, Coeur fled to Rome where Pope Calixtus III chose him to lead a crusade against the Turks.[27] He died at Chios in November 1456.

The Praguerie

Both before and after his coronation at Reims, Charles VII had to deal with a number of important domestic issues. Despite the king's many failings of character, his reign did produce some major reforms which suggest that he may have been more effective than his critics would have us believe. He was also fairly successful in dealing with a powerful and turbulent nobility.

In 1437 Jean d'Alençon, Charles de Bourbon, Jean IV d'Armagnac, princes who had been loyal hitherto, plotted to remove two of the king's councillors, Charles du Maine and the constable, Richemont. The plot was nipped in the bud, but was the prelude of a more serious revolt three years later. Early in October 1439 the Estates-General, meeting at Orleans, denounced pillaging by the *écorcheurs*. The king responded by issuing, on 2 November, an ordinance for the reform of the army, but its application was blocked by princes, led by Bourbon, who did not wish military recruitment to be monopolised by the king and by Richemont. While claiming to be defenders of the 'public weal', the princes were essentially selfish. They were soon joined by Dunois, who feared that the king would not demand the release of Charles d'Orléans from captivity during his talks with the English, and by La Trémoille, who was keen to settle old scores with Richemont. Even the king's son,

Louis, who had been ordered to apply the military ordinance in Poitou, resented the fact that he had not yet been given Dauphiné, although he had reached the age of seventeen.[28]

The revolt, which began in February 1440 at Niort, became known as the *Praguerie* by analogy with recent civil unrest in Bohemia. The rebels planned to expel Richemont from the government, place the king in tutelage, and to hand over effective power to the dauphin and his allies. Alençon even sought the co-operation of the English commander in Guyenne. Charles VII, however, reacted promptly. After recovering Melle, Saint-Maixent and Niort, he pursued the rebels as they retreated towards the Bourbonnais. The local nobility refused to join Bourbon, and towns in the Auvergne shut their gates against him. As Alençon and Bourbon laid siege to Montferrand, Charles received an offer from the duke of Burgundy to mediate with the rebels. Peace talks ensued in which the king insisted on the rebels disbanding their troops for 'all the war of the said kingdom belongs to the king and his officers, and to none other, and there is no one so great in the said kingdom that can levy or retain troops without the authority, commission and command of the king'.[29] The dauphin received Dauphiné along with a pension. Bourbon and Alençon retired to their lordships.

Military Reform

To end the chaos caused by bands of soldiers terrorising the kingdom, Charles VII took a number of important measures. On the one hand, he tried to wean the soldiers from their disorderly ways by assigning them to garrisons close to regions still under foreign domination; on the other, he sought to sever their ties to the great nobles and to attach them exclusively to his service. Thirdly, in 1445–46, Charles selected a number of troops from the general mass and formed them into units known as the *compagnies d'ordonnance*. Each company consisted of one hundred *lances* and each *lance* of one mounted and fully armoured man-at-arms and five attendants (three archers and 2 *coutiliers*) who were also mounted. In all, the king's army consisted of 7200 troops made up of 1800 men-at-arms, 3,600 archers and 1,800 *coutiliers*. Following the truces with Burgundy of 1444, the king did not disband them, as was normal practice: he distributed the companies among various regions, and put the cost of their upkeep on the shoulders of the inhabitants.

In addition to setting up the *compagnies d'ordonnance*, Charles VII tried to improve the quality of his infantry by creating a corps of *francs-archers*, men trained in the use of the bow and crossbow. They were allowed to live at home in peacetime, but were expected to drill regularly and to be ready for action at any time. In return, they were exempted from the direct tax or *taille* – hence their name. Each was paid 4 francs per month while on active duty. But these troops proved disappointing: they were slow to assemble and inclined to desert when the going was rough. The reign of Charles VII was also marked by the development of a more effective artillery. Gaspard and Jean Bureau produced cannon which were more mobile, more accurate and safer for those who used them. The use of iron for cannon-balls instead of stone became frequent in the second half of the reign.[30]

The Expulsion of the English

In August 1449 Charles VII broke the truce with England by invading Normandy.[31] The explanation usually given for this action is that a mercenary captain in English pay had captured the stronghold of Fougères near the Breton border, but a more important cause probably was an alleged attempt by the English to detach Francis I, duke of Brittany, and his brother, Gilles, lord of Champtacé, from their French allegiance. To Charles VII and his advisers, Brittany's obedience to the crown of France was of paramount importance. There was an influential group of Bretons at the French court, including Richemont. By attempting to withdraw Brittany from its French allegiance, England incurred the hostility of those lords who owed their political power and pensions to the French king.[32] Between August 1449 and August 1450 French armies pushed into Normandy from three directions capturing many towns. All contemporary sources speak highly of the excellent discipline and equipment of the royal troops and of their unusual punctiliousness in paying for their victuals. Charles VII regrouped his army outside Rouen, which the English surrendered on 4 November. Despite the late season, the campaign continued, leading to the capture of the Channel ports of Harfleur and Honfleur. Henry VI sent 5000 reinforcements to

Cherbourg in March 1450, but they were crushed at Formigny on 15 April. The reconquest of Normandy was completed by the capture of Caen on 1 July and of Cherbourg on 12 August. In the summer of 1451 Charles VII assembled a large army under the command of Dunois and sent it to reconquer Guyenne. Bordeaux capitulated on 23 June and Bayonne on 20 August. An English army, led by Talbot, managed to reoccupy Bordeaux on 23 October, but the English were defeated at Castillon on 17 July 1453, Talbot and his son being among the dead. After another siege by the French, Bordeaux surrendered on 19 October completing the conquest of Guyenne.

The reduction of Normandy and the conquest of Guyenne were much admired by contemporaries. The churchman and historian, Thomas Basin praised Charles VII for accomplishing so much within his relatively limited means. 'It was with only 1500 lances', he writes, 'that he brought to a conclusion this important and difficult war without calling urgently and forcefully on the armed services of the nobles knowing that a long series of battles had left them poverty-stricken. Many of them, however, joined him spontaneously and without any pressure out of affection for him.'[33] But the conquests of Normandy and Guyenne cost a great deal of money. By asserting his sovereign rights over Brittany, Normandy and Guyenne, Charles VII not only served the crown's interests, but also those of his servants in government. Military force alone did not suffice to hold on to the reconquered provinces. Without the active support of the Norman and Gascon nobility the reconquest would have been much delayed. 'Bribery was an alternative, sometimes a supplement, to military force'. The English made the king pay for going away. The conquests also had to be retained. Writing to James II of Scotland in January 1457, Charles VII observed that he now had to meet the additional cost of watching the coastline and keeping a standing army in Normandy and Gascony.

Once the English had lost all their French possessions, except Calais, one might have expected the *compagnies d'ordonnance* to be disbanded. Some Frenchmen advocated this course of action. Thomas Basin, for example, regarded a standing army as an instrument of tyranny. He also thought it was useless, since the king had the right to mobilise a large force of nobles and their dependents whenever the need arose. Robert Blondel believed that he should avoid using foreign mercenaries by ensuring that the children of nobles and well-to-do people in the towns and countryside were trained in the use of arms, but these suggestions were not followed by the crown. The army created by Charles VII became in effect a standing army which remained roughly the same until 1470. Thereafter it grew rapidly in size.

On 15 April 1454 Charles VII published an ordinance on the administration of justice which rounded off the process of restoring and reunifying the central administration of the kingdom. In 1436, after the reconquest of Paris, a public announcement had been made to the effect that the Parlement and the *Chambre des comptes*, which had been in Poitiers and Bourges respectively, would henceforth be based in the royal palace on the Ile de la Cité, where they had been under the king's predecessors. Twelve Burgundian members were retained under the terms of the peace of Arras, but this did not weaken the monarchy since all the *parlementaires* in 1436 upheld the crown's sovereign rights. However, the Parlement did not recover its 'accustomed form', numbers and organisation until now. The flood of lawsuits, which was symptomatic of the recovery of the kingdom, necessitated a few innovations, notably the division of the *Chambre des enquêtes* into two courts and additional personnel. The ordinance also provided for a clarification and speeding up of legal procedure by launching the codification of customs, an enormous task only to be completed in the sixteenth century.[34]

The Rehabilitation of Joan of Arc

Charles VII could not allow Joan of Arc's condemnation to stand, for it implied that a witch had got him the throne, but this could not be done until he had regained control of Paris and of Rouen where the trial records were kept. He also needed the blessing of the Holy See, for the tribunal that had judged Joan had been set up by the papal inquisitor. It was not until 15 February 1450 that Guillaume Bouillé, a doctor of the university of Paris, was ordered by the king to enquire into the 'faults and abuses' committed by Joan's judges and assessors some twenty years earlier. The enquiry concluded that she should be cleared of heresy and sorcery for the sake of the king's honour. Most witnesses denounced the English for attempting to dishonour Charles VII's title by making him guilty of heresy by association. In 1455 Joan's mother and brothers petitioned Pope Calixtus III to repair the injustice done to her. He responded by appointing three eminent churchmen in France, who cited the inquisitor and promoter of criminal cases in the see of Beauvais to come before them. On 7 July 1456 Joan's condemnation was annulled. She was said to have incurred 'neither mark of infamy nor blemish', but all discussion of her supernatural experiences was omitted. The judges focused instead on judicial technicalities. Although Joan had been sentenced as a relapsed heretic and excommunicate, she had been wrongly allowed on the morning of her execution to confess her sins and to take communion. Her sentence was therefore annulled as invalid, but nothing was said about her orthodoxy. Her relatives received no damages and steps were even taken to prevent a cult of Joan from being established. No 'images or epitaphs' were to be set up in Rouen or elsewhere. Nor was any penalty exacted from her judges and assessors. Charles VII was the main beneficiary of Joan's rehabilitation: it washed his crown clean of the smirch of heresy and witchcraft.[35]

The Treason of Jean d'Alençon

Jean II duc d'Alençon, who had taken part in the *Praguerie* of 1440, became convinced that Charles VII was persecuting him. He believed that the king's mind had been poisoned against him by Charles of Anjou, comte du Maine. Following the *Praguerie*, Alençon had been temporarily deprived of his pension of 12,000 *livres*. He claimed that it was halved when restored. Another of his grievances was the king's refusal to help him recover Fougères which he had been forced to pledge to the duke of Brittany after his capture at Verneuil in 1424. In 1455 Alençon approached Henry VI and Richard, duke of York, in order to arrange another English invasion of Normandy, but the English seemed uninterested, and Alençon's plot was betrayed by one of his tenants.[36]

On 27 May 1456 Alençon was arrested and charged with treason. Charles VII decided to have him tried by the Parlement, by the peers of the realm and by members of the king's council. This *lit de justice*, which met at Vendôme, set the precedent for future trials of peers of France. As Alençon was a member of the Order of the Golden Fleece, Philip the Good was invited at short notice to attend, but declined. Chastellain believed that Charles VII 'intended to frighten the duke of Burgundy,

whom he maintained was a rebel'.[37] Vain attempts were made during
the trial to implicate Philip in Alençon's treason. On 10 October 1458
Alençon was found guilty and sentenced to death, but the king commuted the sentence to imprisonment during his pleasure. The duke lost
his peerage, lands and movables. Alençon, Verneuil and Domfront were
annexed to the royal domain.[38]

Jean Fouquet

The *lit de justice* of 1458 is the subject of a famous miniature by Jean
Fouquet, now universally recognised as one of the outstanding artists of
the fifteenth century. It is the frontispiece of a French edition of Boccaccio's *De Casibus* which describes the workings of Fortune from Adam
and Eve to John the Good. The miniature shows the king presiding over
the assembled peers of France, who sit on benches forming an octagon
beneath the throne, as sentence is passed on Alençon. It evokes not only
the fall from grace of a once great nobleman, but also the king's
triumphant elevation. Mainly known for miniatures illustrating a
number of books of hours and historical books, Fouquet also painted
wonderfully lifelike portraits of Charles VII and members of his court.
A native of Tours, he travelled to Italy in the 1440s taking with him a
portrait of the king as a gift to Pope Eugenius IV, whose likeness he also
captured in paint. Following his return to France, he became associated
with the royal family. He painted portraits of Mary of Anjou, the so-
called 'queen without glory', of Etienne Chevalier, one of four *trésoriers
de France*, and of the chancellor, Guillaume Jouvenel des Ursins. An
Adoration of the Magi shows Charles VII kneeling, surrounded by his
Scottish guard wearing his white, green and red livery. Members of the
royal administration who commissioned works by Fouquet included
the financier, Jean Bureau, who, with his brother Gaspard, created the
new French artillery, and Simon de Varye, the future controller of the
king's stables. By far the best known of Fouquet's works is the set of
forty-five miniatures for the devotional book, known as *Les Heures
d'Étienne Chevalier* (now at the Musée Condé at Chantilly) in which
contemporary French countryside, buildings and people are used to
bring to life biblical stories. Fouquet's art serves to remind us that the
court of Charles VII, though less magnificent than its Burgundian

counterpart, was none the less able to offer employment to an artist of international importance.[39]

Charles VII and the Dauphin

In February 1451 the Dauphin Louis, was accused of 'meddling with the affairs of Jacques Coeur'. He and his father became estranged in 1440 at the time of the *Praguerie*, but they did not fall out completely until 1451, when Louis married Charlotte, the daughter of the duke of Savoy, without paternal consent.[40] Louis was keen to gain a foothold in Savoy where he might mount an operation to gain a lordship in Italy. Charles VII, for his part, wanted to secure the future of his dynasty. He feared that Charlotte, who was only twelve, might not live long enough to give the dauphin an heir. In 1452 Louis was deprived of his pension; and, when he complained of 'evil reports' reaching Charles VII, the last of his lands in France were taken from him. At the same time, the king put pressure on the duke of Savoy to abandon Louis. It was rumoured that Charles intended to disinherit the dauphin in favour of his brother.

Louis sent several embassies to the king. He declared himself ready to obey him, but laid down two conditions: he refused to return to court or to abandon any of his servants. Frightened by the prospect of a French invasion, the duke of Savoy repudiated the dauphin in October. A royal army marched on Dauphiné, but after learning that the English had landed in Bordeaux, it headed for Guyenne instead. The dauphin wrote to his father, offering his services, but in rejecting them Charles VII issued a manifesto in which he denounced his son's 'foolish enterprises'. Louis now joined his uncle, King René of Anjou, in an Italian adventure. While René aimed to reconquer Naples, Louis threatened Genoa, but he was soon persuaded to return to Dauphiné. By the beginning of 1454, with the English out of Guyenne, Charles VII was free to deal with his son. In December 1455, as the king moved to the Bourbonnais with an army, Louis offered to obey him on the same terms as before, but the king had lost patience. The chancellor told the dauphin's envoy: 'This affair has lasted long enough. His Majesty means to see the end of it.' After further exchanges, the chancellor warned Louis that, unless he returned to court unconditionally, the king would proceed against his evil councillors. The dauphin's response was to seek the protection of his uncle, Philip the Good, duke of Burgundy.

On 30 August 1456, as Antoine de Chabannes was about to invade Dauphiné for the king, Louis fled to Burgundy with fifty companions. Next day, he wrote to his father from Saint-Claude, saying that he planned to join Philip on a crusade against the Turks. He expressed the hope that the duke would reconcile him to his father 'the thing which I most desire in the world'. Writing to Chabannes, Charles VII blamed the bastard of Armagnac and Jean de Garguesalle for his son's flight. On 22 December the dauphin wrote to his father, asking for Dauphiné, for a large pension, and for a pardon, but he still refused to return to court. On 8 April 1457 Charles VII resumed the administration of Dauphiné, revoking all his son's grants, yet he was still hoping for a reconciliation. On 9 March 1461 the Milanese envoy at Genappe reported: 'the dauphin has been in close negotiations about reconciling himself with the king of France ... and I fear an agreement will be reached on the part of the king of France, because he is a sick old man, and to an aged father the recovery of a son is a great consolation'. Charles VII's health was failing. He had a leg ulcer as well as a mouth infection which prevented him from eating. Negotiations for a reconciliation continued until March 1461, when Louis's terms were conveyed to his father at Bourges. He asked Charles VII to forget the past and to provide him with a lordship which would enable him to subsist, but the king continued to demand Louis's return to court. Although the dauphin was desperately hard up and his relations with Philip the Good were under strain, he remained in Flanders.[41] He was never to see his father again. Charles VII died at Mehun-sur-Yèvre on 22 July 1461.[42]

6

The 'Universal Spider'

On 17 July 1461, as news reached the Dauphin Louis of his father's rapidly failing health, he moved from Genappe to Avesnes on the French border and instructed his followers to prepare to join him in Champagne. A large military escort was raised for him by Philip the Good, duke of Burgundy, who happily assumed the role of protector of the next king of France.[1] Following Charles VII's death, many French lords and prelates, representatives of the Parlement and university of Paris, and numerous captains and office-holders converged on Avesnes to do obeisance to Louis. Early in August, he set off for Reims. The cost of his coronation and attendant festivities was borne by Philip the Good who entered the city first with a suite of 4000 people. He also brought with him 140 wagons filled with gold coins, precious plate and barrels of wine. Herds of oxen and flocks of sheep, intended as food for the banquets, trailed behind. Philip's nobles were dazzlingly attired in cloth of gold and silver. Louis XI's coronation, on 15 August, was directed by the duke of Burgundy in his capacity as senior peer of France. In Paris, as in Reims, Philip was allowed to enter first, and for a month and a half he treated the inhabitants to festivities and tournaments.[2] He also showered them with gifts. However, Louis soon showed that he intended to be master in his own house.

At the coronation banquet, Philip the Good urged the new king of France to forgive his enemies, which Louis promised to do with a few exceptions, but in the event he proved far more vindictive. He offered large rewards for the capture of Antoine de Chabannes and Pierre de Brézé, who had taken flight, and he dismissed a large number of Charles VII's chief ministers and councillors. Two of the most famous, Guillaume Cousinot and Etienne Chevalier, were imprisoned. As offices fell vacant, Louis rewarded the men who had accompanied him from Genappe. Thus did Jean de Lescun, the so-called 'bastard of Armagnac', become count of Comminges, marshal of France, first chamberlain, lieutenant-general in Guyenne and governor of Dauphiné. Former grooms of Louis became *baillis* and *sénéchaux*. Pierre de Morvilliers, who had been expelled from the Parlement under Charles VII, became chancellor of France. Yet not all of the late king's servants were sacked. The Parlement was more or less spared. The Bureau brothers remained in favour as did Tristan Lermite, who had served Charles VII as *prévôt des maréchaux.*

Louis, moreover, soon saw the error of his ways. He set free de Brézé, Cousinot and Chevalier, restored Guillaume Jouvenel des Ursins to the chancellorship, and appointed Antoine de Chabannes as his chief captain. In short, most of the surviving servants of Charles VII were eventually taken back into his service. As for the 'new men', they were for the most part worthy appointments. Louis liked to seduce the best servants of his great vassals. Among them was Philippe de Commynes, who joined the royal administration in 1472 after serving the duke of Burgundy. Although the king did employ some great lords, like Georges de La Trémoille, he generally preferred lesser nobles or commoners, who could be more easily returned to obscurity if found wanting. Louis was generous to those who served him well. He would act as godfather to their children, give them large handouts, pensions and lands from his domain; he might also marry them off to rich heiresses.[3]

The War of the Public Weal

At the age of thirty-eight Louis XI was old enough to be politically experienced, yet he began his reign by alienating many people. Promises of reform were largely forgotten. A few ill-thought out attempts to rationalise the fiscal system were soon abandoned. Churchmen were affronted by Louis's demand that they should make a property declaration or risk confiscation. The university of Paris was angered by the king's refusal to pressurise the pope into guaranteeing enough prebends for graduates. Many nobles lost their pensions, and courtiers had to abstain from ostentation to avoid arousing suspicion. They were even forbidden to hunt without the king's permission. He set free aristocratic lawbreakers, who had been gaoled by Charles VII, and recalled others from exile abroad. Several princes of the blood were needlessly offended by Louis.

He cashiered Dunois, deprived Jean II de Bourbon of the governorship of Guyenne, took away from Gaston IV comte de Foix the stronghold of Mauléon, and allied in Italy with enemies of the houses of Anjou and Orléans. But it was Francis II, duke of Brittany, who became the chief target of Louis's animosity. The duke retaliated for attacks on his independence by offering protection to Charles VII's former servants. Louis's relations with his erstwhile protector, Philip the Good, duke of Burgundy, soon deteriorated as one of his chief aims was to recover the so-called 'Somme towns'. Philip was persuaded to return them to Louis for 400,000 gold *écus*. At the same time, Louis offered his support to the people of Liège, an independent enclave within the duchy of Burgundy, against their ruler, the prince-bishop Louis de Bourbon.[4]

Responding to Louis XI's provocative policies, a number of powerful noblemen formed a coalition, known as the League for the Public Weal, with the aim, so they said, of restoring good government to the kingdom. They complained that their rights were under attack, that churchmen were being harassed and that the poor were being overtaxed. How they hoped to remedy this state of affairs was left rather vague. They demanded a meeting of the Estates-General, a reduction of taxes and suppression of the *aides*. Their hidden agenda may have been to replace Louis XI by his brother, Charles, duke of Berry, a vain and stupid young man. Among the Leaguers were the dukes of Alençon, Brittany, Bourbon and Lorraine, Charles, count of Charolais, and the count of Saint-Pol, Charles II d'Albret, Dunois and Antoine de Chabannes.[5]

In October 1464 the duke of Bourbon called on his uncle, Philip the Good, to mobilise an army against Louis, but Philip was now too old and feeble to respond effectively. In April 1465, however, his son, Charles, count of Charolais (the future Charles 'the Bold') raised a large army 'for the good and relief of the kingdom'. Hostilities began when Bourbon ordered the arrest of royal officials on his lands and seized royal tax revenues. In a manifesto, Louis XI defended his administration and questioned the rebels' motives. They were, he argued, threatening the kingdom with ruin and encouraging the possibility of a new English invasion. With an army about 30,000 strong, Louis aimed to crush Bourbon before help could reach him and then to march on Picardy. In April, he overran Berry and Bourbonnais. The Burgundians and

Bretons, in the meantime, marched on Paris, but were refused entry. On 15 July Charles of Charolais encountered the royal army at Montlhéry and the ensuing battle was claimed by both sides as a victory. On 10 August, Louis marched on Normandy, while the rebels renewed their attempt to conquer Paris. When the king returned to the capital a fortnight later, he was given an enthusiastic welcome by the inhabitants. He then opened peace talks with the Leaguers and on 29 September, at Conflans, he conceded the demands of the most powerful lords. His brother, Charles of France, was given Normandy in lieu of Berry. Francis II's rights over bishoprics in Brittany were acknowledged. Charolais was given the Somme towns of Amiens, Abbeville, Saint-Quentin, and Péronne. Saint-Pol became constable of France. Bourbon was appointed lieutenant-general in Central France. Jean d'Anjou's claim to Naples and Calabria was recognised. Dunois and Chabannes recovered property that had been confiscated by the crown. Some lords, however, were disappointed. Nemours, Armagnac and Albret went home empty-handed, but the main victims of the War of the Public Weal were the king's subjects who were taxed so that fat pensions might be paid to the rebels. Parts of France had been devastated in the fighting and the kingdom once again fell prey to roving bands of armed men.[6]

Louis XI did not intend his brother, Charles, to keep Normandy, which he regarded as the jewel in France's crown, and he soon found a pretext to snatch the province back from him. Charles fled to the court of Brittany. At the same time, Louis meddled in the affairs of Burgundy by supporting the people of Liège against their lord, Louis de Bourbon. On 15 June 1467 Charles of Charolais became duke of Burgundy. He and the duke of Brittany formed an alliance and sought the friendship of the king of England, Edward IV. On 1 October they allied with Jean II duke of Alençon. In 1468 Louis XI's enemies gained the support of Edward IV whose sister, Margaret, married Charles the Bold. Louis took advantage of the marriage celebrations to extend his truce with Burgundy, thereby gaining time to regain control of towns in Normandy which Francis II had occupied and to invade Brittany. After Louis had forced the duke of Brittany to make peace at Ancenis on 10 September, he was pressed by some of his councillors to fight the duke of Burgundy, but he preferred to discuss peace with Charles the Bold on Burgundian soil, at Péronne. Louis arrived there on 9 October, but the talks made no progress, as Charles refused to abandon his ally, the duke of Normandy. Louis was about to leave Péronne when Charles was informed that a revolt had broken out in Liège. He suspected that it had been instigated by Louis, accused him of treachery and ordered the gates of Péronne to be closed against him. For two days the king was in effect the duke's prisoner. He was only set free on Charles's terms. Louis had to promise to assist him against the Liège rebels. All the disputes arising out of the treaties of Arras and Conflans were settled in Charles's favour. The tribunals in Ghent, Bruges, and Ypres were exempted from the jurisdiction of the Parlement of Paris. Finally, Louis promised to give Champagne and Brie to his brother, Charles.[7]

On 30 October Liège fell to the Burgundians and Louis XI entered the town alongside Charles the Bold. It was then completely destroyed but for some churches. The inferno raged for seven weeks. Following his return to France early in November, Louis XI had the treaty of Péronne registered, but he did not intend to give Champagne and Brie to his brother. They lay too close to Burgundy for his peace of mind. So Charles of France was offered Guyenne instead. Not everyone at the French court favoured this move. Two prelates in particular, Guillaume de Haraucourt, bishop of Verdun, and Cardinal Jean Balue, pressed Charles not to accept the king's offer and were imprisoned in consequence.[8] Charles was eventually persuaded to accept Guyenne and, on 19 August 1469, solemnly promised never to conspire against Louis or to seek the hand of Mary, the only child and heiress of the duke of Burgundy.

Spain

Louis XI loved to spin a fine web in which to ensnare his enemies – hence, the label of 'universal spider' which Commynes attached to his name. Even before his accession Louis meddled in Iberian affairs. When a revolt broke out in Catalonia against King John II of Aragon, Louis offered the rebels his protection. When they refused, he allied with John hoping to force the Catalans to accept his protection. He sent a large army to conquer Barcelona, but a Castilian invasion of Aragon upset his plans. In January 1463 he arbitrated between Enrico IV of Castile and John of Aragon, but his verdict angered both parties. Abandoning John,

Louis made new overtures to the Catalans, but they still would not listen to him They looked instead to Jean, duke of Lorraine, for protection. Hoping one day to obtain Catalonia from the house of Anjou, Louis gave the duke his backing, but the latter died on 16 December 1470, and Louis, who was preparing to invade Burgundy at the time, had to abandon his designs on Catalonia.[9]

Though allied to the Catalans, the people of Roussillon and Cerdagne were unable to fend off French domination. Perpignan fell to Louis XI's army on 9 January 1463. The inhabitants begged the king to uphold their privileges, but he treated them harshly saying that they only had themselves to blame for their fate as they had deserted their lord, the king of Aragon. This provoked a rebellion. In 1472 John II of Aragon seized Perpignan and for two years a terrible war ravaged the country. Louis ordered his troops to destroy everything, but the people fought back, inflicting heavy casualties on the French. In the end, however, they could not save their independence. When Perpignan again fell, on 10 March 1473, Louis wanted to punish the inhabitants severely. He talked of mass expulsions and widespread pillaging, but Boffille de Juge, whom the king appointed to govern Roussillon, managed to gain acceptance by the people.[10]

Louis XI's efforts to control the small Pyrenean kingdom of Navarre alienated Gaston IV de Foix, who claimed its succession, but Gaston died in July 1472 without leaving a son. His inheritance passed to a child, François-Phoebus, whose guardian happened to be Louis's sister, Madeleine. When John II of Aragon died in January 1479, François-Phoebus became king of Navarre and Madeleine acted as regent. Sooner or later, Navarre was bound to be absorbed by France or Castile, each being represented by a faction within the kingdom. François-Phoebus was succeeded in January 1483 by his sister, Catherine de Foix. Soon after the accession of King Charles VIII in France, she married Jean d'Albret, whose ancestors had been loyal servants of the French crown for many years. Thus Navarre passed into the orbit of France.[11]

England and Burgundy

About 1469 both Louis XI and Charles the Bold sought an English alliance. While Charles urged his brother-in-law, Edward IV, to invade

France, Louis offered his support to the rebellious earl of Warwick and to Margaret of Anjou, queen of the deposed Henry VI. With that support, Warwick invaded England in September 1470 and restored Henry to the English throne, forcing Edward IV to flee abroad. Louis XI now looked for Henry VI's help against Charles the Bold. At a meeting of lords, prelates and royal officials at Tours in November 1470, he set forth his grievances against the duke of Burgundy. The assembly formally released Louis from his treaties with him. In January 1471 a royal army invaded Picardy while another entered Burgundy from Dauphiné. 'I am hopeful', Louis wrote, 'that this will be the end of the Burgundians', but his optimism was misplaced, for his brother, Charles, who was dissatisfied with his apanage of Guyenne, was ready to betray him. In March 1471 Edward IV returned to England with Burgundian help and reasserted his authority. Henry VI was again imprisoned and died on 21 May. In the meantime, Charles the Bold set off at the head of an army to reconquer the 'Somme towns', but, after failing to capture Amiens, he apologised to Louis, who readily accepted a truce.[12]

The Last Feudal Coalition

By tearing up the treaties of Conflans and Péronne, Louis XI committed himself to a merciless struggle with his great vassals. During 1471 he had to face a new feudal coalition. In June the alliance of two powerful houses was sealed by the marriage of Francis II duke of Brittany with the daughter of Gaston IV de Foix. In July, Louis XI's brother, Charles, asked the pope to free him from his oath never to marry Mary of Burgundy. Jean V d'Armagnac, who had been dispossessed by Louis in 1469, was recalled from Spain by Charles and given back his lands. He immediately raised an army near Toulouse. John of Aragon and Yolanda of Savoy, Louis XI's sister, pledged their support to the new coalition whose members agreed not to oppose Edward IV if he tried to reconquer the ancient Plantagenet territories in France. On 24 May 1472, however, Charles of France died, and within a few days Guyenne submitted to Louis.

Charles the Bold once said that he liked France so much that he wanted her to have six kings instead of one. After reorganising his army, he launched a new attack on Louis XI on 4 June. On the 27th, after presiding over a massacre at Nesle, the duke laid siege to Beauvais, whose inhabitants put up a fierce resistance. On 22 July Charles lifted the siege and, moving to Normandy, ravaged the Pays de Caux. Hundreds of villages and castles were set on fire and the harvest ruined. Late in October the Burgundian army returned to Flanders, exhausted and hungry. On 3 November the duke signed a new truce with Louis XI. Initially for three months, it was later extended to one year.[13]

Louis XI invariably reserved his hardest blows for his weakest enemies. He invaded Brittany, forcing Francis II to sign a truce on 15 October 1472. Alençon, who was accused of trying to hand over his domains to the duke of Burgundy, was tried by the Parlement and again sentenced to death, but Louis XI pardoned him. Jean V d'Armagnac was less fortunate. Besieged in Lectoure, he surrendered on 11 June 1472. Though allowed to go to the king in order to justify his conduct, he preferred to remain in the Midi and to await an opportunity for revenge. When the royal army withdrew from Lectoure, he recaptured the town, but not for long. When royal troops returned, they sacked Lectoure, and Armagnac was killed. His inheritance – one of the wealthiest in France – was divided between Louis XI's servants.[14] This marked the end of the great feudal coalition. Charles of France and the count of Armagnac were dead; the county of Foix had passed into the hands of a child; Alençon had withdrawn from politics; and the duke of Brittany lay low. As for Charles the Bold, he was now more interested in building up his authority in 'the Germanies' than in fighting Louis XI.

Louis XI and Taxation

Louis XI hardly changed the French fiscal system at all. As dauphin he had called for a drastic reduction of taxation and, soon after his accession, he promised sweeping fiscal reforms. When, in September 1461 the *gabelle* was farmed out as usual, the people of Reims rebelled: they drove out the king's tax officials and destroyed their books. Louis's response was fierce. Nine rebels were put to death while others were mutilated or banished. Yet more troubles occurred at Reims, Angers, Alençon, Aurillac and in Languedoc. In an attempt to repair the damage, Louis launched a bold tax reform. In Languedoc, Normandy and elsewhere, he allowed the provincial estates to redeem all 'extraordinary' taxes (*taille, aides* and *gabelle*) in return for a single annual lump sum; but, when his receipts fell, he reverted to the old system.

By 1465 it was clear that Louis XI would not reduce taxes. This was one of the grievances of the 'League of the Public Weal'. Three years later, the Estates-General of Tours repeated the complaint, but Louis placated them with an assurance that they would not be asked for more money. He even got their consent to his 'doing all that the maintenance of justice requires without awaiting an additional assembly or convocation of estates – since these are not easily brought together'.[15]

Taxes rose from 1.8 million *livres* in 1461 to 4.7 million in 1483. Yet Louis XI was not a miser. He spent little on display but paid good wages to his servants, spoilt the nobility and lavished gifts on religious foundations. His chief vassals received handsome annuities.[16] Louis gave lavish pensions to influential foreigners and tried to buy the neutrality of Brittany and England during his wars with Charles the Bold. He also spent a great deal on the army. In 1483 the *compagnies d'ordonnance* cost 2,700,000 *livres*, the French infantry 944,000 *livres*, and the Swiss mercenaries, 432,000.[17] Louis initiated the regular employment of Swiss mercenaries, paying an annual subsidy to several cantons.

The main sources of royal revenue were the *taille* and forced loans from towns. In 1463 Louis XI required 400,000 gold *écus* to buy back several towns on the Somme from Burgundy. His treasury could only supply half that sum; so he levied a surplus on the *taille*, extorted forced loans from various towns, and seized funds held by the law courts. Later, he forcibly sold titles of nobility and increased the number of venal offices.

Keen to assist France's economic recovery, Louis XI fostered the development of a silk industry at Lyon and Tours and worked hard to build up the fairs at Lyon at the expense of those in Geneva.[18] He also encouraged trade and thought of lowering internal tolls. It has been argued that he deliberately set out to shift the burden of direct taxation from the towns to the countryside, but this is doubtful. He certainly increased the number of towns exempt from the *taille* and consulted them on economic matters, but this was only to make them more receptive to his fiscal demands. Louis regarded rich townsmen as 'a sort of reservoir of wealth to which he could turn when the need arose'.[19] Forced loans amounted to far more than the *taille* from which the towns were exempt.[20]

The end of Louis XI's reign was marked by more fiscal unrest. At Bourges, in April 1474, artisans attacked officials who tried to levy a tax for the upkeep of the town moat. Disturbances also occurred at Le Puy in 1477 and at Agen in 1481, where the ruling oligarchy was accused of fleecing the poorest inhabitants. Near Albret, peasants refused to pay a supplementary *taille* and attacked the tax collectors. If Frenchmen generally accepted the need for taxation, they refused to pay unforeseen supplements – *crues de taille* – which became frequent under Louis XI.[21]

The Black Legend

Louis XI is remembered as a tyrant. The traditional portrait may be summed up as follows. Physically, he was ugly with an excessively long, hooked nose and piercing eyes. His legs were thin and crooked and his walk was ungainly. He dressed shabbily and wore a hat adorned with religious medals indicative of a superstitious nature. Furtive by temperament, Louis liked to roam the streets at night, eavesdropping on his subjects' conversations to find out what they thought of him. Though miserly, he taxed them heavily to pay for his many pious benefactions. Loving to hate, he spent most of his time plotting the downfall of his enemies; if they fell into his hands, he would shut them up in a cage and mock them. Such is the grotesque portrayal handed down by Walter Scott and other Romantic novelists, who allowed their imaginations to play havoc with history.[22]

Fifteenth-century writers, including members of Louis XI's court, were not necessarily truthful. Even Philippe de Commynes needs to be read with caution. Having switched sides from the duke of Burgundy to the king of France in 1472, he needed to justify his change of allegiance by praising Louis's political virtues.[23] Thomas Basin had personal reasons for doing the opposite.[24] Jean de Roye seems to reflect Parisian opinion. He accuses the king of milking his subjects in order to shower gifts, pensions and other favours on churches, ambassadors and the low born. 'He was so feared', he writes, 'that there was not a nobleman, however great, in his realm, even one of his own blood, who slept or rested safely in his house.'[25] Contemporary historians were official panegyrists or chroniclers. The first were few in number, for Louis was not interested in posterity. He appointed only mediocre historians to write about him. As for chroniclers, they were content to record events as experienced by the general public. None seems aware of Louis's efforts to develop France's economy or gives him credit for bringing the Hundred Years War to an end. Burgundian chroniclers were, of course, hostile, although Georges Chastellain shows moderation in judging Louis.[26] Denigration of the king became commonplace under the later Valois. Louis XII's propagandists saw him as the exact opposite of 'the Father of the People'. Claude de Seyssel, who came to France from Savoy after the death of Charles VIII, wrote a book praising Louis XII. He transmits grievances against Louis XI picked up in Savoy and is the first to mention his hat adorned with pious medals. Under Francis I, Louis XI was dismissed as a philistine. Brantôme stresses his drab lifestyle and Montaigne describes him as 'a fickle and changeable being' ('un être ondoyant et divers').[27]

Jean Favier, Louis's latest biographer, offers a more balanced assessment. He stresses Louis's interest in history, his realism, his distrust of intellectuals, his love of intrigue, and his authoritarianism. Above all, he traces the king's development from an inexperienced and impetuous youth, who made costly mistakes, to a mature statesman, who had learnt from experience not to trust anyone. He had also learnt that every man had his price, and that war should only be a last resort. Though well-read in history as a youth, Louis became a man of action. His numerous letters are concerned with practical matters; they show no interest in contemporary intellectual movements or art. Unlike his immediate predecessors, Louis had few thinkers in his entourage. He chose laymen rather than clerics as his secretaries and despised academics. His decisions on matters, ranging from domestic and foreign policy to taxation and military affairs, were his alone. His councillors were simply links in a chain of command which he held. Louis had no chief minister. His instructions frequently use the word *pratiquer*. This means 'knowing' men, 'manipulating', 'persuading' and 'bribing' them. Louis admired the Italians for their ability to respond quickly to a situation. He made it one of his own distinctive skills. Thomas Basin wrote of his 'very quick mind, fertile in expedients, yet very changeable'. He was like a good chess-player several moves ahead of his opponent.[28] These qualities came to the fore in his long struggle with Charles the Bold, duke of Burgundy.[29]

Charles the Bold

The king of France only had to wait for Charles the Bold, duke of Burgundy, to commit a blunder. Insatiably ambitious, Charles wished to shake off his dependence on the king and become a sovereign in his own right. He sought the title of King of the Romans from the Emperor Frederick III and even toyed with the idea of becoming Holy Roman Emperor. Territorially, he planned to unify his Burgundian state which was divided into two blocks separated by Alsace and Lorraine.[30] Soon after his accession, Charles forbade his subjects to appeal to the Parlement of Paris, and, in 1473, he created a Parlement at Malines with a competence extending to the whole of the Low Countries, a move intended to show that he no longer regarded himself as Louis XI's vassal.[31] At the same time, he spared no effort to extend the limits of his state. He annexed Liège in 1468, and virtually completed the unification of the Low Countries in 1473 by conquering Guelders, but, in order to unify the two Burgundian blocks, he needed to acquire Alsace and Lorraine. The nominal ruler of Alsace, Sigismund, duke of Austria, was at war with the Swiss canton of Bern. In order to raise money, he offered to mortgage Upper Alsace to Charles the Bold, who undertook in May 1469 to return it to Sigismund on redemption of the mortgage. But Peter von Hagenbach, whom Charles appointed to administer Alsace, proved highly unpopular. Several towns formed an alliance aimed at checking the progress of Burgundian rule.[32]

In the autumn of 1473 the duke of Burgundy met the Emperor Frederick III at Trier. He asked for the title of King of the Romans and offered the hand of his daughter, Mary, to the emperor's son, Maximilian, but Frederick distrusted the duke and left Trier furtively without conceding anything.[33] Charles then marched into Alsace to support von Hagenbach. He managed to impose his authority, but as soon as his back was turned the Alsatians rebelled. In May 1474 von Hagenbach was overthrown and executed and Burgundian rule in Alsace came to an end.[34] Yet Charles did not stage a comeback. He chose instead to intervene in the principality of Cologne where a violent quarrel had broken out between the archbishop and his chapter. As the duke prepared to invade Cologne, a massive coalition was being formed against him.[35]

Louis XI might have been expected to take advantage of Charles the

Bold's difficulties, but he avoided open conflict.[36] He preferred to cause the duke as much embarrassment as possible by means of bribery and corruption. In the summer of 1473 the Emperor Sigismund turned to Louis for help in recovering Alsace. The king offered his arbitration in the dispute between him and the Swiss, and an agreement was reached in March 1474. In return for a pension from Louis, Sigismund recognised the independence of the cantons. In February 1474 a union of Rhenish towns and eight Swiss cantons formed an alliance, known as the League of Constance, with Sigismund. It was joined in 1475 by René II, duke of Lorraine. Between them, the Alsatian towns and the Swiss cantons raised an excellent army of 40,000 men.[37]

The End of the Hundred Years War

Charles the Bold had allies in plenty, but only Edward IV of England seemed capable of giving him effective support. In 1474 Edward promised to lead an expedition to France before 1 July 1475 and undertook to give to the duke Picardy, Champagne and other territories in full sovereignty. Two thousand English archers were to be sent to Brittany in order to bring Duke Francis II into the war. The rest of the army was to join the Burgundians in Champagne. Edward hoped to be crowned king of France in Reims. This diplomatic build-up helped to stir up some of Louis XI's enemies at home. Jacques, duke of Nemours, negotiated with Charles the Bold, and the count of Saint-Pol promised to admit the English into Amiens, Péronne and Abbeville in return for Champagne. On 16 May 1475 a treaty was signed, committing the duke of Brittany to help Edward IV with eight thousand troops against France The English king also received a substantial subsidy from his subjects to help pay for the war. No pains were spared to raise a powerful army. According to Commynes, it was the largest army ever sent to France by an English king.[38]

Edward IV regarded Charles the Bold's co-operation as essential to the success of his enterprise. In the months before it was launched, he became increasingly wary of the duke's behaviour, notably his intervention in the affairs of Cologne. On 30 July 1474, the duke laid siege to Neuss, a small but well-fortified city. The inhabitants defended themselves fiercely. In the meantime, Louis XI persuaded the Swiss to declare war on Charles and, in November, the forces of the League of Constance occupied Upper Burgundy. The Swiss then invaded Franche-Comté and Savoy. In April 1475 French troops swept into Picardy, Burgundy, Franche-Comté and Luxemburg. Only then did Charles the Bold lift the siege of Neuss. His funds were exhausted and his army was battered. Only a small bodyguard accompanied him when he met Edward IV in Calais. The two men agreed on a strategy: the English were to march through Burgundian territory to Péronne, Saint-Quentin and Reims, but events took an unexpected turn.

Shortly before invading France, Edward IV sent a herald to the French court to present his formal defiance, but Louis XI replied that he might gain more from a settlement with France than he could ever expect from his allies. Louis expected the English to invade Normandy, but Edward chose the safer option of bringing his army to Calais. On 5 August he encamped near Péronne. The count of Saint-Pol offered to deliver up Saint-Quentin, but, on approaching the town, the English were driven off by gunfire. Charles the Bold also refused to admit them into any of his towns. Feeling badly let down by his allies, Edward IV decided to negotiate with Louis. By 18 August truce terms were settled and plans drawn up for a meeting of the two kings. On 25 August the English army appeared near Amiens, and Louis, as a gesture of goodwill, provided the troops with an abundance of food and wine.[39]

At Picquigny, three miles from Amiens, a bridge was built across the Somme with a screen across the middle pierced by a trellis to allow conversation between the two kings. Commynes describes their meeting as follows:

> When he [Edward IV] was within four or five feet of the barrier he raised his hat and bowed to within six inches of the ground. The King [Louis XI], who was already leaning on the barrier, returned his greeting with as much politeness. They began to embrace each other through the holes and the king of England made another even deeper bow. The King began the conversation and said to him, 'My lord, my cousin, you are very welcome. There's nobody in the world whom I would want to meet more than you. And God be praised that we have met here for this good purpose'. The king of England replied to this in quite good French.[40]

Articles of a new treaty were exchanged which the two kings solemnly swore to observe. Louis then invited Edward to Paris where 'he would

dine him with the ladies and that he would give him my lord the cardinal of Bourbon as confessor, since the latter would very willingly absolve
him from sin if he should have committed any, because he knew that
the cardinal was a jolly good fellow'.[41]

The treaty of Picquigny of 29 August 1475, which was to govern
Anglo-French relations for years, contained the following provisions: a
seven-year truce between the kings and their allies; freedom of mercan-
tile intercourse between the two countries; Edward was to leave France
peacefully after receiving 75,000 crowns from Louis; any differences
between the two countries were to be referred to two arbitrators from
each side; neither king was to form an alliance without the other's
knowledge; as soon as they reached marriageable age, the Dauphin
Charles was to marry Edward's daughter, Elizabeth of York, with a
jointure of £60,000 p.a. provided by Louis XI; if either king faced a
rebellion, the other must support him; and Louis XI was to pay Edward
an annual pension of 50,000 crowns.[42]

Edward IV lost no time in carrying out his part of the agreement. As
soon as he had received 55,000 crowns from Louis with a bond for the
rest, he returned to England with his army. Louis boasted that he had
driven the English out of France with venison pasties and fine wines,
but, of course, he had paid a much higher price. In addition to sums
promised and paid to Edward, he had distributed pensions and gifts to
the leading English councillors. Not everyone in England was satisfied
by the treaty, yet Edward did not have to face a revolt.[43] His desire to
retain his French pension and the French marriage planned for his
daughter severely restricted his diplomatic freedom after 1475. He was
obliged to acquiesce in the partial dismemberment of the Burgundian
state by Louis.

Now that the English were off his back, Louis signed a nine-year truce
with the duke of Burgundy on 13 September 1475, which enabled him to
deal with his untrustworthy subjects.[44] High on the list was the count of
Saint-Pol, who had taken refuge at the court of Burgundy. Louis helped
to discredit him with Charles the Bold by planting the count of Contay,
a Burgundian prisoner of war, behind a screen as the duke gave audience to two envoys sent by Saint-Pol.[45] One of them, Louis de Sainville,
described Charles's anger on learning of the treaty of Picquigny and
amused Louis by imitating the duke as he stamped his feet and insulted

the English king. Contay reported everything to Charles, who handed over Saint-Pol to Louis's agents. The count was beheaded in Paris in December 1475. Next to die was Jacques d'Armagnac, duc de Nemours. He was taken to Paris after he had surrendered the fortress of Carlat in March 1476 and executed. The two executions spread terror among French nobles. None, according to a Burgundian secretary, not even princes of the blood, felt able to sleep or rest in peace in their homes. When René, duke of Alençon, thought of fleeing to Brittany, he was arrested and imprisoned in an iron cage so narrow that he lost the use of his shoulder and thigh.[46]

Louis XI was also suspicious of King René of Anjou, who was living in retirement in Provence. In 1474 René had made a will, dividing his inheritance between his grandson, René II of Lorraine, and his nephew, Charles II, count of Maine. Aggrieved at being left out, Louis XI, who was also René's nephew, seized Anjou and Bar. When René spoke of leaving Provence to Charles the Bold, the Parlement decided to prosecute him. This frightened the old king so much that he swore never to ally with the duke of Burgundy, a promise which he duly kept. When René died in 1480, Louis annexed Anjou and Bar to the royal domain. Provence passed into the hands of René's nephew, Charles II, count of Maine, who, dying without issue in 1481, bequeathed Maine and Provence to Louis. Thus, except for Lorraine, all the possessions of the house of Anjou became part of the royal domain. Among the towns acquired by the crown were the ports of Marseille and Toulon. The annexation of Provence marked the submission of the great feudal lordships in the Midi.[47]

The Collapse of Burgundy

While Louis was subduing his vassals, Charles the Bold continued to fight the coalition which had been formed against him. On 11 January 1476 he left Nancy with a powerful army to help the duchess of Savoy reconquer parts of the Pays de Vaud from the Swiss. The two asked Louis XI for help, but he was content to observe events from Lyon. On 22 February Charles captured Grandson, but his army was soon routed by the Swiss. He retired to Lausanne where, on the 6 May, he signed an alliance with the Emperor Frederick III. It provided for the engagement of his daughter, Mary, to the Archduke Maximilian of Habsburg. Meanwhile, René II, duke of Lorraine, began to reconquer his duchy from the Burgundians.[48]

On 27 May Charles marched on Bern. He confided to the Milanese ambassador that he could not live with the disgrace of having been defeated by the Swiss, although he realised that he risked losing 'his state, his life, his everything'.[49] On 11 June he laid siege to Morat (Murten) a small but well-fortified town. The forces of the League of Constance attacked the duke on 22 June, taking him completely by surprise. His army was largely wiped out in 'one of the most decisive and destructive battles in the military history of Europe up to this time'.[50] Louis XI went on a round of pilgrimages in thanksgiving, but his foe was not beaten yet. Turning his attention to Lorraine, Charles laid siege to Nancy which René II had recaptured. This was a risky move: Charles's line of communication along the Moselle valley was insecure and his camp was surrounded by enemy garrisons. On the other hand, René received little support from his friends. Louis XI refused him military assistance and the League of Constance was reluctant to intervene. The Swiss, however, did allow René to raise volunteers on their soil. Charles remained outside Nancy, despite the onset of winter. On 26 December René's Swiss volunteers set out from Basle down the Rhine. After he had been joined by troops from the Lower Union powers and by Lorrainers, he disposed of some 20,000 men. Once again, Charles the Bold was taken by surprise. His guns were pointing the wrong way when the enemy attacked. As the Burgundian troops fled, Charles vanished. Two days later, his frozen body was found among the corpses strewn across the field. His skull had been split by a battle-axe.[51]

News of the duke's defeat and death reached the French court swiftly thanks to the postal service which Louis XI had set up. He was 'so overcome with joy ... that he scarcely knew what attitude to adopt'. He sent for all his captains and important people in Tours to share the good news with them. They rejoiced but 'this may have been', writes Commynes, 'because the King was greatly feared and they were afraid that if he found himself rid of so many enemies he would only want to change several things at home, especially honours and offices ...'[52] Many had cause to feel apprehensive, as they had opposed the king over the Public Weal.[53]

The Burgundian Succession

Mary of Burgundy, the sole daughter and heir of Charles the Bold, was without money or help. Foremost among the neighbours, who greedily coveted her inheritance, was Maximilian of Austria, who could invoke the wishes of her late father. She had accepted Maximilian as her fiancé. On 13 February 1477 Frederick III wrote to Louis XI, claiming the Burgundian lands for his future daughter-in-law. On every side princes were competing to carve up the Burgundian state. Sigismund of Austria and the Swiss wanted Franche-Comté, while the Count Palatine and the duke of Bavaria claimed Holland, Zeeland, Frisia and Hainault. Louis XI wanted 'to undo and destroy this house [of Burgundy] and to dispose of its lordships into several hands'. He did not deign to reply when Mary and her mother-in-law, Margaret of York, wrote, begging Louis for his protection.

After toying with the idea of marrying Mary to the dauphin, Louis preferred a more direct method of seizing her inheritance. He decided to annex the towns of the Somme along with Artois, Flanders, Hainault and the two Burgundies (the duchy and county), and to leave Brabant, Holland and other parts of the Burgundian state to German princes, hoping to win them as allies. He challenged Mary's right to her inheritance and ordered the Parlement to try her father posthumously. Two of Charles the Bold's former servants, Jean de Chalon, prince of Orange, and Georges de La Trémoille, sire de Craon, were commissioned to take possession of the two Burgundies for Louis. 'Now is the time', Louis wrote to La Trémoille, 'to use your five natural senses to place the duchy and county of Burgundy into my hands.'[54] The king tried to overcome potential resistance by distributing concessions to towns and by lavishing pensions and offices on nobles and influential bourgeois. He also lied to them by promising to uphold Mary's rights and to marry her to the dauphin. With much reluctance the Estates of Burgundy, Charolais and Franche-Comté accepted the king's protection, but excesses committed by La Trémoille soon provoked a revolt. It was led by Jean de Chalon and Simon de Quingey. Louis ordered Chalon, if captured, to be burnt and hanged by his feet. In the event, he evaded arrest and was only executed in effigy, but Quingey was captured and imprisoned. Charles of Amboise, who replaced La Trémoille as lieutenant-general, managed to pacify the duchy of Burgundy without much difficulty.[55]

Louis XI speedily conquered the Burgundian towns in Picardy and in the county of Boulogne; he even occupied the imperial town of Cambrai, expelling its bishop. In Artois, however, his task proved more arduous. The people of Arras refused to submit without the approval of Mary of Burgundy. Eighteen burgesses were intercepted by Louis as they went to see her and were promptly decapitated.[56] The people responded by displaying gibbets on their wall from which white crosses, symbol of the royal army, were hung. They defiantly sang: 'Only when rats eat cats will the king become lord of Arras'.[57] On 2 June 1479 Louis ordered their mass expulsion. The town was renamed 'Franchise' and its fortifications were in part dismantled. All the French provinces, except the two Burgundies and Dauphiné, were required to send people to resettle the town, but no good came of the scheme. At the end of his reign Louis allowed the Arrageois to return to their homes, but their trade and industry had been wrecked. The famous tapestry works of Arras never recovered.[58]

Louis XI was especially keen to lay hands on the rich county of Flanders. He hoped to achieve this by deceit. He assured representatives of the local estates that his dearest wish was to see Mary of Burgundy married to the dauphin. He even offered to hand over his crown to them and to go into retirement. At the same time, he stirred up a revolt in Ghent. In March 1477 he showed to the estates a secret letter from Mary which had been handed to him by two of her councillors, Hugonet and Humbercourt. It was her intention, she wrote, not to listen to the estates and to govern only with the advice of the two councillors. But the king's attempt to sow discord between the estates and Mary backfired. The two councillors were arrested by the authorities in Ghent and executed. On 21 April Mary accepted the hand of Maximilian of Austria, and on 19 August they were married.[59]

In June 1477 Louis invaded Hainault, hoping 'to acquire by horror what could not obtain by honour'. He deliberately set out to destroy the countryside. He informed Chabannes, who was attacking Valenciennes, that he was sending him 3000 or 4000 reapers, who were to be set to work and given plenty of wine to drink. After the town of Avesnes had surrendered, it was completely destroyed and all the inhabitants were massacred. Such cruelty, however, merely had the effect of stiffening local resistance. After three months of campaigning, Louis had to sign a truce. He used the winter to impose heavy taxes on French towns and to requisition supplies. Maximilian, for his part, raised a large army, but the campaigns in 1478 and 1479 yielded few results. A bloody battle at Guinegatte on 7 August 1479 proved indecisive.[60]

Following the death of Mary of Burgundy on 27 March 1482, her inheritance passed into the hands of her two children, Philip the Fair and Margaret. The estates of Flanders accepted Maximilian as Philip's guardian, but clearly indicated that Flanders would be ruled in his own name. Louis XI now realised his mistake. He had brought the house of Habsburg into the Low Countries, but he hoped to repair the damage by signing a peace treaty. Talks leading to the peace of Arras of 23 December 1492 were ably conducted for France by the sire d'Esquerdes. Under the agreement, the Dauphin Charles was to marry Maximilian's daughter, Margaret, who was to have Franche-Comté and Artois as dowry. The treaty made no mention of the duchy of Burgundy which remained in Louis's hands. The princess was taken to the French court where she was to be brought up until she was old enough to marry.[61]

The dismemberment of the Burgundian state was now complete. The Swiss had acquired glory and money; René II and Sigismund of Austria had recovered Lorraine and Alsace respectively, but the lion's share of the carve-up had gone to Louis XI. Picardy, the Boulonnais, Artois, Burgundy and Franche-Comté were now part of his kingdom. The duchy of Brittany, however, remained independent and the territorial unity of France could not be regarded as complete until it too had been absorbed. This became a major objective of Louis XI's immediate successors, Charles VIII and Louis XII.

7

The End of Breton Independence

When Louis XI died on 30 August 1483 his son Charles was only thirteen years old – ten months short of the age of majority for a king of France. Among possible regents, two seemed better qualified than the rest: the king's sister and brother-in-law, Anne and Pierre de Beaujeu. Anne was twenty-two years old and Pierre forty-three. They had the custody of the young king and the support of the royal civil service, but could not rely on the military backing of the great nobles. Their main rival was the king's twenty-two-year-old cousin, Louis duke of Orléans. On 15 January 1484 the Estates-General, attended by 287 deputies from all parts of the kingdom, met at Tours.[1] A general *cahier* intended for presentation to the king contained a sweeping denunciation of Louis XI's government and a call for a return to the ways of Charles VII. The assembly exerted little influence on France's future, yet the deputies left reasonably satisfied. The *taille*, which had reached 4.5 million *livres* under Louis XI, was reduced to 1.5 million *livres*. The nobility regained hunting rights on their lands. Only the clergy were disappointed after failing to get the Pragmatic Sanction of Bourges reinstated.[2] Louis of Orléans, annoyed at not having been given the regency, plotted to abduct Charles after his coronation on 30 May, but was foiled by the Beaujeus who carried off the young king to Montargis. Here various supporters of Louis were dismissed from court, while he retired to his *gouvernement* of Ile-de-France.

The 'Mad War'

The minority of Charles VIII was overshadowed by aristocratic revolts known collectively as the 'Mad War'. This was directed against the government of the Beaujeus and erupted in 1487 after a long gestation. A major cause was the independent duchy of Brittany, which offered a haven for malcontents from the French court. Duke Francis II of Brittany had paid 'simple' homage to Louis XI, which entailed none of the obligations towards a suzerain customarily incumbent on a vassal; he had not even gone this far in respect of Charles VIII. His duchy seemed bent on becoming another Burgundy, yet, being poor and militarily weak, it could only hope to defend itself by calling on foreign help, mainly from England. The Bretons, however, were divided. Many nobles chose to serve the king of France and attached themselves to his court. They longed to unite Brittany, where their lands were located, to the kingdom that provided them with offices, honours and wealth. An additional source of Breton weakness was the duke himself. A feckless dilettante, Francis II became senile around 1484. His only offspring were two daughters, Anne and Isabeau. The duchy's affairs fell into the hands of Pierre Landais, the duke's treasurer and a much-hated parvenu.[3]

In October 1484 the Breton exiles in France reached an agreement at Montargis with the French government. They agreed to recognise Charles VIII as their duke's successor, should the latter die without male issue. The king, for his part, agreed to respect Breton privileges and to arrange marriages for the duke's daughters. Francis II's riposte was to obtain an oath from his subjects, acknowledging his daughters as his heirs. On 23 November he also signed a treaty with Louis of Orléans, aimed at freeing Charles VIII from Beaujeu tutelage. Louis simultaneously gained the support of a number of French malcontents. Early in 1483, his evil genius, Dunois, produced a manifesto accusing the government of financial mismanagement. Louis begged Charles to emancipate himself from the Beaujeus and return to Paris. When the king refused, the duke left the capital and began raising troops. He appealed to Francis II and other friends for armed assistance, but the first fires of rebellion were soon extinguished by the Beaujeus. When Charles VIII returned to Paris in February, measures were taken against the rebels. On 23 March Louis of Orléans, who had been deprived of his governorships of Ile-de-France and Champagne, made his submission and was readmitted to the council.[4] But he was only biding his time. On 30 August he issued a new manifesto, criticising the government's financial policy. In league with him were the constable, Jean de Bourbon, the counts of Angoulême and Étampes, Cardinal Pierre de Foix, the sire of

Albret and Dunois. The rebels hoped to have a larger army than Charles VIII, who had just sent troops to England to assist Henry VII, but the king soon put down the revolt. By mid September Louis of Orléans was once again penitent. This time he was forced to accept royal garrisons in the towns of his apanage. The peace of Bourges (2 November) gave France several months of domestic peace.[5]

In June 1486 the King of the Romans, Maximilian of Habsburg, launched a surprise attack on France's northern border, but it soon ran out of steam, for he could not pay his troops. His offensive, however, triggered a new rebellion in France. Louis of Orléans joined Dunois in Brittany in January 1487, but Charles VIII decided to deal first with Charles, count of Angoulême, who led a rebellion in Guyenne. The count surrendered on 19 March and was married off to Louise, the daughter of the duke of Savoy. The future Francis I was their son.[6]

In March 1487 Charles VIII signed the treaty of Châteaubriant with some sixty Breton nobles, led by Marshal de Rieux. He promised them an army of not more than 400 lances and 4000 foot, which was to be withdrawn once the French rebels left Brittany. The king also undertook not to attack Francis II in person or any town where he might be residing. The Bretons, for their part, agreed to serve in the king's army, but the Beaujeus were keen to overrun Brittany before any foreign aid could reach the duke. In May a much larger French army than that envisaged in the treaty invaded Brittany. By 1 June it had reached Vannes, forcing the duke and Louis of Orléans to flee to Nantes. Breaking their word again, the French besieged the city, but on 6 August the siege was lifted, possibly because word had reached Charles VIII of de Rieux's impending betrayal. On 20 February 1488 the Parlement of Paris sentenced Louis to the loss of all his property and punished his accomplices.[7]

Early in 1488 Rieux recaptured most of the Breton towns which had fallen into French hands. In March, Louis de La Trémoille was appointed as the king's lieutenant-general in Brittany. He gathered supplies, arms and troops in Anjou and sent them into the duchy. The campaign took a decisive turn when La Trémoille captured first Châteaubriant, then Fougères, which was reputed to be impregnable. La Trémoille then won a decisive victory at Saint-Aubin-du-Cormier (28 July), capturing Louis of Orléans and many Bretons.[8]

The Breton Wars

The Bretons sued for peace soon afterwards. A majority of Charles VIII's councillors wanted to press on with the war in the belief that the duchy would be conquered within a month, but Charles VIII followed the chancellor, who warned against alienating the Bretons by using violence instead of examining the rights on both sides. Peace was accordingly signed at Le Verger on 20 August. In exchange for the withdrawal of the French army from Brittany, the duke, Francis II, promised to expel all foreign troops from his soil. He also agreed not to arrange marriages for his daughters without Charles VIII's consent, and to hand over four Breton towns as securities, pending an examination of the claims of both parties. A few days later the duke died. As his elder daughter, Anne, was only eleven at the time, the question of her guardianship immediately became a source of friction between the Bretons and the French. Francis II in his will had entrusted his daughters to the custody of Marshal de Rieux and of the sire de Lescun, but, on 18 September, Charles VIII claimed custody for himself by virtue of his kinship with the girls. Matters became even more complex when Anne fell out with Rieux, who was planning to marry her off to Alain d'Albret. While she shut herself up in Rennes with Dunois and a force of German troops, Rieux occupied Nantes, seizing the ducal treasury.[9]

The French threat to Brittany's independence caused serious concern among France's neighbours, who used the respite provided by the treaty of Le Verger to draw closer together.[10] Though indebted to the French government for assistance in gaining his throne, the English king, Henry VII, was unable to resist Ferdinand of Aragon's tempting offer of a matrimonial alliance. This was concluded in 1489 when Ferdinand's daughter, Catherine, married Arthur, Prince of Wales. The English regarded Breton independence as essential to their security. As the archbishop of Sens reported in 1489: 'the English ... told them [the French ambassadors] that Brittany was "Little England". They will send there up to the last man in England in spite of the king'.[11]

On 11 December 1488 France declared war on Brittany and within a few weeks its troops overran the duchy, occupying Brest, Concarneau and Vannes, but the French campaign was not quite swift enough. Troops sent by Brittany's allies – Henry VII, Ferdinand of Aragon and

Maximilian of Habsburg – soon arrived in the duchy. Encouraged by this aid, the Bretons stiffened their resistance. By May, all of Lower Brittany, save Brest, had reverted to the Duchess Anne. Several Breton nobles, however, went over to the French side, while Rieux tried to win power for himself by detaching Anne from her allies. On 22 July 1489 Maximilian signed a treaty with France in which the question of Brittany was referred to a papal court of arbitration sitting in Avignon. A truce, signed in October 1490, brought fighting to an end in Brittany until 1 May 1491.[12]

Rieux now abandoned Albret as prospective husband for Anne and rallied to the idea of marrying her off to the King of the Romans, Maximilian of Habsburg. This project acquired substance in March 1490, when Maximilian appointed four proxies to marry the duchess. The ceremony, which had the approval of the Breton estates, took place in Rennes on 19 December. The marriage was, of course, in breach of the treaty of Le Verger, which had forbidden Anne to marry without the consent of the king of France. It also offended Alain d'Albret, who had hoped to marry her himself. As captain of Nantes, he was well placed to influence events. He entered into secret talks with Charles VIII and, on 2 January 1491, offered him the keys of Nantes. French troops entered the city on 19 March, and Charles made his own entry on Palm Sunday. As soon as the truce expired, the French resumed military operations in the duchy, capturing Vannes and Concarneau. La Trémoille, who had resumed his command, took Redon and Guingamp. Only Rennes and the duchess remained independent.[13]

Charles VIII now mounted a *coup d'état*. Realising that Louis of Orléans might help to settle the Breton question, he pardoned him and ordered his release from prison. Louis was only too glad to be reconciled with the king. On 4 September Pierre de Beaujeu and Orléans also buried their differences. Meanwhile, the war in Brittany drew to a close. In mid June 1491 15,000 French troops encircled Rennes and Duchess Anne, finding herself without money or allies, had to seek a settlement. The Breton estates advised her to marry the French king, but Rennes was the only price that she was prepared to pay for her freedom. On 13 October the town capitulated. Under a treaty it was declared to be neutral and entrusted to the dukes of Orléans and Bourbon and to the prince of Orange. Anne was allowed her freedom.[14]

The Later Valois

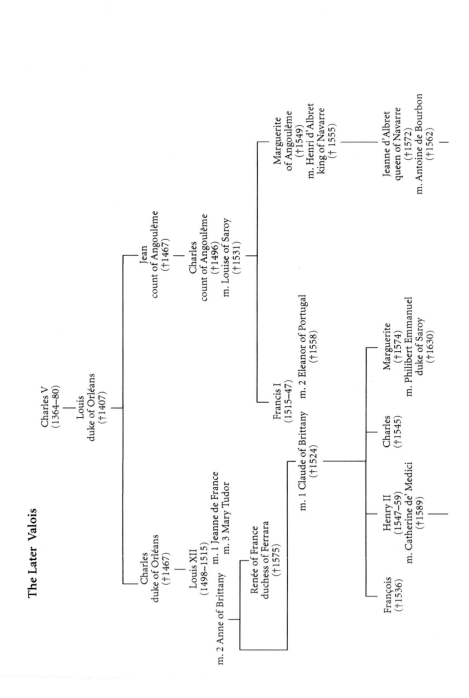

Henry IV
(1589–1610)

Francis II
(1559–60)
m. Mary
queen of Scots
(†1587)

Charles IX
(1560–74)
m. Elizabeth
of Austria

Henry III
(1574–89)
m. Louise
de Vaudémont

François
duke of Alençon
and Anjou
(†1584)

Elizabeth
(†1568)
m. Philip II
of Spain
(1556–98)

Claude
(†1575)
m. Charles III
duke of Lorraine

Marguerite
(†1615)
m. Henri
king of Navarre,
later Henry IV
king of France
(1589–1610)

Isabella,
the infanta

Henri,
marquis du Pont

Charles VIII did not ask for Anne's hand. He offered her instead an escort, should she wish to join Maximilian, and money for her upkeep. He even offered to settle the wages of her mercenaries. But Anne refused to go into exile. Acting as her suzerain, Charles offered to marry her off to a French nobleman of high rank, but she declared that she would only marry a king or his son. Eventually, under strong pressure from her entourage, she agreed to meet Charles VIII. He came to Rennes on 15 November and accepted Anne as his wife. After the betrothal on 17 November, the king returned to Plessis-lez-Tours. His decision to marry Anne of Brittany contradicted a solemn promise made by him in 1483 to marry Margaret of Austria, Maximilian's daughter. Margaret wept bitterly on learning of his betrothal to Anne and kept his portrait for the rest of her life. When Margaret left France, Charles, who seems to have been genuinely fond of her, gave her a valuable chain symbolising eternal friendship.[15] Another worry for the king was Anne's marriage by proxy with Maximilian of Habsburg. Theologians argued about its validity, though they all agreed that an unconsummated union could be easily annulled. The necessary papal dispensation was obtained without difficulty.

Charles VIII and Anne of Brittany were married at the château of Langeais on 6 December 1491.[16] They both renounced their rights of ownership to Brittany. If Charles predeceased Anne, she was to marry his successor. If he died without male issue, she was to regain possession of her duchy. The marriage, which effectively destroyed Brittany's independence, was naturally viewed with concern by France's neighbours. However, Maximilian was too preoccupied in central Europe to react forcefully. He was, it seems, more irritated by the slowness with which the French returned Margaret and her dowry than by the overthrow of his own Breton marriage. Instead of resorting to arms, he tried to turn international opinion against Charles VIII by branding him as an adulterer. Ferdinand of Aragon was also too busy besieging Granada to react strongly to the Franco-Breton marriage. He agreed to hold talks with France on the future of Roussillon. Henry VII of England protested at the marriage and assembled a fleet. He announced his intention in the autumn of 1491 of asserting his claim to the French crown and persuaded Parliament to vote him subsidies. After landing at Calais with a large army on 2 October 1492, Henry besieged Boulogne, but it soon became clear that he had come to bargain, not to fight. Charles VIII was similarly disposed, as his mind was focused on a future invasion of Italy. On 3 November the two kings signed a treaty at Étaples.[17] Apart from its financial provisions, the agreement involved no loss of French territory. The settlement of Brittany's English debts deprived Henry VII of any pretext to interfere in the duchy's affairs.

Union with France

Although Brittany was now effectively part of the kingdom of France, in theory it remained an independent duchy, and Anne of Brittany was determined that it should remain so. When Charles VIII died in April 1498, she asserted her independence as duchess and appointed Jean de Chalon, prince of Orange, to administer Brittany in her name.[18] Louis XII, who succeeded Charles VIII on the throne, was married to Louis XI's deformed and barren daughter, Jeanne de France. He had been forced to marry her by her father as a sinister ploy to ensure the early extinction of the house of Orléans and the incorporation of its lands into the royal domain. Louis XII now decided to get rid of his wife in order to marry his predecessor's widow. Pope Alexander VI was ready to oblige. He issued a brief, listing eight reasons for regarding the king's marriage as null and void, and Louis expressed his gratitude by making the pope's illegitimate son, Cesare Borgia, duc de Valentinois. A papal tribunal was set up in France and Jeanne de France was made to undergo a humiliating public examination before her marriage was annulled. By way of compensation, she was given the duchy of Berry and allowed to devote the rest of her life to the service of God. She died in 1505 and was canonised in 1950.[19]

Louis XII was now free to marry Anne of Brittany, who attracted him mainly for two reasons: she was only twenty-two years old and was capable of child-bearing; secondly, by marrying her he would retain control of Brittany. But the lady could drive a hard bargain. When Louis first proposed to her, she told him that she was not yet free to accept him and thought it unlikely that he would get his own marriage annulled. Anne also declared that, even if this did happen, she was not sure that her conscience would be satisfied. Her religious scruples, however, appear to have been less strong than her desire to remain queen.

On 19 August she and Louis reached an agreement. He promised to hand over to her representatives three Breton towns that had been under French occupation. Anne, for her part, promised to marry Louis as soon as he was free. Shortly afterwards she returned to Brittany.

On 7 January 1499 Anne and Louis signed their marriage contract in Nantes. This laid down that, in the event of issue from the marriage, the second male child, or a female in default of a male, would inherit Brittany. If only one son was born, the heir to the duchy would be his second son. In any event, Anne would administer the duchy in her lifetime; it would then revert to her relatives and heirs exclusively. On 19 January, Louis undertook to respect all the rights and privileges traditionally enjoyed by the Bretons. Meanwhile, on 8 January, he and Anne were married in the château of Nantes.[20] Though often praised for her beauty, Anne had one leg shorter than the other, an infirmity which she concealed by wearing a single high heel. Her first child by Louis was a daughter, Claude, born on 13 October 1499. For eleven years Claude was the only child in the royal nursery and became the pivot of Louis's matrimonial diplomacy. Though plain, she was a desirable match on account of her rich dowry, which included the Orléans patrimony, the duchy of Brittany and the French claims to Asti, Milan, Genoa and Naples.

In the absence of a son, Louis's nearest male heir was his second cousin François d'Angoulême, who in 1500 was six years old. He was being brought up at Amboise by his mother, Louise of Savoy. Both were closely supervised by Pierre de Gié, a marshal of France of Breton origin. He was firmly committed to Brittany's union with France and hoped to see it maintained by a marriage between François and the king's daughter, Claude. Anne of Brittany was determined to protect her duchy's independence and for this reason favoured a marriage between Claude and Charles of Ghent, the grandson of the Emperor Maximilian. Caught in the crossfire between Gié and Anne, Louis XII pursued contradictory policies. In April 1501 he made a secret declaration, nullifying in advance any marriage between Claude and any other than François. In the meantime, the Habsburg marriage for Claude was strongly canvassed by Anne. Claude's dowry was to comprise Milan, Asti, Naples, the duchies of Burgundy and Brittany, and the county of Blois. Had this marriage taken place, France would have been dismembered.

1.   St Michael slaying the dragon, by Jean Fouquet. Illumination from *Heures d'Étienne Chevalier*, *c.* 1452–60. (*Upton House, National Trust*)

2. Banquet offered by Charles V to the Emperor Charles IV, 1378. Illumination from *Les Grandes Chroniques de France*, Bibliothèque Nationale de France, MS Fr. 6465, fol. 444v, *c.* 1460. (*Bibliothèque Nationale/Bridgeman Art Library*)

3. The trial of Jean II, duke of Alençon, at Vendôme, October 1458, by Jean Fouquet. Illumination from a French translation of Boccaccio's *De casibus viro-rum illustrium*, Bayerische Staatsbibliothek, Munich, Codex Gall. 6, fol. 2v. (*Bayerische Staatsbibliothek/Bridgeman Art Library*)

4. Charles VII, by Jean Fouquet, c. 1450–55. (*Musée du Louvre/Bridgeman Art Library*)

5. The triumphal entry of Louis XII into Genoa, *c.* 1508. Illumination from Jean Marot, *Le voyage de Gênes*. Bibliothèque Nationale de France, MS Fr. 5091, fol. 22v. (*Bibliothèque Nationale/Bridgeman Art Library*)

6. Francis I, by Jean and François Clouet, *c.* 1535.) *(Musée du Louvre/Bridgeman Art Library)*

7. Catherine de' Medici, by François Clouet. (*Musée de la Ville de Paris, Musée Carnavalet, Paris/Bridgeman Art Library*)

8. Henry III, by François Clouet, *c.* 1582–86. (*Muzeum Narodowe, Warsaw, Poland/Bridgeman Art Library*)

It is difficult to believe that Louis XII ever seriously entertained such a prospect. He may have simply wanted to extort the investiture of Milan from the emperor and may also have felt covered by the secret declaration he had made in 1501. Be that as it may, the betrothal of Claude and Charles was celebrated in August 1501, and Charles's parents, Philip the Fair and Juana of Castile, came to France in November to see their prospective daughter-in-law.[21]

Early in 1504, as Louis XII fell seriously ill, he was persuaded by Marshal Gié to confirm his declaration of 1501. Gié also took steps to prevent Anne of Brittany returning to her duchy with her daughter in the event of the king's death. The king, however, recovered and Gié came under fire from both Anne and Louise of Savoy. He had to face a number of serious charges. He appeared before the *Grand conseil* in October 1504 and was relentlessly interrogated. A request by Anne for an additional enquiry to be held in Brittany was refused, as was a demand by the prosecution for the death sentence. The case was adjourned and the marshal set free for the time being. In the meantime, Louis XII and Maximilian signed a treaty at Blois which revived the projected marriage between Claude and Charles of Ghent, but the accord was soon upset by the death of Queen Isabella of Castile. She bequeathed her kingdom to her husband, Ferdinand of Aragon, thereby setting aside the rights of her daughter, Juana. Taking umbrage, Philip the Fair assumed the title of king of Castile. He accused Louis XII of betrayal, thereby threatening the proposed marriage between his son and Claude.[22]

In April 1505 Louis XII made a will in which he ordered that his daughter be married to François d'Angoulême as soon as she was old enough, notwithstanding the earlier agreement with Charles of Ghent. He also forbade Claude to leave the kingdom in the meantime for any reason and appointed a council of regency capable of standing up to the queen. Anne was naturally infuriated. When her husband had a relapse, she again withdrew to her duchy and stayed there for five months. Her long absence, however, enabled Louis XII to consolidate his position. In May, he formally announced his daughter's forthcoming marriage to François. He also called an Assembly of Notables consisting of representatives of the Parlements and towns. When it assembled, at Pléssis-lez-Tours in May 1506, the delegates begged the king to marry his daughter to François, who was acceptable to them because he was a

Frenchman. After giving the matter careful thought, Louis graciously conceded their request. By so doing he effectively tore up the treaty of Blois with Maximilian.[23]

In 1513 Anne of Brittany died, bequeathing her duchy to Claude. On 18 May 1514 she married François d'Angoulême, who on 1 January 1515 succeeded Louis XII as king of France. Brittany was now administered by the king of France on behalf of his wife, who remained the duchess. In 1524 shortly before her death, Claude bequeathed Brittany to her eldest son, François, but, as he was a minor, the duchy continued to be administered by the king. When François came of age in 1532, it became necessary to regularise the duchy's status. As a first step, some influential Bretons were invited to Paris They included Louis des Déserts, president of the sovereign court of Rennes, soon to become a Parlement. He advised that the demand for permanent union with France should emanate from the Breton estates and that a few well-placed bribes would achieve this. The advice was duly followed and, in August 1532, the Breton estates debated a possible union with France. Some deputies argued that this would drag Brittany into foreign wars and subject the duchy to heavy taxation; but their opponents pointed to the hardships that had befallen the duchy when it was independent. Even the supporters of union asked for guarantees. They wanted the dauphin to be sent to Rennes as duke and owner of the duchy; its administration and usufruct to be reserved to the king; its rights and privileges to be respected after the union and the dauphin to take an oath to this effect. All four demands were conceded and King Francis I issued an edict annexing Brittany to France. On 12 August the dauphin made his entry into Rennes; two days later, he was crowned as Francis III, duke of Brittany. He was to be the last duke. At his death, in 1536, Brittany became an ordinary French province. A small, independent yet vassal state, which in the past had often called on foreign aid to defend its independence, was no more. From Calais to the Pyrenees, the Atlantic seaboard now belonged to France.[24]

8

The Lure of Italy

In 1494 King Charles VIII of France invaded Italy, unleashing a series of wars, known as the Italian Wars which lasted, on and off, until the peace of Cateau-Cambrésis in 1559, but French interest in the Italian peninsula can be traced back much further than 1494.[1] In April 1379 Pope Clement VII carved out of the Papal States a kingdom, called Adria, which he gave to Louis, duke of Anjou, the brother of King Charles V of France. His aim was to create a friendly lordship in north Italy that would balance the kingdom of Naples in the south. But the plan was foiled by the pope's expulsion from Rome. In June 1380 he persuaded Giovanna, queen of Naples, to adopt Louis of Anjou as her successor in the event of her dying without a direct heir. Her action caused resentment among members of the Angevin house, including Charles III of Durazzo, who seized the Neapolitan throne and had Giovanna put to death.

Louis of Anjou was too busy running the French kingdom to intervene. Even so, the French branch of the Angevin house felt possessed of a solid claim to the kingdom of Naples. In May 1385 Louis II of Anjou was crowned king of Naples at Avignon, and five years later he seized the throne. He kept it until 1399 when, lacking money and support at the French court, he was forced to give it up. Following his death in 1417, his two sons, Louis and René, retained an interest in the southern kingdom. In 1423 by a strange twist of fortune Giovanna II, the daughter of Charles of Durazzo, left her kingdom to Louis III of Anjou. She had previously bequeathed it to Alfonso the Magnanimous, king of Aragon, but had then changed her mind. A struggle ensued from which Alfonso emerged victorious. In 1443 he united Naples and Sicily. The Angevins, however, did not renounce their claim.

Other parts of Italy also attracted the notice of France in the late Middle Ages. In September 1389 Louis of Orléans acquired Asti as a result of his marriage with Valentina, the daughter of Gian Galeazzo Visconti, duke of Milan. Thereafter the alliance with Milan became an essential component of French foreign policy, a possible alternative being an alliance with Florence. During the fourteenth century there were two lobbies at the French court: a Milanese lobby centred on the house of Orléans; and a Florentine one led by the duke of Berry and the counts of Armagnac. In 1393 a quarrel arose between Milan and Genoa over access to the Tyrrhenian Sea. Louis of Orléans was invited to arbitrate, but the dukes of Berry and Burgundy negotiated directly with the Genoese, in 1396 securing sovereignty over the city and Liguria for the king of France. As relations with Milan cooled, the Florentine alliance was strengthened, but the French government clumsily revived a claim to Lucca dating back to 1334, causing Florence to make peace with Gian Galeazzo. Marshal Boucicaut, who administered Genoa for the king of France, used the city to launch crusades against the Turks. In 1405 he ceded Pisa to Florence, which had been seeking a port that would lessen its dependence on Genoa. This caused indignation in Genoa and, in 1409, the French were thrown out of the city. For the next thirty years they kept out of Italy.

When French interest in Italy was revived, its objectives were unchanged. René of Anjou aspired to become king of Naples. Charles of Orléans regained control of Asti and asserted his claim to Milan by invoking the will of Gian Galeazzo Visconti, who had bequeathed the duchy to Louis of Orléans and his heirs should his sons predecease him, which they did. Charles VII remembered Lucca and Genoa, but his attempt to seize the latter in 1446–47 failed.[2] At the end of his reign and at the start of Louis XI's, the French again intervened in Italy. King René had entrusted his Italian interests to his son, John of Calabria. In 1458 he restored French rule in Genoa and, in October 1459, he set off to conquer Naples on his own account, only to be defeated in August 1462 by Ferrante I, the bastard son of Alfonso the Magnanimous. Meanwhile, the Genoese drove the French out of Liguria, except Savona. Louis XI told Florentine envoys in 1461 that his objectives were the same as his father's. His intention, he explained, was to uphold the alliance between Milan and Florence and to defend Francesco Sforza, duke of Milan, against his enemies, thereby implying that he would oppose Charles of Orléans's claim to Milan. However, the king disengaged from Italy after John of Calabria had been defeated in Naples. In 1463 he surrendered to the duke of Milan France's claim to Genoa and seems to have abandoned Naples, but the death of King René of Anjou revived the question of the succession to that kingdom. René and his brother Charles, count of Maine, had left Naples along with the other Angevin domains to Louis XI. This formed the basis of the claim which Charles VIII decided to pursue.[3]

Charles VIII and Naples

Having put down rebellions at home and solved the Breton question, Charles VIII longed to emulate his distant forbear and namesake, the Emperor Charlemagne, who had fought the Saracens in the ninth century. Italy at the end of the fifteenth century was a tempting prey to a more powerful neighbour, divided as it was into several more or less independent states which could be played off against each other.[4] The most important were Venice, Milan, Florence, the Papal States and Naples. The kings of France were particularly interested in the duchy of Milan and the kingdom of Naples. In 1493 Naples was ruled by Ferrante I, the brother-in-law of Ferdinand of Aragon, who was anything but a docile vassal of the papacy. The young Charles VIII had the wills of René and Charles of Maine closely examined to assure himself of the validity of his claim to Naples, but his decision to embark on such a hazardous conquest needs to be placed within a prophetic and visionary context that pointed in the same direction. Charles became king at a time of intense religious fervour prompted by the approach of the 'millennium', which prophets and astrologers were proclaiming to be imminent. 'At the close of the fifteenth century religious faith remained one of the most effective "media" of political action.' (Colette Beaune)

Charles VIII wanted Naples not only for itself, but also as a springboard for a crusade against the Turks who, under Sultan Mehmet II, had expanded their power westward. After capturing Greece and Albania, they had gained a foothold in southern Italy in 1480. Driven out two years later, they remained a threat.[5] The Christian powers were generally agreed on the need for a new crusade with the ultimate aim of freeing Constantinople and the Holy Places. Charles VIII was keen to lead it. He allegedly wanted to follow the example of Henry IV of England, who had planned to lead a crusade to the Holy Land.

He also admired Ferdinand of Aragon for driving the Saracens out of Granada. In planning a crusade, Charles was almost certainly influenced by legends. One was that Charlemagne had freed the Holy Places and handed them over to the emperor in Constantinople; another was that a king of France, called Philip *le despourveu*, had travelled in disguise to Naples in order to rescue the king of Sicily and his daughter from the Saracens. A prophecy popular in the 1490s forecast that a French prince, called Charles, crowned at fourteen and married to Justice, would destroy Florence and be crowned in Rome after purging it of bad priests. He would then sail to Greece, become its king, defeat the Turks and end his life as king of Jerusalem.[6]

Charles VIII was also subject to less fanciful influences. Neapolitan exiles at his court, such as Antonello San Severino, wanted him to help them return to their homeland. He gave them pensions and the use of a fortress in Burgundy until he could raise an army in support of their cause.[7] There were also Frenchmen, like Etienne de Vesc and Guillaume Briçonnet, who could see opportunities of personal enrichment or advancement in Italy. Briçonnet wanted to become a cardinal. Support for a French expedition to Italy existed outside the court as well. The bankers of Lyon and the merchants of Marseille were keen to expand their trade in the Mediterranean at the expense of the Venetians. However, French support for an Italian invasion was far from unanimous. The Milanese ambassador reported: 'it is truly miraculous that the king, young as he is, has persevered in his design in spite of all the opposition he has encountered.'[8] The nobles generally believed that the cost of so far-flung an expedition would not be offset by the results. But the main focus of opposition lay in the towns of northern France, which declined royal demands for a subsidy. Many French people disapproved of Charles VIII leaving his kingdom when his son was still only an infant.[9]

Within Italy, there was support for a French invasion. Lodovico Sforza, the ruler of Milan, urged Charles VIII as early as 1491 to make good his claim to Naples. In Florence, too, the people looked to France to rid them of the arbitrary regime of Piero de' Medici. Savonarola, the fiery Dominican preacher, in his Lenten sermon in 1493, prophesied Charles VIII's coming as that of a soldier sent by God.[10] The Venetians needed French help against the Habsburgs, who, having seized Trieste and Fiume, were entertaining maritime ambitions. Among the Italian cardinals, Giuliano della Rovere hoped to use a French invasion to topple Pope Alexander VI, who had defeated him at the last papal election. He offered to the French the support of the Colonna faction, which controlled the port of Ostia and several castles in the Roman Campagna.

On 13 February 1494, shortly after the death of Ferrante of Naples, Charles VIII travelled to Lyon and took the title of King of Sicily and of Jerusalem. On 29 July he reaffirmed his determination to go to Italy and appointed Pierre de Bourbon as lieutenant-general of the kingdom. Meanwhile, after gathering the necessary funds, the king assembled an army. The heavy cavalry or *gendarmerie* consisted of between 6000 and 8000 troops; the infantry of 4000 to 5000 Frenchmen and about as many Swiss mercenaries. In total, the army was about 16,000 to 20,000 strong. In addition there were a fair number of non-combatants. The artillery, which accounted for 8 per cent of the king's military expenditure, was the finest in Christendom. In 1489 it consisted of 150 pieces, dozens of gunners and a large quantity of gunpowder. Charles VIII was, it seems, the first to use in Italy cannon-balls made of iron instead of stone.[11]

From the moment King Charles VIII crossed the Alps, in August 1494, until his arrival in Naples his march through Italy was a triumphal progress. Wherever he passed, large crowds flocked to acclaim him. He was far from prepossessing physically, being small in stature and having bulging eyes, a hooked nose and a pallid complexion. Italian ambassadors thought he lacked majesty, yet he was not devoid of character: he showed political determination and was politically astute. In each Italian town, an official deputation made up of senior churchmen and local dignitaries would meet him. They would hand him the keys of the town and a length of its wall would be demolished as a sign of subservience. Precious hangings adorned the façades of the houses and temporary monuments, such as triumphal arches, had been erected in the king's honour. Inscriptions comparing him to Caesar or Alexander the Great stressed the sacredness of his mission and his invincibility. Coins bearing his effigy were struck. Wherever Charles was given an entry, he appeared with an impressive military escort. Italians were awestruck by the sheer size of his army and admired the colourful costumes worn by the king and his entourage.[12] The capitulation of so many towns was inspired not only by his reputation as a divinely ordained liberator, but also by fear. Although the French invasion met with little resistance, there were a few incidents, such as the sack of Fivizzano, where the French showed themselves to be, in the words of an observer, worse than Turks or Moors, even than savages. They massacred everyone regardless of age or sex and set fire to everything.

Pope Alexander VI grew fearful as the French advanced on Rome. He did not want to see them permanently settled in Naples, yet could not oppose Charles VIII for fear of reviving the call for a General Council to reform the church in its head and its members. He tried to avoid Charles's presence in Rome by offering to meet him on the way, but the king insisted on meeting him in his own palace. On 29 December the French army entered the Holy City, and two days later Charles made his entry at night by torchlight. On 15 January 1495, he and the pope reached an agreement on various matters, and next day Charles knelt before the Vicar of Christ. On 20 January Alexander celebrated mass at St Peter's before the king and a congregation of 15,000 people.[13] With the pope's blessing, the French resumed their southward march. They captured the fortress of Monte San Giovanni with a savagery which, the king boasted, would serve as a 'great example to those others who might think of obstructing me'. As the French entered the kingdom of Naples, the people revolted. King Alfonso fled to Sicily after abdicating in favour of his son, Ferrantino. On 19 February the French entered the city of Naples, and Ferrantino accepted the offer of an honourable retirement in France.[14]

To the historian Guicciardini, Charles VIII had surpassed Caesar's achievement for he had conquered before seeing. His reputation had preceded him, clearing obstacles in his path. Every town on his march had opened its gates to him making possible the spanking pace of his progress. As Marsilio Ficino said, Charles 'had shaken the world with a nod of his head'. The king, remarked a chronicler, had conquered Naples with a falcon on his wrist. He now set about rewarding the people who had assisted his campaign, showering them with offices and lands. Eleven Frenchmen and only one Neapolitan were appointed to the council of state. Frenchmen were also given major offices. Governorships of provinces and towns were distributed likewise. Thus Etienne de Vesc, one of the main promoters of the Neapolitan expedition, became duke of Nola and Ascoli. The Colonna were rewarded with dozens of fiefs. Profitable marriages were also concluded between French noblemen and Neapolitan heiresses.

The French conquest of Naples was not acceptable in the long term to the Italian states. In March 1495, while Charles VIII and his men were enjoying the pleasures of Naples, four states – Milan, Venice, the papacy and Mantua – formed a league aimed at expelling them from the peninsula. They planned to sever Charles's communications with France. Material aid was promised to the league by the Emperor Maximilian and by Ferdinand of Aragon. Apprised of the danger, Charles VIII wisely decided to return home. He divided his army into two parts: one to defend Naples under Gilbert de Montpensier as viceroy, the other to escort him back to France. He left Naples on 20 May and travelled to Rome. The pope retired to Orvieto in order not to meet him. Meanwhile, in northern Italy, Louis of Orléans, acting on his own authority, attacked the town and imperial fief of Novara thereby giving the Emperor Maximilian a lawful pretext for armed intervention. By-passing Florence, Charles VIII reached Pisa on 20 June. While part of his army moved to Genoa, the bulk crossed the Appenines. Waiting for the French on the north side of the mountains was the league's much larger army under the marquis of Mantua. On 6 July the two armies collided at Fornovo during a thunderstorm.[15] Charles was nearly captured several times during the battle, which was extremely bloody, especially for the league. Although claimed as a victory by the marquis of Mantua, it was really a draw as the French got through, admittedly with the loss of much baggage. Having traversed 200 kilometres in seven days, Charles reached Asti on 15 July. On 9 October a treaty was signed with the league and Charles returned home. Meanwhile, in the kingdom of Naples, the French under Montpensier were subjected to mounting pressure as the Venetians attacked towns along the Adriatic coast, and Ferrantino reoccupied Naples itself. On 5 October Montpensier signed a truce, which paved the way for his capitulation unless he received help by 2 December. However, the death of Charles VIII's infant son, Charles-Orland (named after the Legend of Roland) prevented the king from leading a rescue mission. He was also short of money. Even so, he spent the spring of 1497 trying to organise two expeditions, one to relieve Montpensier; but on 7 April, before any expedition could set off for Italy, Charles hit his head against the lintel of a door at Amboise and died soon afterwards. He was only twenty-seven years old.[16]

Charles VIII's Italian campaign was a disaster for France. It served to demystify the king in Italian eyes. Having looked upon him as a divinely ordained liberator, they had found him to be an ugly little man of doubtful character. He had upset the Florentines by encouraging the Pisans to rebel, and the Neapolitans by the excesses of his entourage. Italians everywhere thought that he had failed in his mission: he had brought them neither freedom nor justice; nor had he reformed the church. Far from leading a crusade, he had aggravated the Turkish threat. His campaign had brought famine and inflation in its wake. The French had behaved like savages, desecrating churches and turning palaces into pigsties. They were to pay a heavy price for their debauches, for they brought home a new and terrible disease, syphilis, which they called 'the Neapolitan sickness'. It was soon claiming victims in many French towns, including Paris.[17]

Louis XII and Milan

On becoming king on 7 April 1498, Louis XII acquired the Angevin claim to Naples, but he was more interested in the duchy of Milan, to which he had inherited a claim from his grandmother, Valentina Visconti. The reigning duke, Lodovico Sforza, was widely regarded as a usurper. Milan was desirable on account of its prosperity and strategic situation. Before embarking on its conquest, Louis prepared the ground diplomatically. He won over Pope Alexander VI by giving a duchy to his son, Cesare Borgia, gained the neutrality of Venice by condoning its annexation of Cremona, and persuaded. Henry VII of England to renew the treaty of Étaples. As for Ferdinand of Aragon, he was relieved to see the new king of France concerning himself with Milan rather than Naples. The Swiss allowed Louis to raise troops in the cantons in return for a pension and an annual subsidy. Philibert, duke of Savoy, allowed the king free passage through his territories in return for an annual pension.[18]

Alongside diplomacy, Louis XII built up an army of 6000 horse and 17,000 foot, but he decided not to lead it himself. He may have regarded it as beneath the dignity of a king of France to measure himself against

a mere Sforza.[19] Tradition also required the king to stay at home as long
as he lacked a direct male heir. The command of the army was, therefore, entrusted to three captains: Gian Giacomo Trivulzio, Stuart
d'Aubigny (soon to be replaced by Charles de Chaumont) and Louis de
Ligny. The vanguard entered the Milanese on 18 July, and a fortnight
later the whole army regrouped in the Lombard plain. Sforza played for
time by offering Louis the succession to Milan, but his proposal was
rejected. The French tried to terrorise the duchy by sacking the small
towns of Rocca d'Arezzo and Annona. At Valenza, they employed a different tactic: by setting free three Italian prisoners of war without
exacting a ransom they hoped to encourage other towns to surrender.
However, Alessandria suffered terribly after resisting for three days. As
Genoa rallied to Louis, the Venetians marched on Lodi and a number
of Lombard towns rebelled. On 2 September Sforza fled to the
emperor's court and, soon afterwards, Milan capitulated.[20]

Louis entered Milan on 6 October, wearing the ducal mantle and
beret. He rode under a canopy carried by four Milanese doctors. The
street decorations included a figure of St Ambrose, patron saint of
Milan, tapestries and coats of arms. A triumphal arch bore the inscrip-
tion 'Louis, king of the Franks, duke of Milan'.[21] Representatives of
various Italian states came to congratulate him. During his stay in the
Milanese Louis tried to win the hearts of the people by severely punish-
ing his troops for any excesses. He also abolished old hunting laws
unpopular with the local nobility. Important families which had been
persecuted by Sforza recovered their privileges and property, while
favours were showered on Sforza's followers in the hope of winning
them over. Humble folk fared less well, as Louis increased indirect taxes
while reducing direct ones. Once he had filled key posts in the duchy
with men of trust and had planted garrisons in various towns, the king
returned to France.[22]

As soon as Louis's back was turned, however, his troops behaved
so badly that the Milanese came to regret Sforza's departure. When
Sforza reappeared in January 1500, they acclaimed him as a liberator. On
25 January the French were thrown out of Milan and had to retire, first
to Novara, then further afield. In March a new French army, under La
Trémoille, invaded Italy and advanced on Novara where Sforza lay
waiting. A battle seemed imminent, but Sforza's Swiss troops refused to

fight their compatriots on the French side. Sforza concealed himself among them after La Trémoille had allowed their return to Switzerland, but he was recognised, taken to France and imprisoned at Loches, where he died a few years later. Georges d'Amboise, in the meantime, pardoned the Milanese and reduced the fine that had been imposed on them. A new French-style government was set up comprising two governors – one military, the other civil – working alongside a senate with a Franco-Italian membership.[23]

Louis XII next turned his attention to Naples, where many of his courtiers had lordships they hoped to recover.[24] He revived the idea, first mooted under Charles VIII, of taking the king of Aragon into partnership. In the secret treaty of Granada (11 November 1500) the two kings agreed to conquer Naples jointly and to divide the spoils. Louis was to get Naples, Campania, Gaeta, the Terra di Lavoro, the Abruzzi and the province of Campobasso, along with the titles of King of Naples and of Jerusalem; Ferdinand was to get Apulia and Calabria and the titles of King of Sicily and duke of Calabria and Apulia. For some unknown reason two provinces – Basilicata and Capitanata – were overlooked in the treaty. In the spring of 1501 Louis raised a new army, placing it under the command of Stuart d'Aubigny. After a general muster at Parma on 25 May, the army marched south across the Apennines. Ferdinand, meanwhile, sent an army under Gonzalo da Cordoba to Calabria and Apulia. In July the French invaded the kingdom of Naples using the same terror tactics as had been used in the duchy of Milan. At Capua, the defenders and population, estimated at 800, were slaughtered in cold blood. When the French entered Naples on 4 August, King Federigo III threw himself on their mercy. He was sent to France, given a a pension and a county, and allowed to spend his remaining years peacefully in the Loire valley.

The period between August 1501 and June 1502 saw the greatest expansion of French power in Italy. Louis XII's territories covered 75,000 square kilometres. No king of France had owned as much since AD 887; none was to have as much again before 1789. But Louis d'Armagnac, duke of Nemours, who was chosen as viceroy of Naples, was a mediocrity unable to stand up to Gonzalo da Cordoba. Squabbles arose between them, a major bone of contention being the two provinces which had been overlooked in the treaty of Granada. The Spaniards claimed them after they had been occupied by the French. Gonzalo expelled the French from Capitanata in 1502 and a long period of desultory warfare ensued in which individual captains did more or less as they pleased. Following Louis XII's return to Italy in the summer, the French invaded Apulia and Calabria. The Spaniards were left with only a few towns on the Adriatic coast including Barletta, where Gonzalo had his headquarters. In April 1503 he launched a counter-offensive, defeating Aubigny at Seminara on 21 April and Nemours at Cerignola a week later. The latter was killed and his army retreated to Capua where it awaited reinforcements, but a relief army under La Trémoille spent three weeks in Rome, supposedly to protect a papal conclave while the French position in the south crumbled away, leaving Gonzalo to occupy Naples effortlessly. He offered the French generous surrender terms which they accepted to Louis XII's dismay. On 31 March 1504 Louis and Ferdinand of Aragon signed a three year truce.

Under the treaty of Blois of 22 September 1504, Louis XII gave up his claim to Naples in return for an indemnity of 900,000 florins while retaining several Italian interests.[25] On 7 April the Emperor Maximilian strengthened Louis's claim to Milan by investing him with the duchy. Louis was also count of Asti and 'protector' of Genoa. He could feel satisfied, but early in 1506 the people of Genoa rose against the French occupation. Louis began by temporising with the rebels, but they set up an administration of their own under a doge and massacred Frenchmen who had taken refuge in a fort. Taking this as a personal affront, Louis gathered a large army and invaded Genoa. The doge fled, the city surrendered, and Louis annexed it to his domain. The city's charters were destroyed and sixty rebels were executed. The king also threatened to impose a huge fine on the Genoese, but later he reduced the amount. A new governor, Raoul de Lannoy, was ordered to run the city humanely and fairly. Being fully aware of Genoa's importance as a commercial and financial centre, Louis XII did not wish to destroy it. He denied his army access to the city, while staging a remarkable entry. Wearing a full suit of armour, a helmet with white plumes and a surcoat of cloth of gold, Louis rode a black charger beneath a canopy carried by four Genoese notables. In the cathedral, six thousand virgins, dressed in white and holding palm branches, sang, imploring his mercy.[26]

Louis XII's conquest of Milan alarmed the Venetians whose *terra firma* abutted the duchy. Relations between them soon deteriorated, and in December 1508 Louis joined the emperor, the king of Aragon and the pope in a coalition against the Venetians.[27] He was promised Brescia as his share of the eventual spoils. On 16 April 1509, three days after declaring war, Louis crossed the Alps to take charge of military operations. For the first time, infantry was placed under the command of noblemen who previously would have considered such a role beneath their dignity. In addition to 20,000 infantry, including 8000 Swiss mercenaries, the king had some 2000 men-at-arms. His captains included veterans, like Gian Giacomo Trivulzio, La Trémoille, La Palice, Chaumont d'Amboise and San Severino. Among younger men were Charles de Bourbon-Montpensier and Gaston de Foix. The Venetian army, which had more cavalry than the French, was led by Bartolomeo d'Alviano and Niccolò Orsini, count of Pitigliano.

On 14 May the French won a resounding victory at Agnadello which they followed up by capturing Cremona, Crema and Brescia.[28] The pope, meanwhile, moved towards Ravenna with an army, but the Emperor Maximilian failed to appear in Italy. Louis thus felt able to return to France. The Venetians knew that time was on their side; they only had to wait for the coalition to fall apart. Early in July they recaptured Padua from the emperor. Louis XII promptly sent a force under La Palice to help Maximilian regain the city. After breaching the wall, he attempted an assault, but the French nobles refused to fight on foot as long as the German nobles remained mounted, whereupon Maximilian angrily lifted the siege and returned to Austria soon to be followed by his troops. La Palice had to fall back on Milan.

Pope Julius II did not wish to see the destruction of Venice, whose maritime cooperation was essential to his plan for a crusade. Nor was he keen to see Louis XII or Maximilan strongly entrenched in north Italy. So, in February 1510, he lifted the interdict on Venice. He then secured the neutrality of Ferdinand of Aragon by giving him the investiture of Naples, and persuaded the Swiss to debar France from raising troops in the cantons. In the summer Julius attacked Ferrara, whose duke, Alfonso d'Este, appealed for help to Louis XII. A French army was promptly dispatched under Chaumont. Fighting around Ferrara continued for more than a year without reaching a decision. When Chaumont died in February 1511, his command passed first to Trivulzio, then to Gaston de Foix, duc de Nemours, who was young, handsome and brave. Under his leadership, the morale of the French rose steeply. They relieved Ferrara, forcing the pope to retire to Ravenna. In October 1511 he formed a so-called Holy League with Aragon and Venice with a view to driving the French out of Italy.[29]

Gaston reorganised his army to face threats from the Swiss in the north, from papal and Spanish forces in the south, and from the Venetians in the east. The Swiss were the first to attack, capturing Bellinzona in December, but Gaston knew that, if he left Milan, its inhabitants would rebel. He therefore remained in the city. In February he relieved Brescia, which was being besieged by the Venetians. Gaston then hoped to draw the enemy into the open by marching on Ravenna. The two armies collided outside the town on 11 April and the ensuing battle was among the bloodiest on record. It was also the first Italian battle in which artillery proved decisive. Although the French emerged victorious, Gaston de Foix was killed.[30] His death, Bayard wrote, made the victory seem like a defeat. Nor did the French gain anything from their success. On 6 May 16,000 Swiss troops, led by Cardinal Schiner, joined the Venetian army outside Verona. Together they marched on Milan, forcing La Palice, the new French commander, to retreat westward from Ravenna with a much reduced army. The retreat then turned into a headlong flight. By the end of June, the French were back in Dauphiné, having lost the Milanese. In December 1512 Massimiliano Sforza, the son of Lodovico Il Moro, was restored as duke of Milan. Soon afterwards, in February 1513, Pope Julius II died.

Louis XII refused to accept the loss of Milan. After coming to terms with the Venetians, he planned a new invasion of Italy. An army 12,000 strong was assembled and placed under the command of Louis II de La Trémoille. It crossed the Alps in May and recaptured Milan with the help of the anti-Sforza faction within the city. La Trémoille next laid siege to Novara which the Swiss had occupied. The town was bombarded and its walls breached, but the approach of a Swiss relief army caused La Trémoille to withdraw. At Trecate, he paused to give his troops some rest, but the Swiss launched a furious surprise attack. The French infantry were almost wiped out.[31] La Trémoille ordered his men to retreat and, by the end of June, they were back in France. Meanwhile, all the towns in the duchy of Milan, except those under Venetian occupation, submitted to Sforza.

Encouraged by the French débâcle in Italy, the English attacked northern France. In mid June a huge army, led by the earl of Shrewsbury and the duke of Suffolk, landed at Calais and laid siege to Thérouanne. Louis XII hurriedly sent an army under the seigneur de Piennes with orders to relieve the town but to avoid a battle. Piennes managed to revictual the garrison, but his men-at-arms were intercepted near Guinegatte as they were returning from their mission. Obeying orders, they avoided an engagement, but their retreat turned into a rout, hence the name 'Battle of the Spurs' given to the action. The surrender of Thérouanne on 23 August was soon followed by that of Tournai.[32]

More misfortunes soon befell Louis XII. Early in September 1513 the Swiss invaded Burgundy and laid siege to Dijon. The governor, La Trémoille, aware that the garrison was outnumbered and that no relief was in the offing, opened talks with the enemy. Acting in the king's name, La Trémoille signed a treaty at Dijon, whereby Louis XII gave up all his claims to Milan and Asti and promised to pay the Swiss 400,000 écus. La Trémoille handed over hostages as security for the treaty's execution and the Swiss returned to their cantons. Dijon and Burgundy had been saved, but Louis XII refused to honour the treaty, a breach of faith not soon forgiven by the Swiss.[33]

The winter of 1513 brought no relief to Louis XII, whose health was fast declining. His queen, Anne of Brittany, died without giving him a son. Her claim to Brittany passed to her daughter, Claude, who married François d'Angoulême, the king's cousin, on 18 May 1514. Eye-witnesses, noting Louis's sickly appearance, did not give him long to live, but he was about to spring a surprise on everyone. After making peace with England in August, he married Henry VIII's sister, Mary Tudor. Public opinion was shocked by this match between an eighteen-year old girl, universally acclaimed for her beauty, and a gout-ridden dotard of fifty-three, but Mary was prepared to pay a heavy price in order to become queen of France. She and Louis were married at Abbeville on 9 October. Within a short time, however, the king began to show signs of wear and tear. The *Basoche*, a company of actors, put on a play showing him being carried off to Heaven or Hell by an English filly. On 1 January 1515 he died at the palace of the Tournelles in Paris and was immediately succeeded by François d'Angoulême, who took the name of Francis I.

9

Valois versus Habsburg

Aged only twenty-one at his accession, Francis I had all the charisma that his three immediate predecessors had lacked, combining a lively mind with a powerful physique. Antonio de Beatis, who visited the French court in 1517, described him as 'very tall, well featured and has a pleasant disposition, cheerful and most engaging, though he has a large nose and in the opinion of many ... his legs are too thin for so big a body'.[1] A Welsh soldier, who observed the king at close quarter in 1520, tells us that he had muscular buttocks and thighs, but legs that were thin and bandy below the knees and feet that were long, slender and completely flat. He had an agreeable voice and a lively conversation marred only by the habit of continually rolling his eyes upwards.[2]

By January 1515 France had lost all her Italian possessions. Massimiliano Sforza had been restored to power in Milan, Genoa was an independent republic and the kingdom of Naples belonged to Aragon. A twofold responsibility rested on Francis: to recover the ground lost by Louis XII and to avenge the humiliation recently suffered by French arms. Veterans of the Italian wars whose reputations had suffered and young noblemen avid for glory looked to him for satisfaction. Francis did not let them down. He began by neutralising his more powerful neighbours. Under the treaty of Paris (24 March 1515) Charles of Luxemburg, the grandson of the Emperor Maximilian I, who ruled the Netherlands and Franche-Comté, was promised the hand of Louis XII's daughter, Renée. In April the treaty of London between France and England was revived. In Italy the Venetians agreed to help Francis militarily in return for assistance against Maximilian; and Genoa reverted to its allegiance. The Swiss, however, refused to desert Sforza, who was also supported by Ferdinand of Aragon and by Pope Leo X.

Francis had the largest standing army in Christendom, but it consisted almost entirely of cavalry. The best infantry were foreign mercenaries. As the Swiss were employed by the enemy, Francis had to turn to German landsknechts, who were brave, but less well disciplined. Mercenaries were also expensive: they insisted on being paid on the nail and were not easily fobbed off. By resorting to various fiscal expedients in addition to normal taxes, Francis raised enough money in 1515 to recruit 6000 cavalry and 31,500 infantry. The army's pride was the artillery made up of sixty large cannon and many lighter pieces.

On 15 July 1515 Francis appointed his mother, Louise of Savoy, to serve as regent in his absence. The Swiss, meanwhile, prepared to defend the Alpine passes. They expected Francis to use either the Mont-Genèvre or the Mont-Cenis pass, but he chose a little-known one, used mainly by local peasants. More than a thousand sappers were sent ahead of the army to remove obstacles and to bridge torrents. On 11 August the French vanguard entered the plain of Piedmont unnoticed and, falling upon the town of Villafranca, they surprised and captured 300 papal cavalry, thereby depriving the Swiss infantry of mounted support. Francis, meanwhile, brought the rest of his army through the mountains. 'We are in the strangest country that any of us has ever seen', he wrote to his mother, 'but I hope to reach the plain of Piedmont with my army tomorrow. This will be a great relief to us, as we are finding it irksome to wear armour in these mountains. Most of the time we have to walk, leading our horses by the bridle.'[3] The descent on the Italian side was so precipitous that guns had to be dismantled and their parts lowered on ropes. A Venetian eyewitness thought nothing comparable had been seen since Hannibal's crossing of the Alps.

On reaching the plain, Francis advanced rapidly eastward. The Swiss, finding themselves outflanked, retreated from the Alpine passes to Lake Maggiore. Francis sent his uncle, René, to treat with them, and a treaty was drafted at Gallarate. The Swiss requested an immediate payment of 150,000 écus, which Francis raised by having a whip-round among his captains. The Swiss, however, were sharply divided: while three cantons – Berne, Fribourg and Solothurn – were ready for peace, the rest, who were inside Milan, decided to continue fighting. On 13 September they mounted a surprise attack on Francis's camp, which by then had moved to Marignano, a village south of Milan. The Swiss swarmed out of Milan briskly and silently, but a cloud of dust that they threw up in the sky alerted the French. As usual, the Swiss advanced in an échelon of three

compact squares of 7000 pikemen each. The first crossed the ditch pro-
tecting the French guns, scattering the infantry. The landsknechts
moved forward, but the Swiss again broke through. A charge by the
French cavalry was thrown back. The fighting continued till midnight.
As the moon vanished, plunging the field into darkness, the armies
parted for the night. Francis seized the opportunity to reorganise his
army. Fighting resumed at dawn and, adapting their tactics to the new
French formation, the Swiss were about to carry the day, when a Venetian army arrived on the field shouting 'San Marco!' Their spirits revived,
the French counter-attacked and by 11 a.m. the Swiss were routed.[4]

Marshal Trivulzio, the veteran of seventeen battles, described Marignano as a 'battle of giants' beside which the rest were but 'children's
games'. The gravediggers reported burying 16,500 bodies. Many French
noblemen were among the victims. Their embalmed bodies were carried
back to France for burial on their estates. Reviewing the battle, Francis
singled out for praise Galiot de Genouillac, the Master of the Artillery.
Legend has it that king crowned his victory by having himself knighted
by the seigneur de Bayard, known as 'the bravest of the brave'. The
immediate result of the battle was the surrender of Milan on 16 September. Sforza was sent to France where he was to remain for the rest of
his life, and Francis entered Milan in triumph on 11 October. He did not
attempt to chase the Swiss out of Italy for ultimately he hoped to enlist
their services. The cantons, as yet, remained divided. Eight signed a
treaty with the king in December, but the other five decided to fight on.

No one was more upset by the French victory than Pope Leo X, who
had backed the wrong horse; but he had nothing to fear, for Francis
needed his friendship. Despite his victory, his position in Lombardy
remained precarious. Faced by a possible coalition between the Swiss,
the Emperor Maximilian and England, he came to terms with Leo. The
two rulers met at Bologna in December and signed a Concordat, which
satisfied a long-standing papal demand for the annulment of the Pragmatic Sanction of Bourges. Curtailments on papal authority over the
French church were removed while Francis's control of episcopal
appointments was legalized.[5]

In March 1516 the Emperor Maximilian invaded north Italy. He
captured Brescia and swept across the Po valley, but on reaching
the outskirts of Milan he suddenly decamped, leaving his troops in the

lurch. His ignominious flight destroyed his credibility with the Swiss with the result that, on 29 November 1516, all thirteen cantons signed the so-called 'Perpetual Peace of Fribourg' with Francis. Francis I agreed to pay them one million *écus*, plus an annual subsidy of 2000 *écus* to each canton. The Swiss, for their part, evacuated the duchy of Milan and promised not to serve anyone against the king of France. In time, this non-aggression pact became an alliance. Francis was now able to raise troops in Switerland.

Marignano was Francis I's finest hour. He was acclaimed as a new Hannibal because of his dramatic crossing of the Alps and as the new Caesar because, like Julius Caesar, he had vanquished the Swiss. The *Commentaires de la guerre gallique*, a beautiful French manuscript of the early sixteenth century, describes a series of imaginary meetings between Francis and Caesar. They meet on different days in a forest as the king is out hunting. Caesar appears to him as a bearded old man in Roman uniform. They compare notes on how best to defeat the Swiss. The author, Demoulins, addressing Francis, writes: 'Your fortune and Caesar's are as alike as two drops of water'.[6]

The Imperial Election

On 23 January 1516 Ferdinand of Aragon died, leaving his kingdom to his grandson, Charles of Habsburg, who already ruled the Netherlands and Franche-Comté. By acquiring Castile, Aragon and Naples, he became France's most powerful neighbour. The situation was complicated by the fact that Francis had inherited the Angevin claim to Naples and that Jean d'Albret looked to him for help in regaining Spanish Navarre, which Ferdinand of Aragon had seized in 1513. But Charles was only sixteen years old and living in the Netherlands. He needed to take possession of his new Spanish kingdom where a powerful coalition of nobles and towns awaited his coming. Only his speedy arrival could ensure his smooth succession. For this, he needed the cooperation of France. Hence the treaty of Noyon (13 August 1516) in which Charles agreed to pay Francis an annual tribute for Naples, thereby implicitly recognising his claim to that kingdom. Charles also promised satisfaction to Catherine de Foix, Albret's widow, for the loss of Spanish Navarre. But the situation changed completely once Charles had secured his Spanish throne. He could not afford to pay Francis the tribute for Naples; nor could he realistically compensate Catherine d'Albret for her loss of Navarre.

In January 1519 the Emperor Maximilian died, throwing open the contest for the succession to the Holy Roman Empire. This was an elective dignity and the seven electors were not bound to choose a Habsburg or even a German. A number of them invited the king of France to stand for election. The empire attracted him as a supra-national dignity commanding enormous prestige. He also feared that Maximilian would be succeeded by his grandson, Charles, whose dominions were already extensive. 'You understand', he wrote, 'the reason which moves me to gain the empire, which is to prevent the said Catholic king from doing so. If he were to succeed, seeing the extent of his kingdoms and lordships, this could do me immeasurable harm: he would always be mistrustful and suspicious, and would doubtless throw me out of Italy.'[7] But Francis stood no chance of being elected. The electors had only invited him in order to elicit bribes from the rival candidates. Francis tried to show that he was richer than Charles, but the odds were stacked against him. The German bankers, who supported the Habsburgs for commercial reasons of their own, denied Francis exchange facilities. He was consequently obliged to send ready cash to Germany instead of bills of exchange, a serious disadvantage at a time when roads were bandit-ridden. Francis also had to win over German public opinion. Habsburg agents used every means to stir up hatred of the French They warned the people that Francis taxed his subjects mercilessly. He countered their propaganda by claiming that he was better able than Charles to defend Christendom against the Turks, but the Germans were not convinced. The electors finally voted for Charles and all of Germany rejoiced.

The imperial election brought France and England closer together. Cardinal Wolsey, who directed Henry VIII's foreign policy, revived an idea, first mooted in 1518, of a meeting between Henry and Francis. Hoping to prevent it or to have it postponed, Charles V visited England and held secret talks with Henry, but the Anglo-French meeting went ahead just the same. It took place in June 1520 at a site between the English town of Guînes and the French town of Ardres. While Henry erected a temporary palace outside Guînes castle, Francis set up a huge and magnificent tent, the tallest of 300 pitched in a meadow. The Field of Cloth of Gold, as the meeting was called, comprised two events: the meeting of the kings on 7 June and a 'feat of arms' which lasted from the 11 June till the 24th. The occasion enabled the two courts to vie with each other in magnificence. Great care was taken to avoid accidents. The kings did not fight each other but headed parallel teams. The story of Henry being worsted by Francis in a wrestling match may be apocryphal. What is certain is that Francis soon tired of the strict etiquette which had been prescribed. One morning he turned up unannounced at Henry's bedside, saying: 'Brother, here am I your prisoner!' Two days later Henry turned up unexpectedly in Francis's bedchamber. On 23 June Wolsey celebrated mass amidst great pomp on the tournament field. The two royal chapels sang hymns alternately and the pope's blessing was conferred on both kings.[8]

The War of 1521

In order to become a fully-fledged emperor, Charles V needed to be crowned by the pope, preferably in Rome. Francis was afraid that, if Charles went to Italy with an army, he would expel the French from Milan. At his instigation two puppet rulers, Robert de La Marck and Henri d'Albret, stirred up trouble for the emperor in Luxemburg and Navarre respectively. Francis disclaimed responsibility for their actions, but Charles was not duped. He accused the king of waging war covertly and responded forcefully. An imperial army threw La Marck out of Luxemburg, while another defeated the French in Navarre. In Italy, too, Francis ran into trouble. On 29 May, Pope Leo X promised to crown Charles emperor in Rome and indicated his willingness to invest him with Naples. Their treaty was kept secret until the French gave the pope a pretext for declaring himself. When the French governor of Milan invaded the Papal States in pursuit of some rebels, the pope made public his alliance with Charles. Francis retaliated by banning the export of ecclesiastical revenues to Rome.

In June 1521 Francis accepted an offer of mediation from Henry VIII, as the emperor threatened France's northern border. A conference met at Calais under Wolsey's chairmanship. Having burnt his fingers, Francis looked for peace or at least a truce, but Gattinara, who led the imperial delegation, wanted neither. His aim was to pin the blame for the war on Francis as the first step towards the formation of an Anglo-imperial alliance. In August, an imperial army invaded Northern France and laid siege to Mézières. Francis prepared to resist while still hoping for a settlement at Calais. In September, the tide of war turned in his favour. Nassau lifted the siege of Mézières; in Italy, Lautrec relieved Parma. Bonnivet also captured Fuenterrabía on the Franco-Spanish border. Francis was no longer interested in peace.

Following Leo's death on 1 December 1521, Francis threatened to sever his allegiance to the Holy See if another Medici pope were elected. In the event, Adrian of Utrecht, Charles V's old tutor, was chosen, taking the name of Hadrian VI. Francis was furious, but Hadrian did not join the anti-French coalition. He wanted to pacify Christendom as the first step towards organising a crusade against the Turks, who were threatening Rhodes, the last Christian outpost in the eastern Mediterranean. Francis was more interested in regaining Milan. In March 1522 Marshal Lautrec laid siege to the city, but, finding it too well defended, turned his attention to Pavia thereby allowing reinforcements to reach Milan's garrison. As the imperial commander, Colonna, emerged from the city, Lautrec lifted the siege of Pavia and marched to Monza. Following at a safe distance, Colonna pitched camp in the grounds of a heavily fortified villa, called La Bicocca. Lautrec saw the madness of attacking it, but his Swiss troops were tired of marching and counter-marching to no purpose. They threatened to go home unless they were given action. The ensuing battle on 27 April was a disaster for France. Some 3000 Swiss were killed and the rest went back to Switzerland humiliated. The only French possesions left in Italy were the castles of Cremona and Milan. On 29 May England entered the war on the imperial side. An army under the earl of Surrey marched out of Calais and tried to provoke the French into giving battle. Within a month the English ran out of supplies and withdrew to Calais. Meanwhile, Rhodes fell to the Turks. The pope urged the Christian princes to sink their differences and to join a crusade, but Francis insisted on Milan being returned to him first. He challenged the pope's right to impose a truce, cheekily reminding him of the fate of his fourteenth-century predecessor, Boniface VIII, when he had opposed King Philip the Fair. He renewed the ban on exports of money to Rome and dismissed the papal nuncio from his court. Hadrian's response was to join the anti-French coalition.

The Treason of Bourbon

On 23 July 1523 Francis I went to the abbey of Saint-Denis to perform the traditional ritual that preceded a military campaign led by the king. He placed the relics of the patron saint on the high altar where they were to remain until the campaign was over. On 12 August he appointed his mother, Louise of Savoy, as regent. Four days later, as he travelled south to join his army in Lyon, he was warned that the constable of France, Charles III de Bourbon, was plotting treason. The information proved correct. Bourbon, a widower since 1521, had been secretly negotiating with the emperor. Charles V had promised him the hand of one of his sisters if he would organise an armed rising against Francis. Henry VIII was a party to the plot. Showing remarkable sangfroid, Francis called on the constable at his château of Moulins, told him of the information he had received, and, pretending not to believe it, asked Bourbon to accompany him to Italy. The constable asked for time to recover from an illness. The king agreed and resumed his journey to Lyon. A few days later Bourbon left Moulins, but instead of joining the king, he met Sir John Russell and formalised his alliance with Henry VIII. Now convinced of Bourbon's treachery, Francis ordered his arrest. The constable fled to imperial territory, soon afterwards becoming one of Charles V's principal lieutenants in Italy. His treason enabled Francis to advance the unification of the French kingdom by annexing the vast Bourbon lands in central France to the royal domain.

Bourbon's plot had failed, yet it served to delay Francis I's return to Italy. He remained in France to oversee the rounding up of Bourbon's accomplices and handed over the command of his Italian invasion to Admiral Bonnivet. The king's caution was vindicated when an English army, led by the duke of Suffolk, invaded Picardy in September. It came to within fifty miles of Paris, causing panic among the inhabitants, but, in December, Suffolk withdrew to Calais. Meanwhile, in Italy, Bonnivet ran into difficulties. After crossing the Ticino, he forced Colonna back to Milan but failed to press home his advantage. By the time he reached Milan, it was too well fortified and he had to withdrew to Abbiategrasso for the winter. In March 1524 Charles de Lannoy, viceroy of Naples, mounted a powerful counter-offensive. Bonnivet again retreated.

Pavia

In May 1524 Henry VIII and Charles V agreed to subsidise an invasion of France led by Charles de Bourbon. He invaded Provence from north Italy on 1 July, meeting little resistance. Assuming the title of count of Provence, he laid siege to Marseille. He needed to capture the town before pushing further into France, but his troops defied his order to launch an assault. Francis, in the meantime, stood by with an army at Avignon. After his captains had dissuaded him from provoking a battle, Bourbon returned to Italy along the coast, leaving the way clear for Francis to effect another Alpine crossing. On 17 October he again appointed his mother as regent and, crossing the mountains in record time, advanced rapidly through Lombardy. The imperialists fell back on Lodi; but instead of pursuing them, Francis laid siege to Pavia. The imperial captain, Pescara, exclaimed: 'We were defeated, soon we shall be victorious!' For Pavia was a hard nut to crack, protected on three sides by walls and on the south by the River Ticino. The garrison consisted of hardened German and Spanish veterans under Antonio de Leyva, one of the best captains of his day.

Though advised to retire to Milan, Francis refused to leave Pavia, thereby condemning his troops to spend a harsh winter in the open. In addition to their main camp, located east of Pavia, the French controlled the large walled park of Mirabello on the north side. Only a small river separated them from the main imperial camp. On 23 February, after weeks of skirmishing, the imperial commanders, who were desperately short of cash, feigned a withdrawal. Under cover of night, they marched their men northward along the outside of the park's wall. Using only picks to avoid making too much noise, sappers breached the wall, and the imperial troops entered the park under cover of a heavy morning mist. It seems that Francis and his troops were expecting them. As the imperial troops advanced, the king led a cavalry charge, but as he did so he got in the way of his own guns, silencing them. After piercing the enemy line, the French came under fire from Spanish arquebusiers concealed in copses near the park's north wall. The French nobles with their plumed helmets and distinctive horse trappings were easily picked off by the snipers. Francis's horse was killed so that he was reduced to fighting on foot. He lashed out with his sword at enemy soldiers who tried to snatch bits of his armour in order to claim a king's ransom. Eventually the king surrendered to the viceroy of Naples. Meanwhile, the battle raged on. The carnage was terrible as rival blocks of infantry collided. Hundreds of Swiss troops were drowned as they tried to ford the Ticino. By noon on 24 February, the battle was over. It had been the biggest slaughter of French noblemen since Agincourt. Some of the king's closest friends were among the dead, including Bonnivet.[9]

After the battle, Francis was taken to the Certosa of Pavia, whence he wrote to his mother the famous lines: 'All is lost save my honour and my life'.[10] He also appealed to the emperor's magnanimity. By accepting a ransom, he said, Charles would turn him into his friend for life; but, unmoved, Charles simply instructed the viceroy to treat the royal prisoner well. For the first three months of his captivity, Francis was held at a castle near Cremona, where he was allowed companionship and visitors. Eventually, he was sent to Spain, where he hoped to exercise his charm on Charles V. On 19 June he reached Barcelona, where he was given a tumultuous welcome. He attended mass at the cathedral and touched hundreds of sick people. In July he was taken to Madrid and given a room in the Alcazar.

Francis I hoped to be released for a cash ransom, but the emperor wanted nothing less than Burgundy and all the other territories formerly owned by his ancestor, Charles the Bold. He also demanded the reinstatement of Charles of Bourbon, and recognition of Henry VIII's claim to the French throne. Francis passed on these demands to his mother, who appointed envoys to negotiate with Charles V. They were forbidden to cede any French territory. When Francis fell gravely ill in September, the emperor hastened to his bedside, evidently afraid of losing his only bargaining counter. Another visitor was Francis's sister, Marguerite, whose presence apparently assisted his recovery. She added her efforts to those of the French envoys to secure her brother's release on reasonable terms, but Charles remained obdurate. In the end, Louise of Savoy agreed to the surrender of Burgundy, and Francis signed a treaty in Madrid to this effect on 14 January 1526.

Charles V's big mistake was to release Francis before securing Burgundy. He merely asked for the king's two eldest sons, François and Henri, to be handed over as hostages pending fulfilment of the treaty. On 17 March 1526 the king was exchanged for them at the Franco-Spanish border. His long captivity had plunged France into a terrible crisis, but Louise of Savoy proved equal to the situation. She had managed to break up the Anglo-imperial alliance by signing a treaty with England in which Francis undertook to pay Henry VIII two million *écus*. Louise also laid the foundations of an alliance between France and the Ottoman empire.[11]

The 'Second Accession'

Francis I's homecoming in March 1526 was accompanied by an almost complete renewal of government personnel coupled with a reassertion of royal authority. The slaughter of so many noblemen at Pavia had created numerous vacancies in the government. Foremost among the new appointees were Anne de Montmorency and Philippe Chabot, who became Grand Master and Admiral of France respectively. The first indication of Francis's future policy was his refusal to ratify the treaty of Madrid. His subjects, he claimed, would not allow such a diminution of his patrimony.[12] Pressing Charles V to release his sons for a ransom, he formed a coalition of European powers, called the Holy League of Cognac, to achieve this end. Charles had again to put off his imperial coronation, but he refused to release Francis's sons for cash. 'I refused money for the father', he declared, 'I will much less take money for the sons.'

Diplomacy now gave way to force. The Sack of Rome (1527) by imperial troops and the consequent captivity of Pope Clement VII offered Francis and his allies justification for renewing hostilities, but they proved disastrous for France. By December 1528 Francis was ready for peace, even if this meant deserting his allies. He avoided embarrassment by getting his mother to negotiate in his name. In August 1529 the so-called Peace of the Ladies was signed at Cambrai. Francis gave up all his claims in Italy but retained Burgundy and recovered his sons for cash. The treaty was sealed by the marriage of Francis with Charles V's sister, Eleanor of Portugal. Charles was at last able to achieve his highest ambition. On 24 February 1530 he was crowned Holy Roman Emperor by Pope Clement VII in Bologna.

Francis and Charles were now brothers-in-law, but their enmity survived. Charles was confronted by two huge problems: the Lutheran Reformation in Germany and Ottoman aggression in the Mediterranean and Central Europe. Francis was only too happy to stir up trouble for him on both fronts. The election of Charles V's brother, Ferdinand, as King of the Romans in 1531 was viewed by many German princes as unconstitutional. They appealed to Francis, who promptly assumed the role of defender of German liberties against Habsburg ambitions. As the Reformation prevented a united opposition to Charles in Germany, Francis also turned himself into a religious peacemaker, but he had difficulty sustaining this role on account of events within France. His persecution of French Protestants after 1534 alienated their German co-religionists, who clearly saw that his policy was self-interested. His credibility beyond the Rhine soon evaporated.

Francis I was also accused of hypocrisy in respect of the Turks. As 'the Most Christian King', he was supposed to defend Christendom against the Infidel, yet he allied with the Turkish puppet, John Zapolyai, who had become king of Hungary, in opposition to Ferdinand of Habsburg. He also established direct links with the Turkish sultan, Suleyman the Magnificent.[13] As Thomas Cromwell remarked, no Christian scruple would deter Francis from bringing the Turk or the Devil into the heart of Christendom if they could help him regain Milan.[14] The king admitted as much himself: 'I cannot deny', he said, 'that I keenly desire the Turk to be powerful and ready for war, not for himself, because he is an Infidel and we are Christian, but to undermine the emperor's power, to force heavy expenses on him and to reassure all other governments against so powerful an enemy'.[15]

In October 1532 Francis I met Henry VIII for the second time. Their talks in Boulogne were ostensibly directed against the Turks but were really about matters nearer home. Francis wanted Henry to share the burden of subsidising opposition to the emperor in Germany, while Henry looked to Francis for support in respect of his divorce from Catherine of Aragon. In January 1533 Pope Clement VII agreed to meet Francis and accepted a marriage alliance between his niece, Catherine de' Medici and the king's second son, Henri duke of Orléans. But Francis's efforts on Henry's behalf were frustrated by the latter's secret marriage to Anne Boleyn, which caused the pope to threaten the English king with excommunication. On 1 September Catherine de' Medici travelled to Villefranche where she was soon joined by Clement. On 12 October the pope entered Marseille escorted by fourteen cardinals.

Next day, Francis prostrated himself at his feet and, on the 28 October Henri and Catherine, aged fifteen and twelve respectively, were married amidst great pomp.[16]

On 1 November 1535 Francesco Sforza, who had ruled Milan since 1525, died without leaving a male heir, thereby reopening the Milanese question. Having renounced his own claim to the duchy, Francis proposed that it should be given to his eldest son, Henri, but he was too close to the French throne to be acceptable to Charles V, who did not rule out, however, the possibility of giving the duchy to Francis's third son, Charles of Angoulême. Matters stood thus in February 1536 when Francis suddenly invaded Savoy. Its ruler, Charles III, who was the emperor's brother-in-law, was too weak to resist, so the French soon overran his duchy. Francis claimed that he only wanted to regain territory that had belonged to his mother, but his real purpose was to gain a bargaining counter in talks on the future of Milan. But the strategy misfired. On 17 April, the emperor denounced the French action in a speech in Rome before Pope Paul III and the Sacred College, and in July he invaded Provence. Francis entrusted the defence of the province to Montmorency, who carried out a scorched-earth withdrawal.[17] The tactic paid off handsomely: after losing thousands of men to hunger and disease, Charles retired to Italy. In the meantime, Francis suffered the loss of his eldest son, the Dauphin François. This gave another twist to the Milanese question, for Alençon was now too close to the French throne to be acceptable to the emperor. By 1537, however, both Francis and Charles were on the verge of bankruptcy, so the war ended in stalemate and the question of Milan remained unsolved.

In 1538 French foreign policy underwent a remarkable change: Francis I decided to become Charles V's friend. Credit for this change belongs to Montmorency, who believed in the feasibility of a peaceful solution to the Milanese question.[18] Pope Paul III, who for reasons of his own wanted the two rulers to sink their differences, persuaded them to meet him at Nice. A ten-year truce was arranged on the basis of the status quo. In June, Francis met Charles at Aigues-Mortes. Observers could scarcely believe their eyes. 'It seems', one of them wrote, 'that what we are seeing is but a dream, considering all that we have seen in the past. God is letting us know that he governs men's hearts as he pleases.'[19] The two sovereigns agreed to defend Christendom jointly and

to bring heretics back into the church. The climax of the new entente
was the emperor's visit to France in the winter of 1539–40. He was
in Spain when a serious tax revolt broke out in Ghent. The quickest
way for him to get there lay through France. Although some of his
councillors advised him against undertaking such a journey, he made
approaches to the French government. Montmorency responded enthu-
siastically, believing that Charles might be persuaded to give up Milan,
but he ruled out any idea of pressing for this during his stay in France.
So the emperor came to France and was splendidly entertained.[20] He was
given magnificent entries in Paris and other towns, 'Peace' and 'Con-
cord' being the dominant themes of the street decorations. In each
town, Charles received a handsome gift. His itinerary had been carefully
planned to show him Francis's artistic achievements, such as the
châteaux of Madrid[21] and Fontainebleau, and no expense was spared to
make his stay memorable.

Though the Milanese question was not broached, Charles did promise to look at it again after meeting his brother, Ferdinand, in Brussels.
Montmorency assumed that he would soon be invited there for talks,
but after a long silence Charles sent a wholly unacceptable proposal. He
offered the hand of his daughter, Mary, to Francis's younger son, the
duke of Orléans on condition that they should inherit the Netherlands,
Burgundy and Charolais. If Mary were to die without issue, her lands
would revert to Charles's heirs in the male line. Francis was asked to
surender his claim to Milan as well as lands taken from the duke of
Savoy, and also to ratify the treaties of Madrid and Cambrai. Montmorency was so stunned by the proposal that he took to his bed for
three days. On 4 April 1540 Francis turned it down flat. The Netherlands, he said, were no substitute for Milan. He refused to ratify the
treaties of Madrid and Cambrai, but offered to hand back his conquests
in Savoy if they could be shown to be unlawful. Later in April he offered
to suspend his claim to Milan if Charles would hand over the Netherlands to the duke of Orléans immediately. He also accepted the
reversion to Charles V if Mary were to die childless, but only if his own
claim to Milan were recognised. The two rulers continued to haggle for
weeks without changing their positions: Milan remained the principal
stumbling-block to any agreement. On 11 October Charles clinched
matters by conferring the duchy on his son, Philip.

The emperor's stance precipitated Montmorency's fall from power. One of his enemies was Francis's formidable mistress, the duchess of Etampes. 'He is a great scoundrel', she said, 'for he has deceived the king by saying that the emperor would give him Milan at once when he knew that the opposite was true.'[22] The duchess had taken a personal dislike to Charles, who had apparently paid her insufficient regard during his stay in France. Under her influence, French policy reverted to its original belligerency. Francis was soon boasting of the troubles that he and the Turks would stir up for Charles. When two French diplomats were murdered by imperial troops in north Italy in July 1541 Francis accused the emperor of breaking the truce of Nice, yet the last thing the emperor wanted at this stage was another conflict with France, for he was about to launch an offensive against the Barbary corsairs in Algeria. Francis abstained from fighting him while Charles was thus engaged; but, as soon as the emperor's expedition failed, he declared war. He launched an offensive on two fronts: in the north, the duke of Orléans captured Luxemburg, while in the south, the Dauphin Henri laid siege to Perpignan. Luxemburg, however, was soon recaptured by the imperialists, and Perpignan held firm. In June Henry VIII of England and the emperor declared war on France.

In the meantime, extraordinary developments were taking place in the Mediterranean. The sultan placed a fleet commanded by Khair-ad-din-Barbarossa at Francis's disposal, and, in August, the combined Franco-Turkish fleets attacked Nice. The sight of Christian fighting Christian with the help of the Infidel was shocking enough, but worse was to come. Francis placed the port of Toulon at Barbarossa's disposal. The presence of Turks on French soil, complete with mosque and slave-market, earned the king universal opprobrium. In December 1543 Henry VIII and Charles V agreed to invade France in person. On 1 July 1544 the imperial commander, Ferrante Gonzaga, issued a proclamation to the effect that the emperor was fighting not to dismember France but to overthrow a tyrant allied to the Turks. While Charles V laid siege to Saint-Dizier, Henry VIII besieged and eventually captured Boulogne. Saint-Dizier proved a tougher nut to crack. It broke the imperial advance towards Paris by holding out for forty-one days. Short of money and needing to settle the religious situation in Germany, Charles had to pull back. So the peace of Crépy was signed in September 1544.

The duke of Orléans was to marry Charles's daughter, Mary, who would receive the Netherlands and Franche-Comté as dowry, or his niece, Anna, who would get Milan. Francis gave up his claims on Savoy and the emperor did likewise in respect of Burgundy The peace got a mixed reception in France. Queen Eleanor was delighted, but the Dauphin Henri was furious, as the peace threatened to rob him of much of his inheritance. He did not need to worry, however, as his elder brother died in September 1545, effectively nullifying the peace.

In July 1545 Charles V declared war on the German Protestant princes. They looked to Francis for help, but five years of conflict had emptied his war-chest. What little was left he needed to recover Boulogne from the English. This now became his first priority; even Milan took second place. In the autumn of 1544 peace talks with England at Calais failed to make headway, as Henry refused to give up Boulogne. The French tried to force a settlement by launching an attack on the south coast of England. They assembled an army in Normandy and a fleet of more than 400 ships at Le Havre. The fleet sailed on 16 July and a few days later entered the Solent as Henry VIII was dining aboard his flagship. An engagement ensued during which the English ship, *Mary Rose*, sank with the loss of 500 men, but not as a result of French action. Later in July, the French landed in the Isle of Wight setting fire to a few villages. Admiral Annebault, who led the expedition, then returned to France without accomplishing anything important. On 7 June 1546 a peace treaty was signed at Ardres in which Francis agreed to pay 2 million *écus* to Henry for the return of Boulogne.

Henry VIII died on 28 January 1547. The English ambassador was told that Francis grieved the loss of his 'good and true friend', yet that same day he was seen 'laughing much and enjoying himself with his ladies'. Soon afterwards he received a reminder, sent by Henry from his deathbed, that he too was mortal.[23] In March, Francis fell gravely ill at Rambouillet, as he was returning to Paris to attend a memorial service for Henry. He prepared to meet his Maker. According to the imperial ambassador, Saint-Mauris, the king admitted to his son that he had made war on trifling pretexts and asked him to repair the injustices done to Charles III of Savoy.[24] He died, aged fifty-two, on 31 March.

Henry II and the Habsburgs

The accession of Henry II in March 1547 and the return to power of
Montmorency produced no startling change in French foreign policy. In
August 1549 the French king declared war on England and attacked
Boulogne. However, the earl of Warwick soon gained power in England,
one of his first moves being to make peace with France. She recovered
Boulogne for a smaller sum than that fixed in 1546, leaving Henry II free
to fight Charles V, whom he had never forgiven for his harsh imprisonment in Spain. On 15 January 1542 he signed the treaty of Chambord
with the German Protestant princes, who, in return for a subsidy,
allowed him to occupy the towns of Cambrai, Metz, Toul and Verdun.
Although France and the empire were effectively at war, Henry did not
embark on his 'German voyage' until April 1552.[25] This began with
Montmorency's capture of Metz and Henry's occupation of Lorraine.
Early in May, the king's army assembled in Alsace. Bypassing Strasbourg, he occupied Haguenau, but when he heard that Maurice of
Saxony, the German Protestant leader, had made peace with Charles's
brother, Ferdinand, King of the Romans, he retreated, and, in July, he
disbanded his army. After reaching a settlement with the German
Protestants, Charles V besieged Metz, but met his match in the duke of
Guise who defended the city. As the siege dragged on through winter,
the imperial forces wasted away. By the time Charles lifted the siege, on
2 January 1553, his army had dwindled to a third of its original size.

In October 1555 at a ceremony in Brussels, Charles V resigned his rule
in the Low Countries to his son Philip, who had recently married the
English queen, Mary Tudor. In January 1556 Philip also received
Charles's Spanish and Italian kingdoms. The Holy Roman Empire
passed to his brother, Ferdinand. Charles V then retired to a Spanish
monastery, where he died in September 1558. His abdication was
swiftly followed by the truce of Vaucelles between Spain and France,
which was meant to last five years, but was soon broken, mainly as a
result of intrigues by the new pope. Paul IV hated the Spaniards on
account of their occupation of Naples and looked to France to assist in
their expulsion. He could count on the support of the Guise faction at
the French court, but not on Montmorency, who was the dominant
influence on Henry at this time. However, the papal legate, Carafa,

worked strenuously to bring France to the papal viewpoint, while Paul
provoked Philip II of Spain by acts of aggression along the Neapolitan
border. In September 1556 the duke of Alba, viceroy of Naples, invaded
the Papal States, whereupon Henry sent Guise to Italy with a strong
army.[26] Ostensibly, the purpose of the expedition was to assist the pope,
but in reality it was to conquer Naples, for Henry had not abandoned
his father's Italian ambitions. Yet it was in northern France, not in Italy,
that the outcome of the war was decided. In August 1557 a Spanish army,
led by Emmanuel-Philibert of Savoy, laid siege to Saint-Quentin. Montmorency marched its relief, but he was heavily defeated on 10 August
and taken prisoner. His removal from Henry's council cleared the way
for Guise, now returned from Italy. Turning his attention to Spain's
English ally, he mounted a surprise attack on Calais, capturing it in
merely eight days. He became overnight a national hero, but mutual
bankruptcy and the rising tide of religious unrest forced the belligerents
to come to terms.

In April 1559 two peace treaties were signed at Cateau-Cambrésis. The
first, between England and France, allowed France to keep Calais for
eight years. It was then to hand the town back or pay for its retention.
The second treaty, between Spain and France, provided for an exchange
of towns along France's northern border, but was mainly concerned
with Italy where France lost everything except a few fortresses in Piedmont. The duchy of Savoy was restored to Emmanuel-Philibert, who
was to marry Henry II's sister, Marguerite. The treaty was also to be
sealed by the marriage of Philip II with Henry II's daughter, Eizabeth de
Valois.

The peace brought to an end the long series of Italian and Habsburg-
Valois wars which had torn Christendom apart since 1494. It put paid
to France's Italian ambitions and marked the beginning of Spain's
ascendancy in Europe.[27] This, however, was also in part the result of a
terrible accident which marred the peace celebrations in Paris. On 30
June a tournament took place in the rue Saint-Antoine. Henry II
appeared in the lists, riding a Turkish stallion given to him by the duke
of Savoy. He vanquished his opponents in the first two rounds, but was
seriously jolted in the third by Gabriel de Montgomery, the captain of
his Scottish guard. Refusing to accept defeat, the king insisted on a further encounter. The two combatants attacked each other fiercely,

splitting each other's lance. As Montgomery's glanced upwards, it lifted the king's visor, driving sharp splinters of wood into his forehead. Some noblemen caught the king as he fell from his mount and carried him, bleedily profusely, to the palace of the Tournelles where he lay for several days. On 10 July he died, leaving only a young boy to succeed him.[28] Henry's death plunged France into one of the worst political crises of her history.

10

A Renaissance Court

The reign of Francis I marked a crucial stage in the development of the royal court. Although still nomadic, as it had been throughout the medieval period, the court grew in size, and its manners, at least on the surface, became more polished; yet it retained a considerable degree of informality. The king prided himself on being readily accessible to his subjects. Except in time of plague, he was extraordinarily approachable and continued to take his meals 'in public'. There was no strict court etiquette regulating the movement of courtiers of the kind that was to develop under Henry III. Anyone decently dressed, or who could claim acquaintance with someone at court, was readily admitted. Such accessibility inevitably carried risks. Thus, in 1530, Francis complained that silver plate had gone missing from his chapel as well as clothes from his wardrobe. In January 1533 three armed strangers were found in his bedchamber at the Louvre, yet his only response was to ask for better policing of the streets of Paris at night.[1]

The court consisted of the king's household, of the households of members of his family, and of a crowd of hangers-on. The king's household was divided into six departments, each with its staff, catering for his bodily and spiritual needs. The staff were paid in money or kind, allowed to eat at court and given allowances of fuel, candles and fodder. The main departments were the *chapelle*, under the Great Almoner, the *chambre* under the First Gentleman of the Chamber and the *hôtel* under the Grand Master, who also had overall control of the court. The *hôtel* was subdivided into three departments concerned with food and wine. There were two kitchens – one for the king – the other for the rest of the court. The *fourrière* was responsible for transporting the court and its furniture. The stables, under the Master of the Horse, cared for the king's horses. Attached to the stables were messengers and a riding school for pages. Two departments – the *vénerie* and *fauconnerie* –

organised the royal hunts. The court also included a body of troops made up of units created in different reigns, the oldest being the Scottish guard which provided the king's bodyguard. There were also three companies of archers, each of one hundred men, the *Cent-suisses* (again one hundred) and two companies of Gentlemen of the household, each of one hundred men. All these troops, except the Swiss, were mounted. Law and order at court were maintained by the *Prévôt de l'hôtel*, who was also responsible for overseeing supplies and ensuring that they were not overpriced. The *chambre aux deniers* administered the court's financial affairs. The court also included many permanent and semi-permanent guests, including princes of the blood, foreign princes, ambassadors and prelates, each with his retainers. Frequent visitors included king's councillors, masters of requests, secretaries and notaries. Among the numerous hangers-on were merchants and artisans, exempted from guild regulations in return for their exclusive services. There were also camp-followers, known as *filles de joie suivant la cour*.[2]

Francis I did not fundamentally alter the structure of the court, but in 1515 he created the title of *Gentilhomme de la chambre* (Gentleman of the chamber) for his closest male companions. They did not always attend the court, as they were employed on a variety of missions, mostly diplomatic. They would, of course, bring back and exchange ideas and impressions which might influence changes at court. A formal visit by *Gentilshommes de la chambre* to the English court in 1518 posed a problem of precedence for King Henry VIII, who solved it by giving his own minions the title of 'Gentlemen of the Privy Chamber'.[3] It was customary for monarchs to exchange gentlemen as a mark of friendship. Thus the English ambassador, Sir Thomas Cheney, one of Henry VIII's closest companions, was invited to enter Francis's chamber as freely as if it were his own master's.[4] Among the duties of the the First Gentleman of the Chamber was the custody of the crown jewels, holding the king's privy purse and signing contracts for work on royal palaces.

The court's population fluctuated wildly. In wartime, as the king and his chief nobles set off on campaign, its nucleus would comprise mainly women, old men and ecclesiastics. Even in peacetime, however, the number of courtiers was variable. As the court travelled about the kingdom, nobles from one area would tag on for a limited time before returning home to be replaced by nobles from another area, again for a short period. As life at court was very expensive, few nobles wanted to stay longer than strictly necessary to the pursuit of their interests; they wanted to capture the king's notice in order to gain some office or other favour. At its fullest extent, the court could number as many as ten thousand people with a corresponding number of horses. Dr John Taylor, who witnessed its arrival in Bordeaux in 1526, reported that stabling had to be found for 22,500 horses and mules.[5] Only châteaux, like Saint-Germain-en-Laye, where the court resided for several weeks at a time, were permanently furnished; the rest remained empty from one royal visit to the next. The court carried around its own furniture, tapestries and gold and silver plate. On arrival at a château, trestle tables and beds would be set up and the walls covered with hangings.

As the kingdom of France grew in size following the annexation of territories such as Brittany, so the court's travels became more extensive. In the winter, when roads turned into quagmires, it tended to stay put, often at Saint-Germain-en-Laye, near Paris, but with the arrival of spring it would take to the roads. The purpose behind this mode of life was partly pleasure and partly political. The king was a dedicated huntsman who liked to explore various forests. At the same time, he needed to impose his authority by visiting as much of his kingdom as possible and getting to know his subjects. Whenever he visited a town for the first time, he was given an entry. This could be a spectacular affair, offering scope for much symbolism and propaganda in the form of temporary monuments and adulatory inscriptions.[6] The king's travels were far from haphazard: each year he would tour a different set of provinces. Some ambassadors, particularly Italians whose masters tended to move within a more restricted space, found Francis I's peregrinations disconcerting. 'Never during the whole of my embassy', wrote a Venetian, 'was the court in the same place for fifteen consecutive days.'[7] Even then one could not be certain of finding the king, for he liked to detach himself from the court in order to hunt, sometimes for days on end, with a small group of companions and his 'fair band' of ladies. He disliked being disturbed when staying at one of his hunting lodges.

Feeding the court could be a problem. In May 1533 its presence in Lyon made great demands on the city's limited supplies, causing food prices to rise sharply. In August 1540, as it travelled to Le Havre, it experienced a serious shortage of fodder for the horses and of wine and cider for the men. As the wells were dry, courtiers took to drinking polluted water, falling seriously ill in consequence. Finding accommodation could also be a problem. Not everyone could share the king's roof. Building accounts for the château of Saint-Germain-en-Laye in the reign of Henry II indicate how rooms were allocated.[8] There were fifty-five apartments within the château and twenty-five in outbuildings. No one except a member of the royal family was allowed to reside above the king, who was on the second floor. His lodging comprised a presence chamber, chamber, wardrobe and closet, and was reached by means of a staircase leading directly from the château's inner courtyard. When an important guest arrived, a guard of honour formed a line from the courtyard to the presence chamber. This was located as far as possible from the chapel in order to allow as many people as possible to see the king as he went to mass each day. Other members of his family and his chief ministers also occupied rooms on the second floor. Strict rules of precedence determined the allocation of rooms in the rest of the building. Ladies, princes accompanied by their wives, and most cardinals shared the king's roof, while single nobles, royal secretaries and household officials were relegated to outbuildings. When the court was on the move an altogether different regime prevailed. Wherever possible the king would stay in one of his own houses; otherwise he would put up at the home of a nobleman, at an inn or a religious house. His courtiers would look for accommodation within a wide radius from the king's person. In extreme cases, they would sleep under canvas. 'Sometimes', writes Cellini, 'there were scarcely two houses to be found and then we set up canvas tents like gipsies, and suffered at times very great discomfort.'[9]

The Châteaux of Francis I

Francis I was a great builder. One of his main legacies was a series of royal palaces built mainly in the Loire valley and in the Ile-de-France. Not content simply to commission them, he participated actively in their design. He was in the habit of making sketches of buildings he wished to see erected.[10] Not all his châteaux were built from scratch. Some were handed down by his predecessors and merely modified to suit his needs. These older châteaux had once been fortresses and retained military features such as moats, gate-houses, towers and machicolations. These features were no longer needed now that the kingdom was at peace internally. Amboise, Blois, Saint-Germain-en-Laye and the Louvre, in Paris, underwent improvements under Francis which displayed the new classical style imported from Italy.[11] In some cases Italian artists were responsible for the work, but the master masons were more commonly French. Initially, classical decoration, such as pilasters, columns of the three Orders and medallions, were applied to the outer surfaces of buildings, which remained structurally Gothic. A good example is the Francis I wing at Blois with its façade of loggias inspired by those which Bramante was building at the Vatican. Its purpose was to allow the king and his entourage to look down on splendid gardens. Inside the courtyard, Francis built an imposing external spiral staircase. The symmetrical plan of the central keep at Chambord, a château built at the heart of a forest near Blois, was probably inspired by that of Poggio a Caiano, a villa built for Lorenzo de' Medici outside Florence in the 1480s. The double-spiral staircase at the centre of the keep, leading to a cupola on the roof, may have been inspired by Leonardo da Vinci, who spent his last years at Amboise.[12]

In 1528, following his return from captivity in Spain, Francis I undertook a massive building programme in the Paris region. At Saint Germain-en-Laye, he added two stories and a flat roof commanding views of the neighbouring forest. The roof was so heavy that the supporting edifice had to be strengthened with large buttresses and iron tie-bars. In Paris, the king demolished the old medieval keep at the Louvre in order to create an inner courtyard. He also began a complete renovation of the old fortress, but much remained to be done at his death. Needing a hunting lodge within striking distance of the capital, Francis built a small château in the Bois de Boulogne which became known as Madrid on account of its similarity with a villa which the king had seen near Madrid during his captivity. Without either courtyard or moat, it was a rectangular building with square pavilions at each end. The elevation comprised two horizontal tiers of open loggias with tall mullioned windows regularly distributed. High-pitched roofs covered the building, but the most unusual feature was the decoration, inside and out, of brightly coloured glazed terracotta made by another Italian, Girolamo della Robbia, of the famous family of Florentine ceramicists, who had settled in France. Significantly, the château contained thirty-two identical apartments, a pattern repeated in Francis's other new châteaux. This suggests that informality ruled when he visited them on his hunting expeditions; his lodgings were the same as those of his companions.[13]

Francis I's favourite château was Fontainebleau, which was again situated in a vast forest where he hunted deer.[14] He incorporated a small oval fortress, which had existed on the site since the Middle Ages, into a much larger complex of buildings. This involved the purchase of an adjacent monastery. Built over a long period starting in 1528, the château underwent a number of radical changes which reflected changes in the royal family. For example, when the king's mother, Louise of Savoy, died in 1531, the distribution of rooms was altered. Francis moved into the lodging formerly occupied by her, while his wife Eleanor took over his old rooms. A monumental staircase, which had been erected in the inner courtyard to provide access to the king's old chamber, thus became redundant and was accordingly demolished. To link the royal apartments in the old building with a new extension on the west side, the king erected a gallery beneath which were kitchens and baths. He commissioned Rosso, a Florentine artist, to decorate the gallery with murals in stucco frames. Such was Francis's pride in his gallery that he kept its key on his person. When John Wallop, the English ambassador, visited Fontainebleau in 1540, the king took him on a guided tour of the gallery and of the baths beneath, where his mistress and other nude ladies were reclining on couches.[15]

Francis I as Patron of the Arts

In addition to being a great builder, Francis I was also an outstanding patron of artists. Even as a boy, he expressed an interest in acquiring a work by the great Mantuan artist, Mantegna, and once he had become king, he attracted many leading Italian artists to his court or collected their works. In 1516 he invited Leonardo da Vinci to settle in France and gave him the Clos-Lucé, a house near Amboise. The artist was sixty-three years old and paralysed in one hand. He could no longer paint, but he could still draw and his French notebooks contain architectural sketches. Some paintings which he brought with him, such as the *Mona Lisa*, eventually found their way into the royal collection.[16] Francis almost certainly talked to Leonardo about art, but the old man did not die in the king's arms, as legend would have us believe. Another early visitor to the French court was Andrea del Sarto, who painted a *Charity* for the king; but after taking money from him for the purchase of works of art in Florence, Andrea failed to return. Even so, Francis continued to employ Italian artists. They included Rosso and Primaticcio, who, with their teams of assistants, decorated much of Fontainebleau. As the king's First Painter, Rosso received a large salary and a house in Paris. In addition to painting murals, he designed costumes for theatrical entertainments as well as tableware, horse-trappings and a tomb. He may also have been an architect. Francis invited Titian to his court, but the artist refused to leave Venice. For portraiture, the king relied mainly on Jean Clouet, an artist from the Low Countries who has left a series of marvellous drawings of members of the court.[17]

The most graphic account of Francis's artistic patronage is contained in the autobiography of Benvenuto Cellini, the Florentine goldsmith and sculptor, who came to France twice, in 1537 and 1540.[18] On the second occasion, he was given a workshop in the Petit Nesle on the left bank of the Seine in Paris, where the king and his courtiers would visit him. The first work produced by Cellini for Francis was a *Jupiter* in silver, six feet tall, like the king. It was intended to be part of a set of twelve statues of gods and goddesses, which were to serve as candlesticks around the royal table, but only *Jupiter* was finished. Another work made for Francis by Cellini was the famous salt-cellar, which has been described as 'an allegory of consummate naturalness ... a paragon of virtuosity'.[19] The only other major work to survive of Cellini's French period is a bronze relief of the *Nymph of Fontainebleau*, which was eventually given by Henry II to his mistress, Diane de Poitiers, for her château at Anet. In 1542 Cellini showed Francis a model for a fountain at Fontainebleau. In the middle stood a male figure intended to rise fifty-four feet above the ground and meant to represent the king in the guise of Mars. Cellini complained that he did not always receive the rewards promised by the king, yet he did not do badly. In addition to cash payments, he received letters of naturalisation exempting him from the *droit d'aubaine*, an onerous duty on foreigners who died in France.

In addition to his building activities, Francis I with the assistance of his agents built up the finest collection of works of art north of the Alps.

Some of the king's agents were French diplomats, like Guillaume du Bellay, while others were Italians, like Battista della Palla or Pietro Aretino, who wished to ingratiate themselves with the king. Della Palla sent various works to Francis which he had secured by hook or by crook in Florence.[20] They included a multi-breasted statue of *Nature* by Tribolo, *Mercury holding a flute* by Bandinelli and a *Hercules* by Michelangelo. The first two can still be seen at Fontainebleau, but the *Hercules*, which was set up there as part of a fountain, vanished about 1714. In addition to recommending Rosso to the king, Aretino sent him two works by Titian, including the famous portrait of the king in profile, now in the Louvre, which was painted from a medal. Aretino was given a gold chain by Francis. In 1540 the king sent Primaticcio to Rome to buy or copy antiquities on his behalf. The artist returned a year later with plaster casts of ancient statues, mostly in the Vatican collection. Some were turned into bronzes by Vignola, the future architect, who set up a foundry at Fontainebleau. Among other works of art in the king's collection were a perfume burner by Raphael, of which only the design survives, and a jewel casket (now in Florence) with crystal panels depicting the life of Christ by Valerio Belli.

'Father of Letters'

Francis I is remembered not only as a great patron of the arts but also as 'the Father of Letters'. One of Rosso's murals at Fontainebleau shows him, sword in hand and a book under his arm, entering the brightly lit temple of Jupiter while in the shadowy foreground blindfolded demons of ignorance lift up their arms in despair.[21] Francis's reputation as a patron of scholars may have been exaggerated. His role in the foundation of the Collège de France, one of the most prestigious academic institutions in France today, may not have been as decisive as was once thought.[22] The contents of two chests of books which Francis I carried around with him pointed to the king's favourite reading. They contained works by Justinus, Thucydides, Appian and Diodorus Siculus as well as romances like the *Destruction de Troie la Grant* and the *Roman de la Rose*. Rabelais, the greatest literary figure of the reign, never held office at court, but Francis knew his work. He failed to see anything reprehensible in Rabelais's *Chronicles* after they had been banned by the Sorbonne. Francis is credited with the creation of a superb library at Fontainebleau, but the evidence for this is inconclusive.[23] The royal library was at Blois until 1544, when it was moved to Fontainebleau. The king added to the stock of books that he had inherited from his predecessors. He commissioned agents in Italy to acquire books in Greek, intended for a library which Francis planned to found alongside a college of three languages, but this was never built. The books, both manuscript and printed, were acquired in Italy by such agents as Georges d'Armagnac, bishop of Rodez, and Guillaume Pellicier. Sometimes they employed scribes to copy rare books for the king. In 1546 it was reported that Francis had established, close to his lodging, a library containing books in Greek, Latin, Hebrew and Arabic. About the same time, he ordered many of his books to be rebound, a task continued more lavishly by his son, Henry II. Despite his lack of learning, Francis was keen to make his books available to scholars. In 1539 Robert Estienne became King's Printer in Hebrew and Latin, and in 1542 King's Printer in Greek. Three special founts of Greek type – the *grecs du roi* – were cut by Claude Garamond at Francis I's expense.

The Cultural Patronage of Henry II

Though less culturally aware than his father, Henry II was no mean builder. He continued rebuilding the Louvre, erected the Château-Neuf at Saint-Germain-en-Laye, added a ballroom to Fontainebleau and carried out improvements at various royal châteaux. He took a close interest in the one built by his mistress, Diane de Poitiers, at Anet. At the same time his ministers and friends built houses fit to receive the court. Anne de Montmorency carried out major works at Écouen and Chantilly, and the cardinal of Lorraine built a famous grotto at Meudon to house his collection of antiquities. Two outstanding architects, Pierre Lescot and Philibert de l'Orme, were employed by the king. Lescot rebuilt the Louvre. He erected a new *corps de logis* two storeys high with a large reception room or *salle* on each floor. A projecting pavilion at each end had three storeys and housed a staircase. Another building, the *Pavillon du roi*, was added at the south-west corner of the Louvre, facing the river. The sculptor Jean Goujon was responsible for some remarkable decoration, both inside and outside, the Louvre displaying a mastery of the classical style. The *salle* on the ground floor contained at one end a gallery supported by four caryatids and, at the other, a *tribunal*, separated from the main room by sixteen Doric columns in groups of four. Elsewhere in the Louvre, Goujon collaborated with the wood-carver, Scipec de Carpi, who gave the king's presence chamber a remarkable coffered ceiling with friezes more correctly Roman than anything previously seen in France. Philibert de l'Orme was a far greater architect than Lescot. He has been called 'the first French architect to have something of the universality of the great Italians'.[24] After spending three years in Rome, studying ancient remains, he returned to his native Lyon and began work for various patrons, including Diane de Poitiers, for whom he built the château of Anet. For Henry II, he designed the tomb of Francis I at Saint-Denis, the chapel at Villers-Cotterêts and the Château-Neuf at Saint-Germain.

The art of painting under Henry II is mainly represented by two artists: Francesco Primaticcio and Niccolò dell'Abbate.[25] Primaticcio continued to be employed at Fontainebleau. By this time he had developed a style characterised by female nudes with long tapering limbs, thin necks and small heads with classical profiles. Between 1552 and 1556 he painted murals in the ballroom at Fontainebleau that betray the influence of Raphael and Parmigianino. More important were his decorations for the *Galerie d'Ulysse*, which was unfortunately destroyed in 1739.[26] Niccolò dell'Abbate came to Fontainebleau in 1552 with a wide experience of north Italian painting, particularly the art of Correggio. Alongside decorative painting, portraiture continued to prosper under Henry II. Its main exponents were François Clouet, who had become royal portraitist in 1541, and Corneille de Lyon, a Dutchman who entered the dauphin's service in 1540 and continued working at court till 1574.

Henry II was keenly interested in projecting his image. In 1547 he appointed a coin engraver to design medals and coins reminiscent of those which had carried the fame of Roman emperors down the centuries. The king's device – a crescent moon – was used by the organisers of his Rouen entry in 1550 to advertise his imperial pretensions. It was said to possess magical properties which guaranteed the king as 'future monarch and emperor of the world'. Royal image-making was powerfully influenced by the cult of ancient Rome that swept through the arts

and literature of mid-sixteenth-century France. Francis I had been identified with Julius Caesar, but it was under Henry II that the essential
prerequisites for the reconstruction of a Roman triumph in art and
poetry were fulfilled in France. This is best revealed by the royal entries.
In 1548 Henry II saw in Lyon a re-enactment of a gladiatorial combat,
which excited him so much that he asked to have it repeated six days
later. The entry itself was a kind of Roman triumph. Henry was met by
160 infantry wearing Roman military uniform. A triumphal arch, nearly
sixty feet high, along the processional route symbolised Honour and
Virtue. Honour, seated in a triumphal car drawn by two elephants, had
a military escort, while Virtue, in a car drawn by two unicorns, was surrounded by nymphs playing musical instruments. However, it was in
Rouen in 1550 that Henry was given the most remarkable entry. He
passed through four triumphal arches. The first showed Orpheus, the
Muses and Hercules destroying the Hydra, the second presented the
Golden Age above Henry's crescent moon, the third showed Hector in
full armour mounted on a platform held up by four caryatids, and the
last displayed an image of Francis I flanked by two columns. The cars
were an even more potent evocation of a Roman triumph. The first,
depicting Fame, was drawn by four winged horses and decorated by
battle scenes, spoils of war and representations of death; the second
showed Vesta enthroned; and the third displayed Henry II holding the
insignia of state and receiving the imperial crown from the goddess
Good Fortune. Each car was preceded by soldiers, cavalry, musicians
and standard-bearers wearing Roman armour. The musical instruments
imitated the long tubular horns and trumpets of the ancient Romans
and, as in Caesar's triumphs, elephants carried the booty. Prisoners of
war followed dejectedly in chains. Then came priests with sacrifical
lambs and Flora and her nymphs scattering flowers. Wave upon wave of
citizens, dressed à la romaine, marched past the king, who viewed the
triumph seated on a throne in a specially constructed gallery.[27]

The trend towards classicism seen in the visual arts under Henry II is
also present in literature, especially poetry. This was when the *Pléiade*, a
group of seven poets, led by Pierre de Ronsard, came into being. In his
Hymne à Henri II de ce nom (1551) Ronsard compares Henry's court to
the deities on Mount Olympus. Jupiter and Henry are shown as mirror
images, reflecting dignity and honour. As the poem unfolds, Apollo

sings the praises of Henry's triumphant majesty. The qualities expected of a prince, and which Henry has in abundance, are extolled. A vivid picture of physical strength emerges as Ronsard praises the king's superiority as a rider and swordsman. His majesty is made to correspond with the energies of his people and the riches of his dominions.

11

Royal Authority

In January 1521 Francis I celebrated Twelfth Night at his court by taking part in a mock battle. He tried to break down the door of a house that was being defended by a group of noblemen. They threw various objects out of the windows, including a smouldering log which fell on the king's head, injuring him grievously. For several weeks his life was in danger. In order to attend to his injury, his head had to be shaved. Feeling conspicuous, he ordered all his male courtiers to have their own heads shaved. The Ferrarese ambassador wrote that he was afraid of undergoing the same treatment if he went to the court.[1] Throughout his reign Francis behaved in a very authoritarian manner.

Although, by the standards of his age, Francis I was not a particularly tyrannical monarch, he showed little regard for existing ordinances, institutions or methods of government. He quarrelled with the Parlement of Paris, the highest court of law in the land, over a number of issues. The Parlement regarded itself as the guardian of the so-called 'fundamental laws', including the Salic law governing the succession to the throne and a law banning the alienation of crown lands. If the king had no cause to break the first law, he was prepared on occasion to flout the second. Francis rejected the parallel which the Parlement liked to draw between itself and the Senate of ancient Rome. He was supported in his authoritarianism by his chancellor, Antoine Duprat, who once said: 'We owe obedience to the king and it is not for us to question his commands'.[2] All authority, he explained, came from the king; otherwise the kingdom would be an aristocracy, not a monarchy.

Policy was decided by the king alone with the advice of his council. This was clearly demonstrated in 1516 when the Concordat of Bologna was imposed on the French people. This was a bargain struck by the king and the pope. In return for the restoration of papal authority in France, which had been seriously curtailed by the Pragmatic Sanction of

Bourges in 1438, the king was given the legal right to control appointments to major ecclesiastical benefices. The agreement was detested by the Parlement, the university of Paris and by the Gallican church; in short, by all the interested parties; yet its registration was roughly forced through. Francis tried to intimidate the Parlement by appointing his uncle, René of Savoy, to attend its debates. The court protested vigorously at this infringement of its liberties but had to give way after the king had threatened to banish some of its members and to replace them by 'worthy men'. Despite René's presence, the Parlement refused to register the Concordat. This enraged the king. He declared that there would be no senate in France, as there was in Venice, and threatened to make the Parlement 'trot after him' like the *Grand Conseil*. Two *parlementaires* who called on him at Amboise were curtly informed that he was inclined to keep them waiting for as long as he had been kept waiting by the Parlement. After they had accomplished their mission, they asked for permission to delay their departure on account of serious flooding in the area, but were warned that, if they had not left by 6 a.m. the next day, they would be thrown into a deep pit and left there for six months. Francis then threatened to set up a rival Parlement in Poitiers. Eventually, the Concordat was registered, albeit with the traditional Latin phrase indicating duress. When the university forbade its publication and appealed to a future General Council, Francis threatened it with banishment and the loss of its privileges. Some of its members were arrested, but released once the king had got what he wanted.[3]

Following the king's defeat and capture at Pavia in February 1525, the Parlement tried to regain lost ground. It presented a wide-ranging set of remonstrances to the king's mother, Louise of Savoy, who governed as regent. She was asked to act more vigorously against heretics, to revoke the Concordat, to suppress evocations to the *Grand Conseil* and to abandon fiscal expedients. She pretended to be impressed by the petition, calling it 'to the honour of God, the exaltation of the faith and very useful and necessary to the welfare of the king and the state'.[4] She even promised to meet its demands and to persuade her son to revoke the Concordat, yet little or nothing was done. By appointing her chancellor, Duprat, as archbishop of Sens and abbot of Saint-Benoît-sur-Loire against the wishes of the chapters concerned, Louise upheld the spirit, if not the letter, of the Concordat. When Francis returned from captivity, he put the Parlement firmly in its place. At a *lit de justice* in 1527, the president, Charles Guillart, addressing the king, said:

'We do not question your authority for this would be a kind of sacrilege and we know well that you are above the laws and that laws and ordinances cannot constrain you and that no coactive authority binds you to them. Yet we wish to say that you do not or should not wish to do all that lies in your power, but only that which is good and equitable, which is nothing else than justice.'[5]

That afternoon, Francis and his council drew up an edict subordinating the Parlement to his authority. It was required to seek annual confirmation of its delegated authority. Moreover, by ordering the Parlement to register the edict in his absence, he prevented it from sheltering under the traditional formula implying duress. The edict marked a turning point in the Parlement's relations with the crown. It continued to remonstrate from time to time till the end of the reign, but never again seriously encroached on the king's authority.[6]

The Parlement of Paris was not the only body of its kind in France. Altogether there were five Parlements in 1515. Each was sovereign within its own *ressort* or area of jurisdiction in respect of the registration of royal ordinances. Thus a law that was registered in Paris was not enforceable in Languedoc unless it was first registered by the Parlement of Toulouse. On the whole, Francis I's relation with the provincial Parlements were good, except for the Parlement of Rouen. The members of this body acquired such a bad reputation that, in 1527, the king threatened to distribute them among other courts and to replace them by worthier men. No action, however, was taken until the Parlement opposed the famous ordinance of Villers-Cotterêts of August 1539. Whereas in Paris it had been registered within a month, in Rouen it was repeatedly obstructed. It was eventually registered, but without sixteen clauses which the Parlement disliked. Early in August 1540 Francis informed the court that he was coming with important things to say. Fearing the worst, the Parlement sent representatives to the chancellor, Guillaume Poyet, who had arrived in Rouen ahead of the king. He reminded them that parlements had been set up as 'an example and a light to others'. A few days later the ordinance of Villers-Cotterêts was registered, this time in its entirety, but this was not enough to assuage the king's anger. He warned the Rouen magistrates he would soon be calling on them, adding 'the worthy members will be pleased and the rest displeased'. They expected a *lit de justice* but were treated instead to a diatribe, lasting four hours, from the chancellor. 'The king', he declared, 'had planted a vineyard with choice plants and had set up a winepress nearby in anticipation of the harvest; but the vines had produced only wild and sour grapes.' On 10 September 1540, the magistrates appeared before the king. He announced that he was cancelling several of their recent decrees and closing down their court till further notice. Later that day, the Parlement surrendered its seal to Francis. But the level of crime in Normandy was such that royal justice still needed dispensing. A commission of Rouen *parlementaires*, known as the *Grands Jours*, was set up at Bayeux, but its impact was limited. Numerous criminals fled from the area as soon as the commission was announced so that effigies had to be used in executions instead of the real culprits. By January 1541, the situation got so out of hand that Francis had to restore the Parlement. Its members were ordered to carry out his wishes diligently in future. They were forbidden to 'contradict, discuss, deduce or allege anything against the registration of the edicts'.[7]

Popular Representation

It has been suggested that the French monarchy in the early sixteenth century was 'popular and consultative' rather than 'absolute'.[8] Yet in many instances the king did not consult his subjects. In 1526, for example, following his return from captivity in Spain, he refused to ratify the treaty of Madrid on the ground that he had been forced to sign it. For a long time historians imagined that he had reached this decision after Burgundian deputies at a meeting of the Estates-General allegedly held in Cognac had proudly affirmed their loyalty to the French crown, but no such meeting ever took place. The decision to break the treaty was taken by the king's council on 10 May, almost a month before the estates of Burgundy met at Dijon. On this occasion they tamely endorsed the decision of the king's council in spite of the fact that Burgundian loyalty to France was far from unanimous.[9] The Estates-General, the main representative body in France under the Ancien Régime, were never called by Francis I, who regarded them as dangerous or at best useless.

They remained in abeyance till 1560, when a combination of religious unrest and royal bankruptcy forced Charles IX to call them. In their absence, the only national body remotely comparable was an Assembly of Notables, called in 1527. Its members were not elected, but chosen by the king, and its procedure was tailored to his needs. It was a sort of enlarged royal council designed to give an appearance of national consultation. The reason for it was the king's need of a large subsidy – two million *écus* – needed to pay the ransom of his two sons left as hostages in Spain under the treaty of Madrid. Francis made it clear to the delegates that he was consulting them simply as an honour, not because he was obliged to do so.[10]

A limited form of popular representation did exist in sixteenth-century France. Representative estates met in a number of provinces, known as *pays d'états*, the principal ones being Normandy, Languedoc, Dauphiné, Burgundy, Provence and Brittany. In most of them the three estates – clergy, nobility and third estate – were represented, but they were not always chosen in the same way, nor was their role always identical. None was truly democratic: the majority of the people, both rural and urban, had no voice. The provincial estates owed their existence to the king: he called them, fixed the date and place of their meeting, appointed their president and determined their agenda. Royal commissioners put forward his demands, negotiated with the deputies and attended to their requests. Usually the estates met once a year, but sometimes more often, their frequency being determined by the crown's fiscal needs. They were sometimes able to negotiate a tax reduction, but the king usually got his way after a haggle. Yet the estates were not insignificant. They often drew the king's attention to economic or administrative matters which required action, and he often responded positively. If contemporary political theorists believed that the king had an absolute authority given to him by God, many were also of the opinion that he should use it sparingly and always in the interest of his subjects. This meant, in effect, respecting their traditional rights and privileges. Francis I put his own gloss on this advice. When the estates of Languedoc claimed exemption from the garrisoning of troops, he replied: 'the kingdom is one body and monarchy'. All his subjects, he explained, needed to be treated alike; if he exempted some, others would have to shoulder a proportionately heavier burden. Equitable as it may seem, this sentiment merely camouflaged the king's self-interest. On another occasion, he was more candid. 'In times of necessity', he declared, 'all privileges lapse, and not only privileges, but common laws as well since necessity knows no law.'[11]

The term 'absolutism' is often misunderstood. It does not imply that the king can do as he pleases. It should not be equated to tyranny. Absolutism means in essence that the king has no superior save God. For all his authoritarianism, Francis was not all-powerful. The enforcement of his policies depended on an administration that was rudimentary in many respects. A comparison of the number of office-holders per head of population in 1515 with the number in 1665 reveals the distance separating Francis's administration from that of Louis XIV. Under Francis they numbered 5000: that is, one office-holder per 3200 inhabitants (assuming a total population of sixteen million) whereas Louis XIV had eleven times as many to impose his will on his twenty million subjects.[12] It follows that if Francis was 'absolute' at all, he was much less so than Louis XIV. He could only point the way towards an absolutism still to be realised. Apart from the limited number of office-holders at his disposal, he had to operate within practical constraints, notably an unsatisfactory tax system and an inefficient fiscal administration.

Taxation

The king depended on two kinds of revenue: the 'ordinary' which he drew from his domain; and the 'extraordinary' which consisted of three main taxes, the *taille*, which was the only direct tax, the salt tax or *gabelle* and the *aides*, which were duties levied on certain commodities. The *taille* was levied annually, the amount being decided by the king's council, but many people were exempt. In addition to the nobility and clergy, several professional groups were exempt, as were a large number of towns, including Paris. Indirect taxes, of course, applied to everyone, but they were subject to all kinds of anomalies. The *gabelle*, for example, was not uniformly levied across the kingdom: some areas did not pay it at all, while others paid in different ways. Francis I incurred heavy expenses from the start of his reign. He inherited a deficit of 1.4 million *livres* from Louis XII, whose funeral had to be paid for as well as Francis's own coronation. But his main expenditure was on the preparation of his first Italian campaign. The peace of Fribourg cost one million *écus* and inaugurated a system of pensions to certain Swiss cantons and individuals. In 1518 Francis paid 600,000 gold *écus* to Henry VIII for the return of Tournai. The imperial election may have cost 400,000 *écus* and the Field of Cloth of Gold at least 200,000 *livres*. All this was onerous enough, but the king's financial predicament grew worse after war with the emperor had broken out in 1521. The hire of Swiss mercenaries was an enormous expense. The tax revenue did not suffice to meet all these demands: it was slow to collect and much of it did not reach the royal coffers. Yet Francis I did not substantially increase the tax burden. His income only rose by an annual average of 1.44 per cent. The *taille* rose from about 2.4 million *livres* in 1515 to some 4.6 million in 1544–45, with a fall to 3.6 million in 1547.[13]

Instances of popular resistance to taxation under Francis I are remarkably few by comparison with the number later on, especially in the early seventeenth century. Foreigners viewed the French as extraordinarily compliant. A Venetian ambassador wrote:

> The king has only to say I want such and such a sum, I order, I consent, and the thing is done as speedily as if it had been decided by the whole nation of its own volition. The situation has already gone so far that a few Frenchmen, who can see a little more clearly than the rest, say: our kings used to call themselves *Reges francorum* [kings of the Franks], but at present they might as well be called *Reges servorum* [kings of slaves]. The king receives all that he asks for and the remainder is at his mercy.[14]

Yet taxation was not always accepted without protest. In 1542 it prompted open resistance in western France. An attempt by Francis to reform the *gabelle* was bitterly opposed by the salt producers of La Rochelle, who feared for their livelihood. They armed themselves and resisted two waves of royal commissioners. Only Francis's personal intervention brought the unrest to a halt. He sat in judgment on the rebels and, after giving them the fright of their lives, pardoned them, but he could not be otherwise than magnanimous at a time when he was fighting on several fronts at once. In the long term, he did not give up his planned reform of the *gabelle*. By 1548 it had become so oppressive as to ignite a new revolt, far more serious than that of 1542. This was savagely put down by Henry II.[15] The magnanimity shown by Francis I to the tax rebels of La Rochelle stands in stark contrast with his treatment of the inhabitants of Lagny-sur-Seine in 1544. They were charged with committing 'acts of disobedience and rebellion' when the king faced an imperial invasion. Francis dispatched an armed force to Lagny under the seigneur de Lorges, who was instructed to sack the town as if it were in enemy hands. Any survivors were denied the right of appeal against any act committed by the troops, and no court in France was allowed to receive such an appeal. The royal decree evidently upset the Parlement of Paris, which registered it only after receiving three *lettres de jussion*. Lagny was wiped off the map for a time and it is unclear if the sack left any survivors.[16]

In order to supplement his tax revenues, Francis I resorted to various fiscal expedients. He borrowed from bankers and private individuals, imposed forced loans on towns, levied clerical tenths, alienated crown lands and sold titles of nobility and offices. A large proportion of the bankers who lent him money were Italians based in Lyon. They normally exacted high rates of interest and Francis soon defaulted on his repayments, thereby destroying his credit. For some time after 1523 he could no longer borrow on the Lyon money market. This crippled his war effort, according to Guicciardini, and led to the peace of Cambrai. Francis also borrowed from his own tax officials, who were always men of substance, or helped himself to the inheritance of a wealthy subject. In 1519, for example, he seized the inheritance of the Grand Master, Artus Gouffier, while promising to compensate his widow with lands.[17] Many towns that were exempt from the *taille* were asked for forced loans. They usually pleaded poverty and were sometimes able to get a reduction of the sum demanded, but they were seldom, if ever, let off completely. The church, too, was fleeced mercilessly. In theory, a clerical tenth was a voluntary gift to assist the king in an emergency and needed the pope's authorisation, but in the course of his reign Francis levied as many as fifty-seven tenths, usually without papal permission. A clerical tenth became, in effect, a regular tax. An expedient much used by Francis was the alienation of crown lands by gift or sale. This was repeatedly opposed by the Parlement as a breach of the 'fundamental law' banning alienations of crown lands, but the king always got his way.

The king also sold titles of nobility and offices. If he sold no more than 150 letters of ennoblement, he was far more prodigal in respect of offices. These were keenly sought by wealthy bourgeois anxious to climb the social ladder, for an *office* was a 'dignity', not just a government post. The more important offices automatically conferred noble status and privileges, such as tax exemption. Sheer greed prompted the king to sell more offices than were administratively necessary. In the long term, venality, as the sale of offices was called, tended to undermine royal authority, for an office-holder who had bought his office regarded it as his personal property and did not feel bound to carry out the public functions attached to it. This danger was enhanced by another expedient much used by the crown. Office-holders were allowed to nominate their successors in return for an additional payment. This, too, was to prove dangerous, as offices became the monopoly of a limited number of families; people rich enough to buy them found themselves excluded from the privileged world of office-holders.[18]

The fiscal administration that Francis I inherited was as defective as the tax system. It was built around the two kinds of revenue: ordinary and extraordinary. The *trésor*, which was responsible for the ordinary revenue, was headed by four *trésoriers de France*, each responsible for an area of the kingdom. Four *généraux des finances* had charge of the extraordinary revenues, each being in charge of an area called a *généralité*. The *trésoriers* and *généraux*, known collectively as *gens de finance*, were expected to reside at court when they were not carrying out tours of inspection. Their main duty was to draw up at the start of each year a kind of national budget based on accounts from each fiscal district. They were, for the most part, closely related and shared common interests. Alongside their royal duties, they ran profitable businesses of their own. Their public and private functions overlapped, offering speculative temptations.[19] An outstanding member of this financial oligarchy was Jacques de Beaune, baron of Semblançay. The son of a rich merchant of Tours, he became the king's chief financial adviser. By 1523 there was not enough money in the king's coffers to pay for the war against Charles V. Francis accused his own fiscal officials of cheating him and set up a commission to audit their accounts. Not even Semblançay, who had done so much to help him out of his difficulties, was spared. Ironically, the commissioners found that it was the king who owed Semblançay money. This sealed the poor man's fate. In January 1527 Semblançay was accused of various malpractices and tried by judges who were his personal enemies. He reminded Francis of his past services, but the king was unmoved. In August the old man (he was over eighty at the time) was found guilty, taken to the gallows at Montfaucon and hanged. A chronicler wrote: 'he was much pitied and mourned by the people, who would have been pleased if the king had seen fit to spare him'.[20] This did not mark the end of the royal persecution of *gens de finance*. During the 1530s a commision called *Commission de la Tour Carrée* continued to harass them. Gaillard Spifame, for example, was imprisoned on a charge of 'having cheated the king of more than three or four hundred thousand francs ... thereby causing the loss of the war and of the battle in which the king had been captured because the men-at-arms had not been paid'.[21]

Local government in early sixteenth-century France was far from tidy. At the top were were eleven governorships (*gouvernements*), but they did not cover the whole of France. Large areas in the centre and west were excluded, presumably because they ranked as apanages, Yet governors were essential to the effective exercise of royal authority. They were recruited from among the princes of the blood and high nobility. Though never more than a commissioner appointed by the king at his pleasure, a governor was commonly accorded quasi-regalian honours, such as a canopy when he first entered a town in his province. He was to all intents and purposes a viceroy. A governor was so often at court or fighting for the king that the performance of his local duties was entrusted to a lieutenant, who was usually a lesser noble or prelate. Yet, even at a distance, a governor could assist his province. He could, for example, ensure that the demands of the local estates were given a favourable hearing by the king's council. His presence at court also gave him unique opportunities for patronage, enabling him to build up a large personal clientèle within his province. This could include soldiers, household officials, servants and local gentlemen. Nearly all governors were captains of the *gendarmerie* – the heavy cavalry forming the core of the army. As such, they controlled recruitment and promotion. A governor's household provided employment for local noblemen and education for their children. This constituted a danger for the crown, as a governor might use his personal clientèle to undermine royal authority, as often happened during the Wars of Religion in the second half of the sixteenth century.[22]

Writing in 1930, the French historian George Pagès wrote: 'Francis I and Henry II were as powerful as any other kings of France; it was at the beginning of the sixteenth century that the absolute monarchy triumphed'.[23] Few historians, if any, would endorse this view today, for it is clear that the French monarchy in the early sixteenth century still had to operate within old-established parameters restricting its freedom of action. The kings certainly regarded themselves as absolute and were encouraged in this belief by contemporary political writers, such as Guillaume Budé, but their absolutism was essentially theoretical. They could rightly claim that the Almighty was their only superior, but in practice they could not do as they wished. The machinery of government, especially the fiscal system, failed to answer the needs of an increasingly unified state. A whole panoply of medieval rights and privileges still had to be treated circumspectly. Policy decisions were taken by the king and his council, but their implementation depended on the effectiveness of a relatively small number of office-holders. Although the Estates-General never met, a certain measure of popular consultation survived in the provincial estates. Above all the king depended on the support of the nobility. Francis I and Henry II were fortunate in getting that support, largely because the nobles were economically content. Recent research has shown that the French nobility as a whole did not suffer economically at this time; if some families became indebted, the majority grew wealthier.[24] The king kept them happy by leading them in war and by rewarding their valour with gifts, offices and titles. This situation was soon to change, as we shall see.

12

The Challenge of Heresy

Probably the gravest challenge facing the Valois monarchs in the six-teenth century was the rise of Protestantism which threatened to destroy the kingdom's unity. Religious toleration was unknown in sixteenth-century France. 'One law, one faith, one king' was the rule that prevailed. The king was seen as God's earthly lieutenant, and his coro-nation endowed him with a semi-priestly character: it was not only a crowning but a consecration performed by the archbishop. Unlike his lay subjects, the king was allowed communion in both kinds. As he was also deemed to possess the miraculous power of healing, thousands of sick people sought his curative touch. At his coronation, he solemnly swore to defend the church and rid his kingdom of heresy. This duty had not been seriously tested in France for three centuries, but in the sixteenth century heresy in the form of Protestantism threatened to tear the kingdom apart. But heresy needed to be recognised. When Lutheranism reached France from Germany in 1519, it was not immedi-ately seen to be a menace, except by the theologians of the university of Paris, commonly known as the Sorbonne.[1] Their doctrinal pronounce-ments commanded enormous respect internationally but were not binding on the monarch.

Sharp differences existed among theologians at the close of the Middle Ages regarding the philosophical foundations of Christian belief.[2] Three currents of thought existed side by side: scholasticism, mysticism and humanism. The most important centre of scholasticism was the university of Paris, whose teaching was drawn from the Vulgate and Peter Lombard's *Book of Sentences*. Its principal exponent in the thirteenth century was Thomas Aquinas, who believed that knowledge of God was attainable through reason with the help of Scripture and the church's teaching. In the fourteenth century, however, the certain-ties implicit in his philosophy were challenged by Duns Scotus and

William of Ockham, who argued that divine truth could only be reached through the teaching of the church. Over time, their brand of philosophy, known as Nominalism, reduced the teaching of theology in Paris to an uncritical acceptance and repetition of the affirmations contained in the *Book of Sentences*. This failed to satisfy the spiritual yearnings of many Christians, who turned to mysticism instead. A mystical tradition had existed in Paris in the fourteenth century, but it was in the Low Countries during the fifteenth century that mysticism became a powerful movement. Known as the *Devotio moderna*, it found its practical expression in the activities of the Brethren of the Common Life, who aimed to followed the precepts laid down by Thomas à Kempis in his *Imitation of Christ*. An important link between this *Devotio moderna* and Paris was John Standonck, who became principal of the collège de Montaigu, one of the university's many colleges. He imposed a harsh discipline on the students in order to elicit from them an active, mystical piety. The third component of Parisian thought was humanism, an import of the late fifteenth century. An early exponent was Guillaume Fichet, who combined respect for scholasticism with a love of ancient literature and philosophy. His disciple, Robert Gaguin, formed a group of scholars who were assisted in their labours by a number of Italian humanists who settled in Paris as teachers. The early Parisian humanists, however, did not know Greek. In 1476 its study was given a boost when George Hermonymos, a Spartan, began teaching in Paris. In 1495 King Charles VIII brought back from Italy Janus Lascaris, an excellent Hellenist. Meanwhile, scholasticism continued to dominate the university's teaching. The first French humanist to break away significantly was Jacques Lefèvre d'Étaples, who combined enthusiasm for Aristotelian philosophy with a strongly mystical Christian faith. The combination of an enthusiasm for the classics with the desire to infuse a more deeply-felt faith into Christian practice animated the movement known as 'Christian' or 'evangelical humanism', whose greatest exponent was Erasmus of Rotterdam. He came to Paris in 1495 to study theology. He entered the collège de Montaigu, but, soon repelled by its austere discipline and scholastic teaching, he joined Gaguin's circle, and in 1499 published a small collection of ancient Greek proverbs. This marked the start of a vast project for the rehabilitation of classical literature to which Erasmus devoted the rest of his life. At the same time, he set out to place the wisdom of the ancients at the service of Christianity.[3]

Francis I was no scholar. Like Shakespeare, he 'had small Latin and less Greek', yet he was an intelligent man interested in books. Like other princes of his day, he was drawn to the occult sciences: astrology, alchemy and the Cabala, which were believed to hold the key to hidden forces animating the universe.[4] He also enjoyed the company of well-educated men, including several humanists. Among them were his secretary, Guillaume Budé, his doctor, Guillaume Cop, his old tutor, François Demoulins, and his confessor, Guillaume Petit. Budé was a Christian humanist who applied his philological expertise to the study of Scripture.[5] At the beginning of Francis I's reign, the greatest need felt by humanists in France was for a college devoted to the teaching of Greek and Hebrew, languages which did not form part of the university curriculum. Francis announced in 1517 his intention of founding such a college, and invited Erasmus to take charge of it. When the Dutchman turned down his invitation, Francis turned to Janus Lascaris. As a first step, he founded a college of young Greeks in Milan, but it soon had to close for lack of funding. Francis I's interest in scholarship, though real enough, was easily supplanted by more urgent matters, such as war. It had to be sustained by tactful reminders from Budé and others. Later in his reign, the idea of a college devoted to the study of Greek and Hebrew, was taken up again. In the 1530s Francis set up royal lectureships in those languages, a move fiercely resisted by theologians of the university, led by the Sorbonne's syndic, Noël Béda. They regarded any departure from their own teaching as heresy, and made no distinction between Christian humanists, like Lefèvre or Erasmus, and the Protestant reformer, Martin Luther.[6]

The Rise of Heresy

Erasmus described France in 1517 as the only part of Christendom free of heresy. Except in Provence, which had been infiltrated by Waldensianism, heresy was confined to a few cranks, but in 1519 Lutheran books reached Paris from Germany. Within a short time they gained converts, especially among the clergy. In 1521 after hotly debating the issue, the Sorbonne formally condemned Luther's doctrine as heretical, thereby posing a problem for the king who had Christian humanists in his entourage. Francis was not obliged to endorse the Sorbonne's pronouncement and resented the faculty's attempts to dictate his own faith or that of his courtiers. For several years the king and the Sorbonne quarrelled over the precise nature of heresy. While repeatedly declaring his hatred of heresy and his determination to root it out, Francis tried to protect members of his entourage from the Sorbonne's campaign to muzzle scholars, like Lefèvre d'Étaples, who favoured a faith firmly rooted in Scripture. The borderline between Lutheranism and Christian humanism was far from clear. Both drew heavily from the writings of St Paul, yet, unlike Luther, Lefèvre d'Étaples never broke with Rome. While sharing Luther's belief in salvation by faith, he continued to hope for self-reform by the church.[7] He counted among his disciples Guillaume Briçonnet, bishop of Meaux, who set about reforming his diocese with the help of a group of evangelical preachers, known as the *Cercle de Meaux*.[8] Another zealous follower of Lefèvre was the king's sister, Marguerite d'Angoulême. She never became a Lutheran, but developed a personal faith seemingly more Protestant than Catholic.[9]

An early sign of trouble between Francis I and the Sorbonne occurred in June 1523 when the faculty began to examine a work by Lefèvre d'Étaples, only to be reprimanded by the chancellor, Antoine Duprat. He ordered the faculty to refer the matter to him and an episcopal commission, including Briçonnet. In July, Francis evoked the matter to the *Grand Conseil*, a judicial body under his direct control. Béda, the Sorbonne's syndic, submitted to the Sorbonne twenty-two allegedly heretical propositions contained in sermons preached by Mazurier and Caroli, two members of the *Cercle de Meaux*. Condemned by the faculty, the preachers were made to recant. In August 1523 the Sorbonne, outraged by the publication of Lefèvre's edition of the New Testament, condemned all editions of Scripture in Greek, Hebrew and French. Francis I reacted by forbidding any discussion of Lefèvre's works. In October 1523 he foiled an attempt by the Sorbonne to condemn Erasmus.[10]

The Sorbonne looked to the Parlement of Paris to enforce its doctrinal pronouncements. In 1523 both bodies decided that the growth of heresy called for more draconian measures than censoring books; they wanted to silence the heretics themselves. Their first victim was a young nobleman, Louis de Berquin. Suspect books were found in his home, including some of his own writings, which the Sorbonne condemned – regardless of an attempt by the king to have them examined by a commission of his own choosing. When Berquin refused to retract his views, he was handed over to the bishop of Paris for trial on a heresy charge. Francis I evoked the case to the *Grand Conseil* and Berquin was set free, though his books were burnt outside Notre-Dame.[11]

Francis I's captivity in 1525–26 gave the Sorbonne and Parlement a chance to assert their authority. They hoped to win the backing of the regent, Louise of Savoy, who was 'the most consistently traditional member of the royal family, the most uneasy about the spread of Lutheranism in France'.[12] The two institutions also exploited a wave of hysteria sweeping through the capital. The Peasants' War had erupted in Germany and rumours of imminent catastrophe were reaching the Parlement daily. The king's sister, who was known for her evangelical leanings, became the butt of popular satire. In March 1525 the bishop of Paris was ordered by the Parlement to set up an anti-heresy tribunal whose four judges (*juges-délégués*) were recruited equally from the Sorbonne and Parlement. When the new tribunal attacked the *Cercle de Meaux*, Francis I wrote from his Spanish prison, ordering the prosecution of Lefèvre, Caroli and Roussel to cease, and any complaints against them to be addressed to the regent.[13] But the Parlement proceeded regardless. As pressure on the *Cercle de Meaux* mounted, its leaders fled or recanted. Lefèvre and Roussel sought sanctuary in Strasbourg. Caroli gained the protection of Marguerite d'Angoulême, and Mazurier recanted after a spell in prison. As for Briçonnet, he reverted to orthodoxy. In January 1526 the campaign against Berquin was resumed. He was rearrested and might have been condemned to death if the king had not returned from Spain. In April 1526, Francis forbade the Parlement to condemn Berquin, and, when he fell ill, ordered him to be transferred to the Louvre. When the Parlement refused to release Berquin on security grounds, Francis had him forcibly removed from the Conciergerie and brought to the Louvre.[14]

Members of the *Cercle de Meaux* likewise benefited from the king's protection. Lefèvre and Roussel returned from foreign exile. Lefèvre became royal librarian and tutor to the king's youngest son, Roussel was appointed as Marguerite d'Angoulême's almoner, and Caroli resumed preaching in Paris. The Sorbonne, however, was not silenced. In May 1526 it condemned Erasmus's *Colloquies*. Soon afterwards Béda published a work, accusing Erasmus and Lefèvre of multiple heresy. Francis banned its sale and forbade the Sorbonne to publish any book without the Parlement's *imprimatur*. Complaining that the king was being led astray by members of his entourage, Béda accused Erasmus and Lefèvre of bringing Lutheranism into France. He suggested that the king would act differently if only he understood the situation.[15]

Francis may well have been confused, for heresy was continually changing its shape. Protestantism was evolving and over time becoming more radical. While Lutheranism continued to believe in the Real Presence of Christ in the Eucharist, Sacramentarianism, a doctrine preached by the Swiss Protestant reformer, Ulrych Zwingli, rejected the Real Presence, arguing that the communion service was a memorial, not a sacrifice. Calvinism, another Protestant variant, took up the same position. Francis I had to make sense of this ideological muddle. Little is known about his personal faith, save that he attended Mass each day. But he could not abstain from a religious debate which had grave political implications. The king, it seems, opposed any religious dissent likely to provoke public unrest.

By 1528 Protestants began to think that Francis I was coming round to their views. Wolfgang Capito wrote to Zwingli: 'the king favours the Word'.[16] But Francis was simply asserting his authority as it was being challenged by the Parlement and Sorbonne. When, in December 1527, the French clergy called on him to extirpate 'the damned and insufferable Lutheran sect', Francis said that he was determined to act as 'the Most Christian King' in word and deed. Shortly afterwards, Berquin was rearrested, tried for heresy, and sentenced to life imprisonment. Instead of accepting his fate, he unwisely appealed, only to be sentenced to death. In the king's absence from Paris, Berquin was taken to the Place de Grève and burnt.[17] In June 1528 a statue of the Virgin and Child at the corner of a street in Paris was vandalised. This deed, one of the earliest instances of iconoclasm of the French Reformation, greatly upset the king. He offered a substantial reward for any information about the iconoclasts and commissioned a replacement. He then led a solemn procession to the scene of the sacrilege and placed the new statue in its niche.[18] A synod of the French clergy, meeting at Sens later that year, took stringent measures for the suppression of heresy. In 1529 Francis was blamed for the Parlement's decision to ban all French translations of Scripture. Guillaume Farel, a member of the *Cercle de Meaux*, wrote to Capito: 'I cannot see what progress can be made among the French under so insane a sovereign who has allowed the New Testament to be forbidden to the people, so that there remains no way of making the truth known'.[19] The Swiss reformer, Oecolampadius, was equally despondent. Writing to Zwingli in May 1530, he wrote:

It is getting too late for France to turn to Christ for persons who arrived here [Basle] at Easter brought news that the bishops and theologians are extremely hostile to those who profess Christ, and that the king is not merely silent about this but actually threatens the most learned Gérard Roussel and Jacques Lefèvre and others with burning if they don't dissuade his sister from the beliefs they have induced her to embrace.[20]

In August 1530, however, following the peace of Cambrai, Bucer informed Luther that the Gospel was making good progress in France. He hoped that Christ would soon be received by the people, 'for the king is not opposed to the truth, and now that he has recovered his children, he will cease to be so dependent on the pope and the emperor'. Bucer praised 'that most Christian heroine', the king's sister, adding that in part of Normandy so many people were professing the Gospel that it was being called 'little Germany'.

Meanwhile, Francis I continued to clash with the Sorbonne as it sought to impose orthodoxy on his sister, Marguerite. In Lent 1531 the faculty accused her almoner, Roussel, of preaching heresy at the Louvre. The king satisfied the faculty by ordering the preacher to give advance notice of the content of his future sermons, but in 1533 the accusation levelled at Roussel was renewed. Six theologians were ordered to preach against Lutheranism in Paris, but they angered the king by attacking Roussel personally. Francis was also offended when a theologian accused his brother-in-law, Henri d'Albret, of being a heretic. He banished Béda and other theologians from Paris, thereby provoking several days of street demonstrations for and against the victims. In October 1533 students of the Collège de Navarre put on a play attacking Marguerite. She was shown preaching heresy and tormenting anyone who would not listen to her. The college was searched by the *prévôt de Paris* and two of its principals were arrested. Later that month, a poem by Marguerite was blacklisted by the university. When the king demanded an explanation, the rector, Nicolas Cop, asked all the faculties to dissociate themselves from the list. The theologian responsible for the ban denied that any offence to Marguerite had been intended. He explained that her poem had been banned because it had been published without his faculty's *imprimatur*. It was now removed from the blacklist and an apology sent to the king.[21]

On 1 November 1533, while Francis was meeting Pope Clement VII in the south of France, Cop preached a sermon before an academic audience in Paris in which he poured scorn on the idea of salvation by good works. 'Who could be so obtuse', he asked, 'as to think and assert that eternal life is a repayment for our good deeds, or that our good deeds are worthy of eternal life?' Detecting Luther's influence in the sermon, some of the audience complained to the Parlement, whereupon Cop called a meeting of the entire university. He claimed that he had been misrepresented and asked for his critics to be called to account, but, failing to get support, he fled from Paris. Three months later he turned up in Switzerland. Another fugitive was his friend, John Calvin, the future reformer, who took refuge in Angoulême. Meanwhile, in Paris, the Parlement made a number of arrests and the Sorbonne began a process of self-examination. Both bodies warned the king, who was in Lyon, that heresy was making headway in the capital. 'We are angry and displeased to learn', he replied, 'that ... this damned heretical Lutheran sect is flourishing in our good town of Paris.' He ordered counter-measures and the publication of two papal bulls against heresy.

Foreign policy helped determine Francis I's attitude to the Protestant Reformation. Although he had made peace with the emperor and was now his brother-in-law, he continued to plot against him. He courted Pope Clement VII while seeking the support of German princes, but their religious divisions hampered the formation of a united opposition to Charles V. Francis accordingly set himself up as religious peacemaker in Germany. His principal agent was Guillaume du Bellay, seigneur de Langey, who tried in May 1534 to persuade the princes that a recent meeting between Francis and the pope had produced a climate favourable to a reunification of the churches. He informed the diet of Baden that Clement VII had shown a desire to review outdated church institutions and to accept some of the views of the German Protestants.

Francis was made to hope that the religious schism in Germany could be healed but an event in France shattered that expectation.

The Affair of the Placards

On the morning of Sunday 18 October 1534, Parisians were startled to find that placards or broadsheets had been put up overnight in a number of public places. Each placard contained the same message: the Mass is not the sacrifice claimed by Catholics since Christ's sacrifice on the Cross cannot be repeated; Christ is not present in the host, since Scripture tells us that He is with God the Father till the Day of Judgment; transubstantiation is a human invention without the sanction of Scripture, and the Eucharist is a memorial, not a miracle. In addition to being a succinct statement of the Sacramentarian doctrine, the placard was also extremely abusive. Transubstantiation was denounced as 'a horrible and execrable blasphemy', an act of 'public idolatry', and 'the doctrine of devils'. Priests were condemned as 'miserable sacrificers', 'false antichrists', 'ravening wolves', 'brigands', 'lewdsters' and 'enemies of God'.[22]

Hysteria swept across Paris as a rumour spread that Protestants were about to sack the Louvre, burn down the churches and massacre Catholic worshippers. Reports that identical placards had been found in a number of provincial towns heightened the panic. One had even appeared on the door of the king's chamber at Amboise. Within twenty-four hours of their discovery, the Parlement ordered a procession in the capital and a search for the unknown bill-posters. The prisons soon began to fill up and on 10 November the first sentences were passed. Three days later, a shoemaker's son was burned and he was followed at the stake by a rich draper. By the end of the month four more people had been burnt. Francis I was blamed for the repression. The Protestant martyrologist, Jean Crespin, tells us that the king 'vomited rage through his eyes and mouth' after the placard had been found on door of his bedchamber. But the repression was initiated not by the king, who was absent from the capital at the time, but by the Parlement and municipal authorities. Be that as it may, the Affair of the Placards played into the hands of the Sorbonne and Parlement. For years they had been trying to silence religious dissenters, only to be repeatedly hindered by the king. Now they had him in their power. He could not dispute the gravity of the affair, which demonstrated the existence of an underground movement more radical than any hitherto seen in France. Far from being merely an attack on Catholic beliefs, the placards called on the general public to reject the church and all its practices. Even if he had wished otherwise, Francis would have had no option but to endorse the repression. On 9 December 1534 he backed the punitive measures so far taken and soon afterwards appointed commissioners to try suspects. His new-found zeal earned him a vote of thanks from the Sorbonne.

On 13 January 1535, soon after Francis I's return to the capital, some copies of Marcourt's *Petit traité* – an elaboration of the doctrine of the placards – were found in Paris. Such an act of defiance called for a royal response. Francis accordingly banned all printing till further notice. At his instigation a public procession, one of the most spectacular ever seen in Paris, took place on 21 January, bringing together the court, the Parlement, university, religious orders, municipal government and trade guilds. Countless relics were brought out for the occasion. Pride of place was given to the Blessed Sacrament, which was reverently carried by the bishop of Paris under a canopy borne by the king's three sons and the duc de Vendôme. Francis walked immediately behind, bareheaded, dressed in black and holding a lighted candle. To an accompaniment of church bells, intrumental music and hymn-singing, the huge cortège wound its way from Saint-Germain l'Auxerrois to Notre-Dame cathedral. At various points along the route, it stopped to allow the sacrament to be placed on a temporary altar. The sight of the king praying allegedly drew tears from the spectators. Now and then someone would shout: 'Sire, do good justice!' and he would reply with a reassuring sign. After Mass and a banquet at the bishop's palace, Francis made a speech in which he urged his subjects to inform on all heretics, even relatives and friends. The day ended with six public burnings. On 24 January a royal proclamation called on seventy-three so-called 'Lutherans', including the poet Clément Marot, to give themselves up. Five days later, harbourers of heretics were made liable to the same penalties as the heretics themselves. Informers were to get a quarter of their victims' property.

The campaign of persecution seriously damaged Francis I's reputation in Germany. Imperial agents pointed to the contrast between his harsh treatment of Christians and the warm welcome he had extended to ambassadors from the Ottoman sultan. In a manifesto addressed to the imperial diet on 1 February 1535, Francis tried to justify himself. Punitive measures, he explained, had been taken for political, not religious, reasons. Their aim had been to suppress sedition. He added that he was being slandered by men who wanted to play the Habsburg game by sowing discord between the French and the Germans. But words alone could not win back the trust of the German Lutherans; deeds too were required. On 16 July 1535 Francis issued the edict of Coucy, which halted the religious persecution on the ground that heresy no longer existed in France. All religious prisoners were to be released and religious exiles allowed to come home. Both were promised a pardon, but the edict specifically excluded 'sacramentarians' from the amnesty. Dissenters were also required to abjure within six months on pain of hanging. On 31 May 1536 the pardon was extended to all religious dissenters, including sacramentarians, but they were still required to abjure within six months.[23]

The edict of Coucy encouraged reformers to hope that Francis remained open to persuasion, a hope eloquently expressed by Calvin in the preface to his *Institutes of the Christian Religion*, published in Basle in March 1536. Addressing the king, he explained that French evangelicals had been falsely charged with sedition and that their cause – the cause of Christ – had been mercilessly trampled upon. 'This has happened', Calvin explained, 'as a result of the tyranny of certain Pharisees rather than by your will.' He urged Francis to listen to what evangelicals had to say in self-defence. 'Although your heart is at present alienated from, even inflamed against us', he continued, 'I trust that we may regain its favour, if you will only read our confession once without indignation or wrath.'[24]

By 1540 it had become clear to the crown that the growth of heresy in France would only be checked by giving the Parlements more powers. On 1 June they were accordingly given overall control of heresy jurisdiction by the edict of Fontainebleau. The preamble recalled the measures so far taken to extirpate 'evil errors' from the kingdom. Having been purged, they had now reappeared. They were allegedly being spread by religious exiles who had returned, and by other dissidents who had hidden during the recent repression and were being helped by people in high places. All the king's subjects were instructed to help fight heresy, 'as each is bound to run in order to put out a public fire'. In July, Parisians were ordered to hand over to the Parlement within twenty-four hours all books banned by the court. Measures were also taken to control the book trade.[25]

Throughout the 1540s 'Lutherans' (they were still called thus even though their views were often more extreme than Luther's) were reported from almost every part of France. In May 1542 the president of the Parlement of Rouen claimed that the church had never been in such danger since the days of the Arian heresy. Having contaminated the lower orders in Rouen, heresy was receiving support from 'the chief families'. In August 1542 the king admitted that the evil was still growing. He questioned and reduced to silence François Landry, a Parisian priest, whose sermons had provoked a public outcry, but other preachers remained troublesome. Protestantism was especially rife among the lower clergy and the urban middle and lower classes. The nobility were not as yet greatly affected, though some members of the court, including the king's mistress, the duchesse d'Etampes, were said to harbour 'Lutheran' sympathies. The peasantry, in general, was not affected. Francis urged the courts to intensify their efforts to stamp out heresy. Meanwhile, the Sorbonne issued clear doctrinal guidelines. In 1543 it published an index of sixty-five forbidden books. Between 1541 and 1544 six Parisian booksellers or printers were put on trial: one was tortured and two were burned.

The last years of Francis I's reign saw a steep rise in prosecutions for heresy by the Parlement. Victims included the scholar-printer, Étienne Dolet, who was burnt in August 1546. In 1545 five commissioners were given full powers to hunt down heretics in the Parlement's area of jurisdiction. Among the most zealous was Nicole Mangin, who arrested forty-seven men and seventeen women at Meaux in September 1546. Of these, fourteen were burnt in front of a huge crowd.[26] Religious persecution in the rest of France varied in intensity; some Parlements being more severe than others. The fiercest were those in areas of Roman law. The Parlement of Toulouse, for example, waged a fierce campaign in Languedoc. In Provence, the Parlement forced the king's hand in respect of the Waldensian heresy.

The Vaudois were mainly peasants living in villages and small towns spread out along the Durance valley. Substituting their own apostolic forms for the authority and practices of the Catholic church, they regarded spiritual probity as essential to the administration of the sacraments. They rejected the doctrine of purgatory, the cult of the Virgin and saints, and did not think worship needed to be focused on a church. Outwardly, however, little distinguished the Vaudois from their Catholic neighbours. Their spiritual needs were served by wandering pastors, called *barbes*, who would meet once a year in a remote Alpine valley. In 1532 they decided to adhere to Calvinism. In May 1540 Francis endorsed a draconian decree against the Vaudois of Mérindol, but pardoned them after Guillaume du Bellay had given them a favourable report. Later, Francis changed his mind before issuing a new pardon and ordering an enquiry. Such vacillations on his part point to the reliance that he placed on hearsay evidence that was sometimes contradictory. The appointment of Jean Maynier, baron d'Oppède, as president of the Parlement of Aix-en-Provence was the signal for a renewed attack on the Vaudois which culminated in several villages being wiped out by royal troops in April 1545. The number of victims may have run into thousands. Francis, who had again changed his mind, showed no remorse. When congratulated on his zeal by the papal nuncio, he reaffirmed his determination to uphold respect for the Catholic faith and for the pope.[27]

Henry II and Heresy

By March 1547, when Henry II succeeded to the throne, Protestantism was firmly entrenched in France and the monarchy was committed to its suppression. Henry was less concerned than his father had been to distinguish between evangelicalism and heresy. Though Calvin had yet to give cohesion to French Protestantism, heresy had become easier to recognise. Henry also had less reason to placate the German Protestant princes following their defeat by the emperor at Mühlberg in 1547. He was allegedly encouraged to persecute dissenters by his mistress, Diane de Poitiers, and by his chief minister, Anne de Montmorency, a noted hawk. Unlike Francis, who never witnessed an *auto-da-fé*, Henry did so more than once. In April 1547 he legislated against blasphemers and, in October, set up a special tribunal in Paris to deal with heresy cases. It became known as the *Chambre ardente* (Burning chamber) on account of its severe sentencing. Between May 1548 and March 1550 it handed down 37 death sentences, representing 17 per cent of the 215 cases which it heard.[28] Of the people who were not executed, only thirty-nine were acquitted; the rest were given various punishments. Twenty-one had their property confiscated and were banished from the kingdom.

The *Chambre ardente* was opposed by the ecclesiastical courts which, except in cases involving clerics, had lost their traditional jurisdiction. In November 1549 they were allowed to judge cases of 'simple heresy', that is to say, cases in which the accused had not voiced their opinions publicly. Yet clashes over jurisdiction continued to occur, causing Henry to issue the edict of Châteaubriant in June 1551. Henceforth, only the Parlements and the recently created presidial courts were allowed to judge heresy cases without appeal. Cases of 'simple heresy' were left to the church courts. In the light of reports that the judiciary itself was being infiltrated by Protestantism, the Parlements were required to examine their personnel every three months. All aspects of literary censorship were covered by the edict. Informers were to receive a third of property confiscated from their victims. Magistrates were ordered to seek out heretics and to search houses for banned books. Outward conformity ceased to guarantee safety. All teachers were to be good Catholics. The property of religious exiles was to be confiscated. Attendance at church became obligatory. Bishops were instructed to reside in their dioceses and to read out every Sunday the articles of faith laid down by the Sorbonne in 1543.[29]

One effect of the new wave of persecution was to swell the ranks of people fleeing to Geneva, where Calvin was trying to establish a city 'governed by God'. They may have numbered as many as 10,000 and included several printers, who helped to produce Calvinist propaganda for dissemination in France. The war between Henry II and the Emperor Charles V facilitated the progress of heresy in France. In April 1556 Henry admitted to the imperial ambassador that other business had prevented him from dealing with the menace. He denounced Geneva as 'the source of much evil because many heretics are received there and thence disseminate their errors throughout France'. In 1555, Calvinist missionaries trained in Geneva began to slip across the border. Henry, who had always assumed that Protestantism was confined to the lower orders of society, was horrified to learn that it was gaining ground among the nobility. Louis, prince of Condé, for example, visited Geneva between 1555 and 1559 and asked to hear a Calvinist sermon.[30] Other French nobles came not merely as visitors but as immigrants. By offering them shelter, the Genevan authorities became embroiled in French politics. Some of the future military leaders of the Huguenot cause were indoctrinated alongside the pastors who would become its spiritual leaders.

Henry II was aware of the threat to his authority posed by the Genevan missionaries. On 24 July 1557 the edict of Compiègne increased the penalties for heresy. The preamble blamed the failure of earlier legislation to restore religious uniformity on conflicts over jurisdiction and the undue leniency of judges. The death penalty was now mandated for a wide range of offences.[31] Henry warned that he would use force of arms in addition to the law courts to put down heresy, which he now identified with sedition; but bitter opposition from the Parlement and the French defeat at Saint-Quentin prevented the edict's application. The Genevan missionaries were thus able to continue making converts in France. They tried at first to operate in secret, holding services in private houses or secluded woodland, but they were sometimes discovered.[32] On 4 September 1557 an angry mob broke up a Calvinist meeting at a house in the rue Saint-Jacques in Paris. 132 people were arrested, including women and children. Some were put on trial; three were burnt.[33] The German Protestant princes pleaded with Henry II to show clemency, but he told them to mind their own business. In May 1558 Calvinists held a mass demonstration, lasting several days, in the Pré-aux-Clercs, a meadow close to the Louvre. It was attended by Antoine de Bourbon, king of Navarre, whose support, as a prince of the blood, the Calvinists were keen to enlist. Henry II banned access to the Pré-aux-Clercs on pain of death, and numerous arrests were made, but he could not afford to stir up trouble at home just as he was about to launch a new military campaign against the emperor. He promised, however, to cause blood to flow and heads to roll once the war was over.[34]

A matter of grave concern to Henry was the fact that even the Parlement of Paris was being infiltrated by Protestantism. He did not want to interfere with the court's judicial procedures, but he expected its members to purge heretics from their midst. In March 1559 the sentence of death passed on three heretics was commuted by the Parlement to banishment. This led to a special meeting or *mercuriale* being called, which the king attended on 10 June. He was shocked by the opinions expressed by some of the younger councillors. Anne du Bourg, for example, proposed the suspension of all heresy trials pending a meeting of a General Council. He also deplored the leniency shown by the courts to murderers, blasphemers and adulterers, when persons whose only crime was to invoke Christ's name were burnt. Taking the charge of adultery personally, Henry flew into a rage. He asked to see the minutes of earlier sessions of the *mercuriale* and ordered du Bourg's arrest. Later, he ordered more arrests. During his imprisonment du Bourg wrote a pamphlet attacking a monarch who tried to force his subjects to live in a manner contrary to God's will. The king's resolve to stamp out heresy may have been stiffened by an attempt on his own life. A chancery clerk, called Caboche, attempted to stab the king as was leaving the Sainte-Chapelle. Henry wanted to question his assailant, but Caboche was eliminated before the king could do so. The Calvinists were suspected of having killed Caboche to stop him disclosing their secrets.[35]

In May 1559 the French Calvinists or Huguenots held their first National Synod in Paris. The meeting took place in two private houses and was chaired by a Parisian pastor. The delegates were mostly pastors from ten other French churches. They drafted a Confession of Faith closely modelled on that drafted by Calvin in 1557 for presentation to the king.[36] They also drew up an Ecclesiastical Discipline similar to the Genevan ordinances. Strict rules were laid down governing the choice of ministers, and Calvinists were forbidden to publish any religious book without the permission of two or three pastors of proven orthodoxy. Nearly every provincial synod which met after 1559 endorsed these decisions. The Calvinist churches in France were thus 'welded into a single instrument under the indirect but real control of Geneva' (Kingdon).

The peace of Cateau-Cambrésis of April 1559 enabled Henry II to give more time to heresy. It was said that he would soon lead an army against Protestant strongholds in the kingdom, but fate intervened. On 30 June, as we have seen, he was seriously wounded in a tournament. For several days he lay in the palace of the Tournelles as doctors struggled to save his life. Their efforts proved vain. On 10 July the king died. The Huguenots, who had suffered so much at his hands, acclaimed his death as a divine punishment.

13

Mother and Sons

The untimely death of King Henry II in July 1559 plunged his kingdom into a major political crisis, for his eldest son, Francis II, was only fifteen years old and in precarious health. Officially, he was old enough to rule, but he lacked political experience. Effective power inevitably passed into the hands of his mother, Catherine de' Medici, who, from now until her death in 1589, became the dominant figure in French political life. Three of her sons, Francis II, Charles IX and Henry III, became successively kings of France; another, François, duke of Alençon, is mainly remembered as a trouble-maker. None, with the possible exception of Henry III who did strike out on his own, was as politically significant as Catherine.

Catherine owed her life and marriage to Francis I. Having conquered and lost the duchy of Milan, he spent the rest of his reign trying to regain it. He enlisted the support of two popes, Leo X and Clement VII, both members to the Florentine family of Medici. In 1516 Leo's nephew, Lorenzo, became head of the Florentine republic. Congratulating him in September 1517, Francis wrote: 'I intend to help you with all my power. I also wish to marry you off to some beautiful and good lady of noble birth and my kin so that the love I bear you may grow and be strengthened'.[1] Such an offer must have seemed irresistible to Lorenzo, a mere citizen of Florence, albeit a privileged one. He therefore accepted the hand of Francis I's chosen lady, Madeleine de La Tour d'Auvergne, countess of Boulogne, a princess of royal blood. The marriage, celebrated at Amboise in April 1518, was followed by ten days of rejoicing. After touring Madeleine's estates in Auvergne, the newly-weds returned to Italy. A year later, on 13 April, Madeleine gave birth in Florence to a daughter, christened Caterina. But Madeleine died soon afterwards and was soon followed to the grave by her husband. Catherine was brought up as an orphan in Florence and experienced hard times during the emperor's siege of the city.[2]

In November 1523 Catherine's uncle, Giulio de' Medici, was elected pope, taking the name of Clement VII. In October 1530 he arranged for her to join him in Rome and, from this time onward, she became a useful pawn in his diplomacy. In 1531, seizing an opportunity of drawing closer to the pope, Francis I offered his own younger son, Henri, duke of Orléans, as a possible husband for Catherine. Thrilled by the prospect of uniting his family with the royal house of France, Clement readily accepted the offer. Catherine began to learn French about this time and may have been able to speak it by the time she left Florence two years later. A Venetian ambassador described her as small and thin, without fine features and with bulging eyes. In 1533, as the date of her marriage drew nearer, Catherine was showered with gifts by the king of France and the pope. Her trousseau was paid for in part by a forced loan levied on the city of Florence. She left Florence on 1 September and travelled by sea from La Spezia to Villefranche-sur-Mer. She was joined on 9 October by the pope, who had arranged to meet Francis I. This meeting took place at Marseille a few days later and, on 28 October, Catherine and Henri were married amidst great pomp. That evening the newly-weds, both aged fourteen, were taken by Queen Eleanor and her ladies to a nuptial chamber where they allegedly consummated their union in the presence of Francis, who declared that 'each had shown valour in the joust'.[3]

Catherine spent fourteen years at the court of Francis I. She admired her father-in-law and in later years cited his court and government as examples for her children to follow. Francis, for his part, liked Catherine, who shared his love of the great outdoors. She was an excellent rider and accompanied him as one of his 'fair band' of ladies. She was also noted for her intellectual gifts. Her knowledge of Greek won praise from a Florentine envoy, but it was her expertise in geography, physics and astronomy which was later to impress the poet Ronsard.[4] Catherine adapted well to her new environment, but her marriage was fraught from the start. She was despised as 'a merchant's daughter' by Francis I's courtiers. By forming an alliance with Clement VII, Francis had hoped to enhance his prospects in Italy, but the pope died in September 1533, to be succeeded not by a Medici but by Paul III, who belonged to the house of Farnese. Catherine's marriage thus lost its political *raison d'être* and was seen by many French courtiers as even more of a *mésalliance*.

She would have been in a stronger position had she given her husband an heir, but the first ten years of her marriage proved barren. Her position was weakened further by the death of Francis I's eldest son, the Dauphin François, which brought her husband one step nearer the throne. Francis I came under pressure to repudiate his daughter-in-law, but he refused to do so. Catherine's best safeguard, however, was to become pregnant. Fortunately for her, she gave birth to a son, François, on 20 January 1544, and he was soon followed by a daughter, Elizabeth. In September 1545 Francis I's second son, Charles, died, leaving the way to the throne clear for Catherine's husband, Henri. When Francis I died on 31 March 1547, Henri became king of France.[5]

Catherine was twenty-eight years old when she became queen of France, but, as yet, she was allowed no political influence. Henry II looked to others for advice, notably, his mistress, Diane de Poitiers, and his chief minister, the Constable Anne de Montmorency. Catherine's role was essentially to perpetuate the dynasty. She produced eight more children: Claude in November 1547, Louis in February 1549 (he died in October 1550), Charles-Maximilien (the future Charles IX) in June 1550, Edouard-Alexandre (the future Henry III) in September 1551, Marguerite (the future 'reine Margot') in May 1553, Hercule (the future François d'Alençon) in March 1555 and twin daughters, Jeanne and Victoire, in June 1556. So many confinements within a short period did not allow Catherine much time for other activity. She was called upon twice to serve as regent during her husband's military campaigns, but was required to share her authority with others.

Catherine was devastated by the death of Henry II. She remained in mourning for the rest of her life, a shattered lance becoming her emblem. Henry's death left a power vacuum at the heart of government. The new king, Francis II, was only fifteen and in need of guidance. This was supplied by two of the late king's ministers, François, second duke of Guise, and his brother, Charles, cardinal of Lorraine. Pushing aside Montmorency, the brothers joined the king at the Louvre. Within a few days the English ambassador reported: 'the house of Guise ruleth and doth all about the French king'. The cardinal was described by a Florentine envoy as both pope and king in France. The Guises were related to the king in several ways. They were the uncles of Francis II's queen, Mary Stuart, and the duke was married to Anne d'Este, Louis XII's granddaughter. Yet many Frenchmen regarded the Guises as foreigners, for their origins lay in the duchy of Lorraine, which was still part of the Holy Roman Empire.[6] They failed to see by what right the Guises controlled the government instead of Antoine de Bourbon, first prince of the blood. But Antoine was in Guyenne when Henry II died and took so long to reach the court that, when eventually he arrived, he was admitted to the king's council but excluded from the inner circle of ministers who decided policy.[7]

Two major problems faced the government of Francis II in 1559: a serious financial crisis and the rise of Protestantism. Both were vigorously tackled by the Guises. Faced with the choice of increasing taxes or curbing expenditure, they chose the latter. A number of highly unpopular measures were taken: royal troops were disbanded, the payment of their wages deferred, pensions suppressed, past alienations of royal lands revoked, and the interest on royal debts curtailed. Many people suspected that these measures were being taken, not in the national interest, but for the benefit of the Guises themselves. Royal account books for 1560 are filled with gifts of money, payments of arrears and reimbursements of loans to relatives, clients and servants of the Guises.[8] They also tightened up the laws against heresy. In September 1559 a law ordered houses used by Huguenots for meetings to be razed to the ground. Two months later, the death penalty was prescribed for anyone attending such meetings.[9] A victim of the repression was Anne du Bourg, who had been arrested under Henry II. The Protestant minister, François Morel, appealed on his behalf to Catherine de' Medici, who was thought to be sympathetic. She promised to help Huguenots as long as they 'lived secretly and without scandal'. With a singular lack of tact Morel warned Catherine that, if du Bourg were executed, God would punish her and her children as he had punished her husband. This sealed du Bourg's fate: he was burned on 23 December.[10]

In March 1560 a serious attempt was made to topple the Guises. A group of lesser noblemen led by Jean du Barry, seigneur de La Renaudie, a Protestant adventurer, plotted to seize control of the court when it was at the château of Amboise, but news of the conspiracy leaked out and the plotters were ambushed by royal troops before they could act. Those who were not killed outright were summarily executed and their bodies left to hang from the château's battlements. This grisly spectacle was watched by the king and the rest of the court.[11] Yet surprisingly the event did not lead to a hardening of royal policy towards Huguenots. The king had already offered an amnesty to all peaceful reformers, and the idea was now mooted of calling a national council to restore the kingdom's religious unity. Catherine may have been partly responsible for this softer line. She is usually given credit for the edict of Romorantin of May 1560 which entrusted heresy cases only to ecclesiastical courts. Had this been applied, it would have mitigated the persecution of Protestants, since the church courts could not impose the death penalty, but the measure was bitterly opposed by the Parlements and proved ineffective.[12]

The Search for Peace

At this point, Catherine was looking for a peaceful solution to France's religious problem. She was assisted by Michel de l'Hôpital, a learned jurist, who became Chancellor of France, in June 1560. He wanted to reform the judiciary and the church and it was to achieve this that an Assembly of Notables met at Fontainebleau in August 1560. Catherine called on the members to act in such a way that the king would keep his sceptre, his subjects would be relieved of their sufferings and the malcontents would be satisfied. In the course of the meeting, Gaspard de Châtillon, seigneur de Coligny and Admiral of France, presented two petitions – one to the king, the other to his mother – from the Huguenots of Normandy. They asked for an end to persecution and for the right to assemble for worship and to build churches. Catherine was invited to follow Esther's example by freeing God's elect from the perils facing them, but the assembly failed to reassure the Huguenots, who took to arms in various parts of the country. Louis of Bourbon, prince of Condé, was accused of raising troops, arrested, put on trial and found guilty of *lèse-majesté*. At this juncture, Francis II fell seriously ill. Physicians had no cure to offer for a fistula in his left ear and, on 5 December, he died. Condé's life was accordingly spared.

Charles IX, who became king on 5 December 1560 at the age of ten, was too young to rule. His mother consequently became regent and the Guises had to give up the reins of power. Catherine was forty-one years old and without commitment to either of the two rival houses of Guise and Bourbon. 'My principal aim', she wrote to her daughter, the queen of Spain, 'is to have the honour of God before my eyes in all things and to preserve my authority, not for myself, but for the conservation of this kingdom and for the good of all your brothers.'[13] She presided over the king's council, initiated and controlled state business, directed domestic and foreign policy, and appointed to offices and ecclesiastical benefices. Her energy was astounding. Catherine was the first to receive and open dispatches and to read letters patent before they were signed by the king. Each of his replies was accompanied by a letter from his mother. She also gave herself a great seal. Her chief concern was to restore peace to the kingdom. In January 1561 she ordered the release of all religious prisoners and suspended all cases of heresy. Her stance, however, was misconstrued by the Huguenots, who imagined that she was coming over to their side. They became more militant than ever, thereby provoking a Catholic backlash spearheaded by the Parlements. On 7 April Montmorency, the duke of Guise and marshal Saint-André formed a coalition, known as the Triumvirate, in defence of the old religion.[14]

Catherine still believed that the religious crisis in France could be settled by compromise. She told the emperor that she would never agree to a change of religion in France, but believed that a national council, by reforming the church, would bring back the sheep that had strayed from the fold. A colloquy, held at Poissy in September 1561, brought Catholics and Protestants face to face. The Calvinist delegation was led by Calvin's lieutenant, Théodore de Bèze, but the discussions that ensued merely served to underline intransigence on both sides. Catherine failed to understand the depth of feeling aroused by a doctrinal issue such as the Eucharist. In the end, the colloquy proved a dismal failure.[15] After consulting senior members of the sovereign courts, the regent issued the Edict of January. This allowed Huguenots to gather for worship, but only outside walled towns and during the day, pending a decision by the General Council meeting at Trent.[16] This, however, merely confirmed the main tenets of the Catholic faith. Its disciplinary decrees restored to the church many powers of jurisdiction which, in France, had long been taken over by the crown. The Council of Trent effectively completed the schism of Christendom.

On 1 March 1562 the duke of Guise was travelling through Champagne when he stumbled on some Protestants worshipping in a barn at

Wassy. A skirmish soon became a massacre as the duke's men entered the barn and began shooting. According to one account seventy-four Protestants were killed and 104 injured.[17] News of the massacre was greeted with jubilation by Catholics, while the prince of Condé, who had become leader of the Huguenot movement, left Paris. Guise, Antoine de Bourbon and a thousand cavalry descended on the court at Fontainebleau and persuaded Catherine and the king to return with them to the capital. Condé, meanwhile, joined Coligny at Meaux. They then marched south with an army and seized control of Orléans. On 8 April 1562 Condé issued a manifesto claiming that he, not the Guises, was upholding the law. He and other Huguenot nobles signed a declaration setting themselves the aim of liberating the king, his brothers and the queen mother and of safeguarding freedom of conscience. Catherine could not allow the Huguenots to mount a rebellion. She tried one last time to negotiate, but the Huguenot leaders refused to give up the free exercise of their faith. Despairing of peace, Catherine told them: 'Since you rely on your forces, we will show you ours'. The religious wars had begun.

The First Religious War

The first war, which began in 1562, was one of the bloodiest of a long series. An early victim was Antoine de Bourbon, who was fatally wounded at the siege of Rouen. In December the royal and Huguenot armies met near Dreux. 'Each one', wrote François de La Noue, 'braced himself for battle, contemplating that the men he saw coming were neither Spanish, English nor Italian, but French, indeed the bravest of them, among whom could be found his own comrades, relatives and friends, and that within the hour it would be necessary to start killing one another.'[18] The ensuing battle was indeed terrible. Both sides suffered heavy casualties, including a large number of nobles. Marshal Saint-André was murdered after he had been captured. The constable Montmorency and Louis de Condé were taken prisoner. Overnight the political situation was transformed: the only member of the Triumvirate to survive was the duke of Guise, who took over command of the king's army. Catherine still hoped for a religious compromise, but hawks on both sides pressed for the war to continue.

In February 1563 Guise was murdered as he laid siege to Orléans. His assassin was Poltrot de Méré, a Huguenot nobleman. This event sent new shock waves through the kingdom, for Guise was a Catholic hero. His widow, Anne d'Este, and her family blamed Coligny for the murder and swore to avenge it, regardless of the crown's efforts to clear his name. For the time being, however, the house of Guise lost its political influence, as the duke's son, Henri, was only a child, and the cardinal of Lorraine, was at the Council of Trent. Catherine was therefore able to secure peace in March 1563, using Montmorency and Condé as nego- tiators. The treaty of Amboise of March 1563 tried to remove the causes of civil war by means of a compromise. Freedom of conscience was allowed for everyone, though Protestant worship was severely restricted. The settlement, however, in attempting to be fair, pleased no one. While Huguenots regretted losing the freedom of worship given to them by the Edict of January 1562, Catholics viewed the peace as too generous to the losing side in the war. The Parlement of Paris endorsed the settlement, but only provisionally.

Catherine was anxious to have her son proclaimed of age, as a king commanded more authority than a regent and a female one at that. Although Charles IX was only thirteen, his council decided that he was old enough to rule. On 17 August 1563 he went to the Parlement of Rouen accompanied by his mother, the princes of the blood, the constable and marshals of France and a throng of nobles and royal councillors. The young king announced that he would tolerate no disobedience among his subjects now that he was of age, ordered them to observe the recent edict of pacification, and forbade them to have dealings with foreign powers without his permission or to raise taxes except by his command. The chancellor, L'Hôpital, explained that the king wished to be regarded as major in all things and in respect of everyone save his mother to whom he reserved the power to command. Catherine then announced that she was handing over the government to her son. As she took a few steps towards him, he left his throne, came forward cap in hand, saying that he would govern and command as much, if not more, than she had done. The princes of the blood, cardinals, great officers of state and noblemen then walked up to Charles, each in turn making a deep bow and kissing his hand. The doors of the chamber were then flung open and a proclamation read out, confirming the peace and ordering all the king's subjects to give up their arms.

Catherine now took Charles IX on an extended progress through France which began in Paris on 24 January 1564 and lasted until 1 May 1566. The court moved on 201 days out of 829 and stayed put on 628. The total distance covered was 907 leagues (one league equalling 4.83 kilometres). One aim of the progress was to ensure that the edict of Amboise was being enforced. Royal officials were expected to account for their activities to the king and to receive his instructions. Another aim was diplomatic: Catherine hoped to meet her son-in-law, Philip II of Spain, in order to clear up differences. She looked forward to seeing her daughter, Elizabeth, now Philip's queen, and to arrange marriages for two of her children. The court, consisting of several thousand people, was accompanied by a multitude of horses and a veritable army. The king and his mother travelled either by coach or litter or rode horses, as did most of the nobles. The rank and file travelled on foot. Where rivers were navigable, boats were used. The pace of travel, leisurely by modern standards, was determined by factors such as weather, the state of the roads, feast days and the king's health (he fell ill twice). In overall charge was Montmorency: he maintained discipline, issued instructions to town governors and rode ahead of the main party to ensure that everthing was in order for the king's reception.[19]

After stopping at Sens, the scene of a recent massacre of Huguenots, the royal caravan moved to Troyes, where a peace treaty with Elizabeth I of England was signed. The local judges were accused of not pulling their weight and told that the king would replace them if they did not mend their ways. At Bar-le-Duc, Catherine attended the baptism of her first grandchild, the son of the duke and duchess of Lorraine. On 22 March Charles IX entered Dijon, whose governor, Gaspard de Saulx-Tavannes, staged a military pageant of alarming verisimilitude. More than a hundred formal urban entries were held during the progress. Their programmes drew themes from classical mythology, the Bible or French history. Charles IX was often compared to St Louis, who had been guided in his early years by his wise and prudent mother, Blanche of Castile. At Dijon, the chancellor made sure that the Parlement had duly registered the edict of Amboise. Wherever the king passed, he tried to strike a fair balance between the religious parties. In the course of the progress nobles tagged on or dropped off as they pleased. Political or religious affiliations determined their movements. Thus, in territories where the Guises were dominant, Huguenots made themselves scarce. At Lyon, a city with a large Huguenot population, Montmorency took charge of the fortification, artillery and keys before introducing a royal garrison. Protestant services were banned during the king's visit. A plague epidemic forced the court to move on to Crémieu, where an important edict concerning French towns was issued on 14 July under which the choice of municipal magistrates in the chief towns was left to the king.

After visiting Roussillon and Romans, the court travelled to Montélimar, Orange and Avignon, where it was hosted by the papal vice-legate. On 16 August Catherine and her son called on Nostradamus at Salon de Crau. The old man prophesied that the king would live as long as Montmorency; in fact, Charles was to outlive him by seven years. On 23 October the royal caravan reached Aix-en-Provence, where the Parlement refused to register the Edict of Amboise. Charles IX suspended the court, replacing it by a commission of Parisian *parlementaires*. The next stage of the progress was less contentious. At Brignoles, the king watched young girls dance the volta and martingale; in Provence, he admired the distinctive flora and fauna and visited Roman remains, including the Pont du Gard. At Toulon, he took a trip out to sea on a galley; and, at Marseille, he took part in a mock naval battle. After spending forty-six days in Toulouse, the court resumed its travels, reaching Bordeaux on 12 April, where Charles IX held another *lit de justice*. The Chancellor once again reprimanded the local *parlementaires*. 'All this disorder', he declared, 'stems from the contempt in which you hold the king and his ordinances which you neither fear nor obey except at your pleasure.'[20] He reaffirmed the king's determination to impose the Edict of Amboise.

For Catherine, the climax of the 'Grand Tour' was a reunion with her daughter, Elizabeth, queen of Spain, in Bayonne.[21] She would have liked to meet her son-in-law, Philip II, but he refused to come and sent in his place the duke of Alba, a noted Catholic hawk. He had been instructed to urge Charles IX to revoke the Edict of Amboise in favour of a policy of renewed religious persecution in France. The duke's presence at

Bayonne bred fears among the Huguenots of a secret Franco-Spanish plot for their extermination. Politics apart, the summit enabled Catherine to show that France, in spite of her domestic problems, was still capable of staging a magnificent spectacle. A banquet held on the Ile d'Aigueneau, on 23 June, was particularly lavish. Guests were taken there in splendidly decorated boats. On the way, they saw fishermen harpooning an artificial whale which spewed red wine from its wounds. They also encountered six tritons, sitting on a large turtle and blowing conch shells, Neptune in a chariot pulled by sea-horses, Arion riding on two dolphins and sirens singing their praise. On the island, they were treated to regional dances performed by girls dressed as shepherdesses. The banquet was followed by a ballet of nymphs and satyrs. Next day, a tournament was fought by so-called 'British' and 'Irish' knights, led by the king and his brother Henri. The event, in a special enclosure, was accompanied by music and musical recitation.

The return leg of the progress took the court to Angers, Blois and Moulins, where it stayed for three months. The government had planned to cap its programme of administrative and judicial reform with a major ordinance and it was to this end that an Assembly of Notables was called. The occasion brought the Guises and the Châtillons face to face for the first time since 1564. Catherine worked hard to heal their enmity. Charles IX formally acquitted Coligny of any part in the assassination of François de Guise, and the admiral and the cardinal of Lorraine were persuaded to kiss each other.[22]

The 'Surprise de Meaux'

Catherine imagined, in March 1565, that the progress had largely succeeded in bringing peace to the kingdom. 'All things are as peaceful here', she wrote, 'as we may hope: the further we go, the more is obedience established, and the damage caused by disorder and confusion to the minds of the people is purged and cleansed, so I hope that with God's help all things will revert to their original state.'[23] That was still her hope when the court returned to Paris on 1 May 1566, but she was in for a rude awakening. In 1566 a serious revolt broke out in the Netherlands, and Philip II sent an army under the duke of Alba to suppress it. Setting off from the duchy of Milan, the Spanish army marched north, skirting the eastern border of France. No one knew its destination exactly. The Huguenots suspected that they might be the intended victims of the expedition. Their suspicions were heightened when Charles IX hired 6000 Swiss mercenaries and failed to disband them once Alba had reached Brussels. Catherine assured Condé that her son, as long as he listened to her, would abide by the Edict of Amboise, but, taking no chances, the Huguenots decided on a pre-emptive strike. They had four objectives: to seize some key towns, to raise a strong army; to 'cut to pieces' the Swiss troops; and to expel the cardinal of Lorraine from the court. As they assembled at Rosay-en-Brie, Catherine and her son, who were relaxing at Montceaux, moved to the neighbouring walled town of Meaux and sought the added protection of the Swiss troops. They then returned to Paris but had to shake off a Huguenot attempt to intercept them. Charles IX swore never again to allow anyone to frighten him, and to pursue the rebels into their houses and even into their beds. Catherine was equally indignant. She wrote to the duke of Savoy: 'I could not have imagined that such ambitious and unfortunate designs could have entered the hearts of the subjects regarding their king'. The unprovoked rebellion, known as the Surprise de Meaux, was in her judgment the 'greatest wickedness in the world'.[24]

After daring to pursue the royal family to Paris, the Huguenots compounded their offence by blockading the capital and destroying windmills on its periphery. Parisians rushed to take up arms and broke into Protestant homes looking for arsonists. From his pulpit, Simon Vigor denounced the Huguenots as traitors. Their religion had been established by the sword, he ranted, and would be destroyed by the sword. On 7 October, as Paris began to feel pangs of hunger, the king sent a herald to the Huguenot camp at Saint-Denis to call on the leaders, Condé, Coligny and d'Andelot, to surrender or be classed as rebels. They offered to serve the king if their freedom to worship and their personal safety could be safeguarded. Encouraged by these words, Montmorency attempted to negotiate, but he upset the Huguenots by describing the Edict of Amboise as provisional and by declaring that the king would never accept two religions in his kingdom. The talks were broken off and, on 10 October, the old constable (he was seventy-four years old) rode out of Paris at the head of a huge army. The ensuing battle, fought on the plain of Saint-Denis, proved indecisive, but

Montmorency was fatally wounded.[25] Charles IX appointed his own brother, Henri, duke of Anjou, as commander-in-chief of the royal forces. After the battle, Condé lifted the blockade of Paris and dashed to Lorraine, hoping to link up with German mercenaries, led by John Casimir of the Palatinate. Anjou's army prepared to go in pursuit, but its sheer size prevented it from keeping up with the enemy. Moving south, Condé besieged Chartres, but the town was too well defended. As both sides were impecunious, they resumed talking. The result was the peace of Longjumeau (March 1568), which restored the Edict of Amboise in full, but the treaty was less favorable to the Huguenots than it seemed. La Noue called it 'this wicked little peace'.[26] While the Huguenots agreed to disarm and hand over the towns which they had seized, Charles IX was allowed to retain his army for the time being. Coligny saw the flaw, but had to fall in with Condé's wishes and those of most Protestant leaders.

Historians are divided over their interpretation of royal policy at this time. Some believe that Catherine de' Medici was still working for peace; others think that she was no longer interested in a compromise with the Huguenots. The fact that Michel de l'Hôpital was dismissed as chancellor in September 1568 and replaced by René de Birague, a notorious hardliner, seems significant. The cardinal of Lorraine, who had returned from the Council of Trent, also became dominant in the king's council. Events moved rapidly towards a resumption of hostilities. As Condé and Coligny were resting at their respective homes in Burgundy, they learnt that royal troops were closing in on them. Fearing a trap, they suddenly left with their families and, gathering a large number of supporters on the way, took refuge in the strongly fortified Atlantic port of La Rochelle. On 13 March 1569, the main royal army under Anjou and the Huguenot one, led by Condé and Coligny, met on the field of Jarnac.[27] In the ensuing battle, Condé surrendered only to be murdered by a member of Anjou's guard. According to Brantôme, Anjou humiliated Condé by having his body carried off the field on the back of a donkey, 'his arms and legs dangling'. It has been suggested that Condé's death was part of a comprehensive policy by the government to wipe out the Huguenot leadership.

Admiral Coligny now became the sole commander of the Huguenot forces. Jeanne d'Albret presented Condé's son and her own son, Henri, aged fifteen and sixteen respectively, to the Huguenot army as its new leaders. Everyone knew, however, that they were only 'the admiral's pages', but, as princes of the blood, they gave the Huguenot cause legitimacy. After Jarnac, Coligny linked up with a German army commanded by Wolfgang of Zweibrücken, and in October the rival armies fought another battle, this time at Moncontour. Anjou was once again the victor.[28] The Huguenots suffered huge losses. Catherine de' Medici thanked God for allowing her son to be the instrument of such a great deed, but Charles IX was less pleased. Jealous of his brother's military successes, he lost no time in joining his army to share in the glory. Coligny now marched to the south of France, where he was joined by thousands of troops. After wintering in those parts, he mounted a new offensive designed to force the government to negotiate by bringing the war nearer to Paris. The tactic succeeded, and, in August 1570, a new peace treaty, less one-sided than that of Longjumeau, was signed. The peace of Saint-Germain ceded to the Huguenots four security towns for two years. They were granted freedom of conscience everywhere and freedom to worship where they had done so before the war, in two towns per *gouvernement* and in the homes of nobles with superior rights of justice. But Protestant worship was still banned in Paris and at court.[29]

The Massacre of St Bartholomew's Day

Historians generally believe that the peace of Saint-Germain was a genuine attempt by the crown to bridge the religious division of France, yet it lasted only two years and no one knows exactly what lay in the mind of the king and his ministers. Whatever Catherine's motivation may have been, she took advantage of the peace to arrange marriages for her children. Charles IX married the Emperor Maximilian II's younger daughter, Elizabeth of Austria. This made him the brother-in-law of King Philip II of Spain, who had taken Elizabeth's elder sister, Anna, as his fourth wife following the death of Elizabeth of Valois in October 1568. The marriage took place at Mézières in November 1570. The union of two great dynasties, both claiming descent from Charlemagne, was seen as an event of enormous significance that might lead to a universal peace. Charles IX made his belated entry into Paris on 6 March 1571.

The programme of the entry, devised by the poet Ronsard and others, and the monuments designed by famous artists, such as Niccolò dell' Abbate and Germain Pilon, celebrated the themes of Empire and Peace. Another theme was the religious peace achieved by Catherine, who was portrayed as Juno.[30] On 11 March, the king addressed the Parlement: 'After God', he said, 'I am most obliged to my mother. Thanks to her tenderness towards me and my people, her application, her zeal and her prudence, the affairs of the state have been so well managed when I was too young to attend to them myself that the storms of civil war have not damaged my kingdom.'[31]

Two other marriages planned by Catherine proved more difficult to arrange. She had hoped to marry her daughter Marguerite to the king of Portugal, but he seemed uninterested, so she turned to Henri de Navarre, a leading Protestant. Catherine may have calculated that the marriage would bring him back into the Catholic fold or serve to unite the two religious camps in France. Henri was at that moment at La Rochelle with his mother Jeanne d'Albret. If he were to marry Marguerite a papal dispensation would be needed on account of his religion and of consanguinity between the parties. Jeanne, who was herself a zealous Protestant, was opposed to the match. She disliked the French court and its morals, and suspected that Catherine's proposal was a ruse intended to separate a prince of the blood from the Huguenot party. The other marriage envisaged by the queen mother was that of her favourite son, Henri, duke of Anjou, with the English queen, Elizabeth I. This too was controversial. As the daughter of Anne Boleyn, Elizabeth was viewed by the Catholic world as a heretic and a bastard. At thirty-seven she was also much older than Anjou, who was only seventeen. Moreover, she had been excommunicated by the pope. Her flirtation with the earl of Leicester had caused mirth at the French court, and Anjou did not think his honour would be enhanced by a marriage to a 'whore', as he liked to call her. When it became clear that he would never accept Elizabeth as his wife, Catherine put forward her youngest son, François, duke of Alençon. Misshapen, pock-marked and only sixteen years old, he was not much of a catch for Elizabeth. She began by declining Catherine's offer on account of the age difference, but later indicated that she might marry Alençon but only if she could see him first.[32]

On 4 April 1572 Jeanne d'Albret at last consented to the marriage of
her son, Henri, to Charles IX's sister, Marguerite. A few days later the
bishop of Macon wrote to the papal nuncio: 'Your Reverence can be
assured that we will soon see the Prince returning to the bosom of Holy
Church'. The wedding took place at the cathedral of Notre-Dame in
Paris on 18 August. It drew to the capital a large number of Protestant
and Catholic noblemen who were still at heart bitter enemies. The capital itself was a hotbed of Catholic fanaticism, which had already given
rise to several major incidents. Tension was heightened by the warm
weather which brought everyone out into the streets. The wedding was
followed by several days of festivity. The balls, masques and tournaments had been devised by Anjou, and legend has it that he devised
mock battles in which the Huguenots were to be deliberately humiliated.
Coligny would have been wise to leave Paris soon after the celebrations,
but various pressing matters, notably the plight of his co-religionists in
the Netherlands, kept him at court. He tried to persuade Charles IX to
send them military aid. On 22 August, however, as Admiral Coligny was
walking back to his residence from the Louvre, he was hit by a bullet
fired from an upstairs window of a house. The assailant has been identified with the seigneur de Maurevert, a client of the Guises. The admiral
was only wounded, but his companions called on the king to take
appropriate action.[33] Writing to his ambassador in England, Charles
blamed the Guises for the crime: 'This wicked deed', he wrote, 'has
come from the enmity between the houses of Guise and Châtillon'. The
attempt on Coligny's life was followed two days later by the Massacre of
St Bartholomew's Day in which thousands of Huguenots in Paris were
slaughtered in cold blood by a mob. The government, it seems, was
partly responsible. The failed attempt on Coligny's life had caused panic
at court. On 23 August the king and his council had decided that a
renewal of civil war was inevitable. They thought 'it preferable to win a
battle in Paris, where all the leaders were, than to risk one in the field
and to fall into a dangerous and uncertain war'. Coligny was among the
first victims of the massacre, which was soon repeated in a number of
provincial towns.[34]

The massacre seriously weakened the Protestant cause. Many
Huguenots who could not believe that God would have allowed such a
slaughter, abjured their faith. Even the two young princes, Navarre and

Condé, the nominal leaders of the Huguenot movement, were received into the Catholic faith; but, unlike many of their co-religionists, they did so under duress. Many chose exile abroad, mainly to England. The massacre also had a devastating effect on relations between the Huguenots and the crown. During the first three religious wars, their leaders had repeatedly proclaimed their loyalty to the crown. They focused their rebellion on the king's so-called 'evil advisers', but this fiction could no longer be sustained once Charles IX had admitted responsibility for the murder of the Huguenot leaders. Huguenots, who had so far adhered to the doctrine of non-resistance preached by Calvin and other reformers, now had to look for another justification for armed opposition to the crown.

Although seriously weakened by the massacre, the Huguenot party had not been destroyed. It survived in the west and south where it controlled a number of fortified towns, the most important being La Rochelle. After the inhabitants had refused to admit Armand de Biron as governor, Charles IX decided to use force. A huge army under the command of Henri of Anjou was sent to besiege the town. This operation dragged on through the spring, the town's resistance being stiffened by the arrival of refugees from the recent massacres. At times, the entire population was mobilized, including women who pelted the royal troops from the ramparts with stones. La Rochelle had to endure a fierce bombardment by Anjou's guns and repulsed eight assaults.[35] Curiously, the town was saved by an event in eastern Europe. On 7 July Sigismund-Augustus, king of Poland, died, bringing the Jagiellon dynasty to an end. Catherine, who had tried unsuccessfully to marry Anjou to two queens, now put him forward as a candidate for election to the Polish throne. But a difficulty needed to be overcome. The duke was reputed to be a fanatical Catholic and also the main instigator of the St Bartholomew's Day massacre. Poland, by contrast, was the only European country where religious toleration existed under the constitution. But Anjou's main rivals – the Russian tsar, Ivan the Terrible, and the Austrian archduke Ernest – were even less attractive to the Polish electors. So, on 10 May, after nearly a month of intensive electioneering, Anjou was elected king of Poland. He received the news on 29 May in his camp outside La Rochelle. Though he cared little about Poland as such, he liked the idea of being king in his own right instead of living in the shadow of his elder brother. His elevation also gave him an honourable pretext for lifting the siege of La Rochelle and coming to terms with its inhabitants. On 19 August a large and distinguished Polish embassy arrived in Paris. The inhabitants laughed at their bonnets and bulky fur coats, but the French court was dazzled by their learning and command of languages. On 22 August they obtained from Anjou a formal promise to respect the religious peace in Poland. He tried to put off his departure for Poland for as long as possible, but was eventually obliged to leave by Charles IX who wanted him out of the way. The court escorted him to Blamont in Lorraine whence he travelled across Germany to his eastern kingdom.[36]

Anjou's departure left the way clear for his younger brother, François of Alençon, to assert himself. He hoped to succeed Anjou as lieutenant-general of the kingdom but was opposed by the Guises. This suited Catherine, who feared that Alençon might try to seize the throne if Charles IX were to die during Henri's absence in Poland. She had every reason to feel anxious, for Alençon was implicated in two plots discovered about this time at the French court. His status, as prince of the blood, made him attractive to groups of aristocratic malcontents seeking a leader. The chancellor, Birague, wanted Alençon and Henri de Navarre executed, but Charles IX refused to take such a step.[37] He merely had the two princes put under a heavy guard and made to take an oath of loyalty. On 30 May 1574 Charles IX died and Catherine de' Medici declared herself regent pending her son's return from Poland. He now became King Henry III. Meanwhile, the kingdom fell prey to yet another religious war as Huguenots in the Midi formed an alliance with Henri de Montmorency-Damville, the disgruntled Catholic governor of Languedoc.

14

The Last Valois

Henry III was in Cracow when news reached him of his elder brother's death. He decided to return to France at once in response to an urgent call from his mother, Catherine de' Medici. Ditching his Polish ministers and subjects without even bidding them farewell, he fled in disguise under cover of night. He reached the Austrian border in the nick of time, evading the Polish chancellor who had set off in pursuit.[1] Once across the border, Henry was magnificently received by the emperor. An even grander welcome awaited him in Venice. The king entered the city on board a galley escorted by the *Bucintoro* and hundreds of gondolas. Splendid entertainments were laid on for him, including fireworks, regattas, banquets, concerts, a *Te Deum* at the basilica of San Marco, balls and a visit to the Arsenal. With such a display of power and magnificence, the Venetians hoped to enlist the support of France against the threat of Spanish hegemony, felt elsewhere in Italy. Easily seduced, Henry spent lavishly on jewels and perfumes by day and enjoyed the company of Venetian courtesans by night. From Venice he made his way across northern Italy, reaching Turin on 12 August.[2]

Catherine de' Medici and the French court met Henry in Lyon on 6 September 1574. The most urgent matter requiring his attention was the continuing religious unrest in France. Montmorency-Damville, the Catholic governor of Languedoc who had recently joined forces with the Huguenots, was ordered to disband his army or retire to Savoy. His reply was a manifesto blaming the king's foreign councillors for all the kingdom's woes. Catherine tried to negotiate with Damville, but, suspecting that she was only trying to detach him from his Huguenot allies, he continued to defy the king. Meanwhile, the Huguenot leader, Henri, prince of Condé, sought military assistance in Germany and financial help in England.

On 13 February 1575 Henry III was crowned at Reims. The next day he married Louise de Vaudémont, a princess of the house of Lorraine. In April he tried to bring peace to France. He explained that he had returned from Poland with open arms, intending to embrace all his subjects equally without religious discrimination, but he refused to accede to Damville's sweeping demands. He and the Huguenots laid down two preconditions for future peace talks: freedom of worship for Protestants throughout France and the release of marshals Montmorency and Cossé, who had been imprisoned following a plot in 1574. In the meantime, fighting continued in various parts of France. Large armies were no longer involved. Instead, forces, each of a few thousand men under a captain, launched surprise attacks on towns and villages, springing ambushes or causing mayhem in the countryside. Pillage, rape and exacting ransoms became the order of the day.

A Troublesome Brother

In September 1575 the king's younger brother, Alençon, escaped from court and, at Dreux, issued a manifesto echoing Damville's demands. He demanded the removal of foreigners from the king's council, a religious peace pending a church council and a meeting of the Estates-General.[3] In the meantime, the threat of foreign invasion grew after Condé had signed a military alliance with the Elector-Palatine, John-Casimir. Henry III was afraid that Alençon, as first prince of the blood, would give the opposition an appearance of legality if he put himself at its head. To avert this danger, he sent his mother, Catherine, to negotiate with the duke. On 21 November she signed a seven-month truce with Alençon at Champigny.[4] He was granted five towns by way of security, but two of the town governors refused to cooperate. The duke, moreover, had no control over the actions of Condé and John Casimir. In January 1576 they invaded northern France, taking Henry III completely by surprise. He watched helplessly as the invaders swept through Burgundy, leaving a trail of destruction in their wake. Catherine hoped that Alençon would stay neutral, but, in December, he accused the chancellor, Birague, of trying to poison him and made this a pretext for breaking the truce and siding with the invaders. In February 1576 the crisis deepened for Henry III when Henri de Navarre escaped from court and reverted to his original Protestant faith.

Soon afterwards Navarre, Alençon, Condé and Damville presented a lengthy set of demands to the king, and on 9 April 1576 Alençon issued the following declaration: 'We have decided to exploit the means given to us by God in order to win by force the peace and tranquillity that we could not achieve with reason'.[5] Lacking the means needed to resist the coalition, Henry relied once more on his mother's diplomatic skills. She met the princes near Sens and virtually conceded all their demands in a treaty, commonly called the Peace of Monsieur (the title given to the king's younger brother) because everyone guessed that it had been forced on the king by Alençon. Huguenots were now given for the first time freedom of worship throughout France, except within two leagues of Paris and the court. They were also allowed to build churches or *temples* and were admitted to all professions, schools and hospitals. Bipartisan courts, comprising Catholic and Protestant judges, were set up in every Parlement. The massacre of St Bartholomew was described as a 'crime' and the families of victims were exempted from taxation. Coligny was rehabilitated posthumously and his children recovered their property. Eight surety towns were given to the Huguenots: two each in Languedoc, Guyenne, Dauphiné and Provence. Henry III promised to call a meeting of the Estates-General within six months.[6] Alençon acquired the title of duke of Anjou.

The Peace of Monsieur was denounced as a 'sell-out' by Catholics, and Henry III was reviled for having signed it. Writing to the pope, he admitted his distress and powerlessness. Many Catholics began to see that only by forming a party would they be able to defend their faith effectively. Already under Charles IX armed associations or confraternities had been set up by Catholics in various provinces and towns. The Catholic League was a response to the Peace of Monsieur, which had granted the governorship of Péronne in Picardy to the Huguenot leader, Condé.[7] The town's existing governor, Jacques d'Humières, refused to hand it over and formed an armed association of Picard nobles. He called on all French princes, nobles and prelates to unite against heresy. From Picardy, the League spread to the rest of the kingdom. While Henry reprimanded Humières for his initiative, Guise demanded the restoration of all the rights, franchises and liberties which the French had enjoyed under King Clovis. He invited all Catholics to join the League and to follow any leader chosen to accomplish its sacred mission. Before publishing its programme, the League sent a lawyer, Jean David, to Rome in order to get the pope's approval, but he was murdered on his way home. A memorandum found on his body outlined a plan to depose the Valois dynasty in favour of the Guises. The Huguenots claimed it as a set of minutes taken at a papal consistory. This was patently absurd, but Henry III was alerted to Guise ambitions. The tenor of the document was clear: the Valois were a discredited dynasty and the Guises were perfectly suited, physically and spiritually, to rule the kingdom.[8] The League, meanwhile, gathered support with the help of mendicant friars and Jesuits. From the Hôtel de Guise in Paris, a web was spun across the kingdom, the soul of the new movement being Guise's sister, Catherine, duchess of Montpensier, who had never forgiven Henry III for jilting her in favour of Marie de Clèves. She inspired much of the League's propaganda which mercilessly lampooned Henry III and his favourites or *mignons*.

In an attempt to defuse the opposition, Henry III created a league of his own. He laid down the rules in December 1576. In every province an armed force was to be set up and funds set aside for its upkeep. The governor would be assisted by six noblemen of sufficient substance. Catholics who failed to join the new association would be classed as enemies of God, king and country, and treated accordingly. The freedom of conscience and property of peaceful Protestants would be respected provided they complied with decisions to be taken by the Estates-General, which had begun to meet at Blois.[9] The success of Henry's policy depended on the outcome of this assembly. He hoped that it would provide him with the funds necessary to enforce the peace on his own terms rather than on those of the Guises. But the estates proved anything but helpful. Under pressure from the Guise lobby, the clergy and nobility backed a proposal for the establishment of an executive body whose decisions would be binding, even without the king's consent. Henry countered this attack on his authority by inciting the estates to call for the restoration of religious unity in the kingdom. He hoped to provoke a new civil war and that the estates would feel morally bound to grant him the means to fight it. In the end, they voted for the suppression of Protestantism but were extremely reluctant to assist the king financially. Left in the lurch, Henry could neither pay his Swiss troops nor maintain his extravagant lifestyle. The clergy did offer him

450,000 *livres*, but, when he tried to raise more money by selling off crown lands, the third estate objected strongly. 'They won't help me with their [money]', Henry complained, 'and they won't let me help myself with mine; it's too cruel.'[10]

War, in the meantime, had broken out in Provence and Dauphiné. This was deeply discouraging for Henry III. He had opted for war not out of religious fanaticism but in the hope of effacing the humiliation of the Peace of Monsieur, of standing up to the Guises and of extracting money from the estates. All he was left with was war, uncertain support from the League and virtually no money. Catherine de' Medici, who believed that he should treat with the Huguenots, persuaded him to sink his differences with Damville in March 1577. Despite his chronic penury, Henry managed to raise an army, but could only afford to keep it in the field for a month. Without the support of Damville or Anjou, the Huguenots had become vulnerable, except in the south. Anjou recaptured La Charité in May earning for himself a hero's welcome at court. Catherine laid on a festive banquet at Chenonceau in which beautiful ladies appeared topless and with flowing hair 'like brides'. The king, trimly corseted and heavily perfumed, wore a pink and silver gown sparkling with jewels.[11] Later that year, Anjou added to his laurels by sacking Issoire in Auvergne. 'Most of the town', according to de Thou, 'and all its riches were reduced to ashes.'[12] Countless women were raped. This earned the duke another hero's welcome at court. In Huguenot eyes his hands were now as bloody as those of his brother and mother. They never trusted him again. As the war dragged on, the royal army dwindled in size and began to run out of munitions. Henry was only too glad to sign the Peace of Bergerac on 17 September 1577, which reduced the number of concessions granted to the Huguenots by the Peace of Monsieur. Catholic worship was restored throughout France and all leagues banned. The settlement was an attempt by the king to reassert his authority. He called it 'his peace', as distinct from the earlier one which had been Monsieur's.[13] Anjou was left to pursue his ambitions in the Netherlands by siding with the Dutch rebels against Spain, but the last thing Henry III wanted was to be dragged into a conflict with Spain by his brother. He tried to stop him marching north with an army and Catherine lectured him on the dangers facing France should he persist in his enterprise, but Anjou would not listen. In July he arrived at Mons and offered the Dutch States-General his assistance. In exchange for his military assistance, the Dutch appointed him 'Defender of the liberty of the Netherlands' against the Spanish tyranny, but the hopes they had placed in him were soon dashed when his unpaid troops deserted, ravaging the countryside on their homeward march.

Although France was theoretically at peace in 1579, the true situation particularly in the south was closer to anarchy. As Henry III disliked travel, he asked his mother to help restore his authority in the south. She signed a treaty with the Huguenots at Nérac in February and presided over the estates of Languedoc. Wherever she went, she pressed for mutual understanding, while stressing the need to obey the king above all, but the situation in the Midi remained precarious and the Huguenots were soon given another pretext to renew hostilities. In the north, Condé seized the border town of La Fère in November, and in the south Navarre first made his mark as a military leader by storming Cahors. Yet the majority of Huguenots in the Midi wanted peace, as did Anjou, who had still not given up his ambitions in the Netherlands. In November 1580 he negotiated the Peace of Fleix which confirmed the treaties of Bergerac and Nérac. He seized Cambrai in August, but was soon forced back to the Channel coast by the Spaniards. In October he visited England, but Elizabeth made clear that she had no intention of marrying him. Returning to the Netherlands he assumed the title of duke of Brabant. However, his attempt to seize Antwerp in January 1583 ended in disaster. In October he returned to France for good.

An Enigmatic Monarch

Henry III's character bewildered contemporaries. As duke of Anjou, he had been a successful soldier, but his Polish experience seems to have changed him. He appeared indolent and pleasure-loving. Intellectually, he was probably the most gifted of the later Valois. His former tutor, Jacques Amyot, compared him to his grandfather, Francis I. They were, he thought, equally bright, but Henry was the more studious. He had learnt Latin and Italian, read a great deal and was a fine public speaker. Far from being indolent, he would spend several hours each

day examining state papers, writing numerous letters, reading and taking notes. He liked to invite scholars to debate questions of moral and
natural philosophy in his apartment at the Louvre. These meetings,
which became known as the Palace Academy, brought together most of
the literary and scholarly personalities of the day.[14] The essential purpose of the meetings was to equip the king intellectually and morally for
the tasks of kingship. Speech at the Academy was relatively free, for
Henry wanted instruction, not flattery. Although interested in astronomy, he did not share his mother's enthusiasm for astrology. Generally,
speeches before the Academy were strongly Christian in tone, yet
humanism dictated the choice of topics and the ponderous classical
allusions made by the speakers. Although basically an intellectual, Henry
III did not renounce the outdoor life. A good but temperamental
sportsman, he would hunt intensively for a few days, then stop. He
would also play tennis or another ball game, albeit spasmodically. His
other hobbies were equally fitful: after losing 30,000 *écus* gambling in
1579, he never gambled again and expelled a courtier for being an incor-
rigible gambler. More lasting was the king's fondness for lapdogs. In
1586 there were at least three hundred in his household. Unlike Charles
IX, Henry disliked animal fights.[15]

In one important respect Henry III was quite different from his predecessors. Whereas they had boasted of their accessibility, he tried to
distance himself from his subjects. He set up a barrier around his table
to keep spectators at bay when he ate 'in public', and issued household
regulations designed to control access to his chamber according to social
rank.[16] This was reflected in the design of royal palaces by the insertion
of a long sequence of rooms through which courtiers were only allowed
to move at a given signal.[17] As Henry spent much of his time in Paris,
he visited other towns less than his predecessors, leaving entries to the
provincial governors who were, in effect, viceroys. The king preferred to
take part in solemn services of thanksgiving – *Te Deums* – which symbolised the close rapport which he assumed to exist between the crown
and the Almighty.

Henry disliked crowds and took part in only four town entries as
against Charles IX's 108.[18] The first took place at Orléans on 15 November 1576 when Henry had to listen to four speeches. They referred to the
sadness felt by his subjects when he had gone to Poland and of their joy

at his return. The speakers stressed the fact that Henry had been merely elected as king of Poland whereas France was his by divine right, as manifested in the hereditary succession. An interesting parallel was drawn by one speaker between Henry and two earlier rulers – one Roman, the other French – who had gained the title of Augustus. Both, like Henry, had had to overcome political opposition at the start of their reigns, but God had smiled upon them by giving them forty years of peace and prosperity. Like the Roman Augustus, Henry might one day boast that he had turned France from a kingdom of earth to one of gold. However, the bishop of Orléans warned him that this would depend on his restoring the Catholic faith to its original glory and strength. He implied that the subjects' obedience was conditional on the king continuing to fight the Huguenots.[19]

Henry's Catholicism was never in doubt. On his journey back from Poland in 1574, he had several conversations with Carlo Borromeo, archbishop of Milan, who made a deep impression on him. The future saint may have persuaded Henry of the need to appease God's wrath by a new outpouring of religious fervour. The king was also much influenced by Spanish writers, like Luis de Granada, whose works were well represented in his library. As early as 1575, after the first major political crisis of his reign, Henry took refuge in prayer, visiting one church after another. As from 1582, he undertook a series of pilgrimages aimed at securing his succession. He travelled from Paris to Notre-Dame du Puy in Auvergne accompanied by Jesuits and by the dukes of Joyeuse and Épernon. Penitential confraternities sprang up in Paris under his sponsorship. In 1583 he set up a confraternity of White Penitents who staged public processions. They wore a robe of white cloth shaped like a sack and a hood covering the head and face, but for slits for the eyes and mouth. Henry was a member of this confraternity, as were many of his courtiers. He also set up at Vincennes a confraternity of 'Hieronymites' consisting initially of twelve courtiers and ecclesiastics. They were given cells in the forest in which to make occasional retreats. On such occasions, they wore a friar's habit and observed a strict rule. Sacred oratory was an important activity of the Hieronymites and the king himself preached on the feast of St Jerome. Another important manifestation of his distinctive religiosity was the foundation of the Order of the Holy Spirit in December 1578. Its members were expected to serve as 'a mirror and example' to all the king's other subjects.[20]

A disturbing contrast existed between Henry III's austere religiosity and his foppishness. His court became noted for sartorial excess. Courtiers liked to cover themselves with jewels, embroidery and other accessories. About 1590 they took to wearing doublets with four sleeves, two for use and two for display as wings. At the Estates-General of 1576, Henry wore a doublet and breeches covered with gold and silver braid. Later, he abandoned bright colours in favour of black or grey. The attention which he gave to his personal hygiene, in particular to his hair, was mocked by contemporaries as effeminate. Today, Henry is perhaps best remembered for his favourites or *mignons*, who were young noblemen of his generation.[21] They were not homosexuals, as is often assumed. Far from being effeminate, they were skilful swordsmen, who risked their lives in duels.

Henry wanted his court to become a place dedicated to the daily exaltation of his own majesty. In 1581 he marshalled all of its resources – poets, artists, musicians and mechanics – to celebrate the marriage of his favourite, the duke of Joyeuse with his sister-in-law, Marguerite de Lorraine. The festivities, described as 'magnificences' lasted for about a fortnight, a different spectacle being offered daily.[22] They combined elements drawn from the world of medieval chivalry with the rather self-conscious learning and refinement of the Renaissance. A fête on 24 September consisted of tournaments in allegorical settings, a water fête, an equestrian ballet and a wonderful fireworks display. Elaborate temporary buildings, designed by the best artists of the day, were erected in the streets and squares of Paris, and the various shows were accompanied by music, acclaimed as 'the most harmonious that had ever been heard'. The most famous of the Joyeuse 'magnificences' was the *Ballet comique de la reine* whose theme was the transference of power from the enchantress Circe to the royal family. Circe was defeated by an alliance of the virtues and Minerva with the celestial world, expressed through ballets based on geometrical figures and danced by the queen, the bride and other ladies. A clap of thunder and the descent of Jupiter sitting on an eagle brought the show to a climax. A musical accompaniment reminded spectators that the god had come to protect France from the horrors of war and to strengthen and bless her monarchy.

The End of the Dynasty

Henry III suffered from chronic ill health.[23] He was above all afraid of the stone, which usually led to an extremely painful and almost invariably fatal operation. To avert this fate, he underwent thermal treatment. In 1579 he developed an ear abscess which burst of its own accord, leaving him partially deaf. This and other abscesses which developed on his hand and leg were almost certainly tubercular. Henry was not impotent but, for whatever reason, he failed to produce any progeny. In 1582 he had a sort of nervous breakdown after convincing himself that the kingdom would be plunged into a succession crisis that would destroy all his efforts to give it peace. Many Frenchmen hoped that Anjou would eventually succeed to the throne, but he died of consumption in June 1584. This left the Huguenot leader, Henri de Navarre as heir presumptive, a prospect which filled Catholics with alarm. This grave situation led to the formation of a new league for the defence of the Catholic religion.

In September 1584 Henri duke of Guise, his brothers, Charles duke of Mayenne and Louis cardinal of Guise, and two other noblemen formed an association at Nancy aimed at excluding Navarre from the throne. In December, the new league signed the treaty of Joinville with Philip II of Spain. The parties undertook to defend the Catholic faith and to extirpate Protestantism from France and the Netherlands. Navarre's uncle, Charles, cardinal of Bourbon, was recognised as heir to the throne. The decrees of the Council of Trent were to be treated as 'fundamental laws' in France. Philip II agreed to subsidise an armed rising by the League, and soon afterwards its forces seized a number of important French towns.[24]

A manifesto published by the Leaguers at Péronne on 31 March urged Catholics to prepare for civil war. They were warned of the dangers facing them in the event of a Huguenot becoming king. While preparing to defend himself, Henry III again relied on his mother's good offices to avert another armed conflict. She met the leaders of the League at Épernay in April, and three months later signed the peace of Nemours with them.[25] This was deeply humiliating to her son. He undertook to pay for the League's troops and conceded a number of surety towns. The lion's share was given to Guise, whose clients also received favours, pensions and governorships. An edict arising from the treaty banned Protestant worship and ordered all pastors to leave the kingdom without delay. Their flocks were allowed six months in which to abjure or go into exile. Huguenots were debarred from all public offices and were to surrender their surety towns. Setting aside the Salic Law, the edict deprived Henri de Navarre of his right to the throne. He was so shocked by the treaty that half his moustache is said to have turned white on hearing about it. In August 1583 he, Condé and Damville renewed their alliance. In a joint manifesto they accused the house of Lorraine of seeking to supplant the house of France. Reaffirming their loyalty to the crown, they explained that they had no option but to fight the League.

Henry III had never been in so much danger. Guise had the support of the Catholic nobility and of several towns, including Paris. Popular support for the League is easily explained. Catholics were genuinely frightened by the prospect of a Huguenot monarch. The League seemed to them like the realisation of a Christian ideal as well as bringing hope of a change of regime. Despite a reforming ordinance of 1579, the kingdom remained in turmoil: justice was badly administered, taxes were heavier than ever and civil war was endemic. A doubling of the price of bread since 1576 caused severe hardship among the urban poor. All this, plus the personal unpopularity of Henry III and his *mignons*, played into the hands of Guise and his followers. Among the towns supporting the League, Paris was the most radical. It had its own league which was set up late in 1584 by a group of Catholic zealots. Its central committee was known as the Sixteen, after the number of districts from which its members were elected. From the beginning, a close understanding existed between them and Guise. While building up a store of arms, the League infiltrated all the main institutions in the capital and unleashed a virulent propaganda campaign. Hundreds of printed pamphlets warned the people that the Huguenots were planning a massacre as well as Navarre's accession to the throne.[26]

In September Pope Sixtus V issued a bull depriving Henri de Navarre of his right to the French throne and, in October, Henry III issued a new edict which branded Huguenots as traitors and ordered the confiscation of their property. Navarre responded in kind. Writing to Catherine de' Medici, he denounced the pope's bull and warned her that Henry might be the next to be deposed by the Holy See. Both sides appealed to public opinion before coming to blows. In March 1586 Henry sent three armies to fight the Huguenots, one of them commanded by Guise, but the king was not keen to fight. He tried to disarm criticism by giving commands to his two favourites, Joyeuse and Épernon, but he lacked the means to fight a war. Whenever he tried to raise funds, he encountered resistance. Parisians reacted angrily when in June he tried to force the Parlement to register twenty-seven fiscal edicts. Navarre, for his part, secured a promise of financial help from England. This money was used to pay for German *reiters* whom John Casimir had raised for an invasion of France in support of the Huguenots.[27]

As the threat of a German invasion grew apace, Catherine again resorted to diplomacy. She met Navarre at Saint-Brice, near Cognac, in December 1586, but he was only interested in gaining time pending the arrival of help from Germany. The queen mother returned home empty-handed. Meanwhile, the League opposed any peace move. At a meeting at Ourscamp abbey in September, Guise and the cardinals of Guise and Bourbon had decided to reject any settlement with Navarre. In February 1587 Henry III shut himself up in the Louvre after learning of a plot by the League to kidnap him and force him to hand over power. He was, in effect, no longer in control of the kingdom. The Guises were doing as they pleased. In March news of the execution of Mary Queen of Scots inflamed Catholic opinion in France. Henry III was reviled for not saving her life. A rumour circulated in Paris to the effect that thousands of Huguenots were lurking in the suburbs waiting for the signal to avenge the massacre of St Bartholomew's Day. Early in July 1587, Henry met Guise at Meaux. The duke made a great show of obedience, but his real master was Philip II of Spain. 'I regard His Catholic Majesty', he said, 'as the father of all Catholics and of myself in particular.'[28]

In August 1587 Henry III announced that he was ready to lead his army. He took up a position on the Loire in order to prevent a link-up between the German relief army, which by now had invaded France, and the Huguenots. Joyeuse was sent to fight Navarre in the west, but on 18 October he suffered a crushing defeat at Coutras, which also cost him his life.[29] Navarre, however, did not follow up his victory. The German relief force, in the meantime, failed to cross the Loire and began to fall apart. As the Germans retreated, they were twice defeated by Guise. Early in December, they surrendered to Henry, who returned to Paris in triumph, but everyone knew that the real victors of the war had been his enemies: Guise and Navarre. Henry now provoked the League's fury by giving to Épernon offices previously held by Joyeuse, including the governorship of Normandy which Guise had coveted as a reward for his victory over the Germans. Épernon also became Admiral of France and governor of Angoumois, Aunis and Saintonge. As Étienne Pasquier noted, Épernon's elevation lost the king more nobles than Coutras. The favourite was also accused of robbing the kingdom. He may not have been as rich as the Leaguers imagined, but his fortune had been built up in a decade. A pamphlet compared him to Piers Gaveston, Edward II's ill-fated favourite.[30] While a vitriolic campaign of propaganda continued to be waged by the duchess of Montpensier, Henry seemed bent on scandalising public opinion. According to L'Estoile, he attended the fair at Saint-Germain every day, seeing and condoning misbehaviour against women and girls by his *mignons* and courtiers. Every night he attended parties in various parts of the city and held masquerades and balls as if there was no war and no League.[31]

Early in 1588 the leaders of the League, meeting at Nancy, drew up a set of demands for the king. They asked for the dismissal of Épernon, acceptance of Guise's tutelage in the fight against heresy, and publication of the decrees of the Council of Trent. A sharp rise in the price of food and an influx of hungry poor from the countryside aggravated political tension in Paris. Relations between the king and Guise were severed in May, when the duke accepted an invitation from the Sixteen in defiance of a ban on his entering the city. Henry chose not to arrest him, but brought troops into Paris at night and posted them in various strategic places regardless of the capital's traditional right of self-defence. Pouring into the streets, crowds erected barricades. The king's troops came under attack. Guise did nothing at first, but eventually he toured the streets at the king's request and ensured the troops' safety. On 13 May, the so-called Day of Barricades, Henry slipped out of the capital unnoticed and fled to Chartres.[32] Fearing that they might be classed as rebels, the Parisians sent deputations to him, but he would not receive them. Meanwhile, Guise tightened his hold on the capital. A new governor, devoted to him, was appointed and the king's supporters on the town council fled or were ousted. The leader of the Sixteen became mayor and took an oath of loyalty to Guise as the representative of the cardinal de Bourbon, the League's chosen heir to the throne.[33]

Eventually, Catherine de' Medici persuaded Henry to concede nearly all
the League's demands in a new Edict of Union: he dismissed Épernon,
reaffirmed the treaty of Nemours, recognised the cardinal of Bourbon
as his heir presumptive, bestowed new governorships on the Guises and
appointed the duke as lieutenant-general of the kingdom. Henry's
humiliation seemed complete, yet he was only playing for time. In September, he surprised everyone by sacking his ministers and replacing
them by young, hard-working men devoted to himself. He also called a
meeting of the Estates-General. He tried to influence the elections, but
most of the deputies chosen supported the League.

The League was easily able to exploit the king's financial weakness.
His failure to pay the salaries of office-holders or the interest owed to
the *rentiers* or holders of government annuities caused much public
resentment. Revenues which would normally have served those ends
had been used by Henry to fund his war against the League. As complaints were aired at the Estates-General, Henry conditionally agreed to
some of their demands, but this only made the Third Estate more truc-
ulent. It argued that kings owed their authority to the estates and
objected to the king's council overriding their decisions. Henry suspected that they were being manipulated by the League. He also saw the
hand of Guise in a recent invasion of the marquisate of Saluzzo by the
duke of Savoy. He accordingly decided that the time had come to assert
his authority. On 23 October Guise was lured into the king's chamber
at the château of Blois and hacked to death by the 'Forty-five', Henry's
personal bodyguard. Next day, the duke's brother, the cardinal of Guise,
was also murdered. Other prominent Leaguers, including the cardinal
of Bourbon, and members of the Guise family were thrown into
prison.[34] The meeting of the Estates-General came to an abrupt end in
the wake of these violent events.

Henry III visited his mother shortly after the murders in Blois. 'Please
forgive me', he said,

> M. de Guise is dead, and will not be spoken of again. I have had him killed.
> I have forestalled him in the plot which he had conceived against me. I
> could no longer tolerate his insolence although I tried hard enough to do
> so for I did not want the stain of his blood on my hands ... Nevertheless,
> as I was aware of, and had at every moment evidence that he was sapping
> and menacing my authority, my life and my State, I resolved upon this

deed which I have long contemplated ... I want to be a king and not a prisoner or a slave as I have been since the 13th May and now I begin to be king and master.[35]

Catherine's response is unknown, but on 26 December she wrote to Bernardino d'Osimo: 'Oh! The poor thing, what has he done? Pray for him – he has more need of it now than ever. I see him on the brink of his ruination and I fear that he will lose body, soul and kingdom'.[36] Henry certainly could not have committed a worse mistake. Overnight his subjects turned against him. Nowhere was the reaction to the murders in Blois more violent than in Paris, where preachers called for vengeance on 'the new Herod'. Pamphlets poured from the presses exalting the Guises as martyrs. The town council repudiated its allegiance to the blood-soaked tyrant of Blois. Releasing them their obedience, the Sorbonne called on all Frenchmen to take up arms. In one procession, little children drawn from various parishes marched from the Cemetery of the Innocents to the church of Sainte-Geneviève. Each carried a lighted candle and at the entrance to the church trampled it underfoot 'as a sign that the cursed tyrant [Henry III] was excommunicated'. Taxes were imposed on the rich 'for the defence of the Catholic religion'. The murder of the cardinal of Guise was, of course, seen by the Holy See as a particularly heinous crime.[37] In May, Pope Sixtus V summoned Henry to Rome to explain his conduct under threat of excommunication. As the Sixteen tightened their hold on the capital, mobs attacked royal images. In the church of the Augustins, a picture of Henry III and the Order of the Holy Spirit was destroyed, as were the tombs of Anne de Joyeuse and his brother in the church of Saint-Paul. The Parlement also came under fire. In January a mob broke into the *Grand' Chambre* and carried off the first president and two of his colleagues before throwing them into the Bastille. Their places were filled by Leaguers. In February 1589 Guise's younger brother, Charles, duke of Mayenne, entered the capital in triumph at the head of an army and was appointed lieutenant-general of the kingdom, but he set up his own administration rather than allow free rein to the Sixteen.

On 5 January 1589 Catherine de' Medici died, leaving Henry III isolated.[38] He was caught between the League's forces in the north and east of France and those of the Huguenots in the south. The king controlled Bordeaux, a few towns in the Loire valley and two provinces, but his shortage of money was such that he was reduced to pawning crown jewels. In February 1589 he managed to get a loan of 1,200,000 *livres* from the Elbene bank, but his credit was too low to attract larger loans. Only by allying with Navarre could he hope to carry on the fight. On 26 April the two Henrys signed a truce that was soon followed by an accord. Combining their armies, they laid siege to Paris, setting up their headquarters at Saint-Cloud and Meudon respectively.

In the meantime, a frenzy of anti-Valois feeling exploded in the capital. As processions were staged, invoking the Almighty's protection, preachers denounced Henry III as the agent of Satan and called for his extermination. Among those who heard the call was a Dominican friar, called Jacques Clément. He told his fellow friars of a vision in which an angel had appeared to him brandishing an unsheathed sword. 'I am a messenger of the all-powerful God', said the angel, 'who comes to tell you that, by your hand, the Tyrant of France must be put to death.'[39] On 1 August the friar made his way to the king's camp, claiming that he carried a message from some of Henry's friends in the capital. He was admitted to the royal presence, even though Henry was sitting on his close stool at the time. He invited Clément to come nearer, whereupon the friar stabbed him in the abdomen. A few hours later, Henry died. He was the first king of France to die at the hands of one of his own subjects and his death may be taken as a sign that the mystique of monarchy had collapsed.[40] Yet the institution itself survived. It was the Valois dynasty which stood discredited in the eyes of most Frenchmen. News of Henry III's assassination caused wild rejoicing in Paris. For many Catholics, it marked the completion of the sacred mission of Catholic purification which the Massacre of St Bartholomew's Day had only accomplished in part. Henry's demise seemed to remove the last obstacle in the path of a Catholic triumph in France. Clément was canonised by the League's propagandists. In the words of Jean Boucher, the curé of Saint-Benoît, 'a new David has killed Goliath; a new Judith has killed Holofernes'.[41] One of Henry III's last acts was to recognise Henri of Navarre as his heir and to warn him that only by becoming a Catholic would he gain the throne.

15

Assessment

Each of three royal dynasties – the Capetians, the Valois and the Bourbons – contributed to the making of the French kingdom. As territorial princes, the early Capetians (987–1108) were not powerful. They sought to enlarge their principality, centred on Paris and the Ile-de-France, by encroaching on the lands of their neighbours. Yet the king's sacred and judicial attributes, and his role as overlord were generally recognised. His coronation and anointing set him apart from his people. On a practical level, he was supported by his domain and by his ecclesiastical and secular rights. A primitive machinery of government, centred on his household, ensured that his authority was effective at least in the lands which he controlled in person.

By 1226 the royal lands had been enlarged to include the duchy of Normandy, the counties of Maine and Anjou, most of Poitou and substantial holdings in Languedoc. The king's legal suzerainty was acknowledged and generally obeyed and his power over the French church was considerable. The remarkable expansion of royal power after 1200 under Philip Augustus (1180–1223) and his son Louis VIII (1223–26) was assisted by social and economic changes including population growth, land clearance the spread of markets, fairs and trade, an increasing prosperity and an economy more dependant on coinage than in the past. Some of these changes undermined the nobility's economic standing. Philip-Augustus successfully exploited the weaknesses and divisions of his enemies.

Rebellions during the minority of Louis IX (1226–44) showed that royal power was still not firmly entrenched throughout the kingdom, but the king managed to consolidate the conquests of his father and grandfather. The machinery of government also became more effective. The *baillis* made their appearance. At first they were itinerant officials with judicial and fiscal duties, sent out in groups of three or four on temporary missions to hold inquests and assizes, but they were soon given authority in specific areas, known as *bailliages*. The great expansion of royal lands made the king wealthy. The royal court of justice – the Parlement – gradually emerged from the *curia regis*, reaching its maturity in the early fourteenth century. In 1248 the judicial sessions of the king's council became fixed in Paris. The prestige of monarchy reached great heights under Louis IX (1244–70), partly as a response to vastly increased royal power and wealth, and partly as a reflection of the king's reputation for piety and justice. Royal power in France reached its medieval apogee during the reign of Philip IV 'the Fair'(1285–1314) under whom a flood of lawsuits reached the Parlement of Paris. The king's judicial ordinances were in many cases effective throughout the kingdom. Philip could call on all his vassals for military service and sometimes levied taxes throughout the kingdom for its defence. Any opposition to his feudal and sovereign powers was firmly punished, and, in his dealings with the church, Philip was strong enough even to humiliate the papacy. He and his sons were able to impose their authority far more widely and effectively than the early Capetians had been able to do.[1]

Turning to the second dynasty, the Valois, we are faced with an amazing story of survival followed by recovery and consolidation. The Hundred Years War with England very nearly brought the French monarchy to its knees. Not only was King John the Good defeated and taken prisoner at the battle of Poitiers, but his grandson, Charles VI, was assailed by a crippling mental breakdown which left him at the mercy of his entourage. The defeats suffered by the French armies at Poitiers and Agincourt were traumatic, and alongside these disasters the French kingdom experienced a catastrophic loss of population as a result of the Black Death. While the English king occupied Paris, his French counterpart was relegated to Bourges, a provincial city south of the Loire. He became derisively known as 'the King of Bourges'. Yet with the miraculous assistance of Joan of Arc, King Charles VII managed to be crowned at Reims. The English were then driven out of France, except Calais, which remained an English foothold on the Continent till 1558. The overmighty subject ceased to be an immediate threat to the French crown when Charles the Bold was killed on the battlefield of Nancy in 1477. His death offered King Louis XI, one of the ablest of the Valois kings, the chance to annex Burgundy. Later in his reign, in 1481, he

acquired Provence and with it the port of Marseille, offering a valuable
opening on the Mediterranean and access to trade with the Levant. This
left only the duchy of Brittany as a major independent fief. This too was
drawn into the royal orbit by the marriage of its duchess, Anne, to King
Charles VIII. Much as Anne would have liked to uphold her duchy's
independence, it was eventually annexed by France in 1532.

By 1494 the French monarchy had become so powerful at home that
it could envisage conquests abroad. As yet, the notion that France was
bounded by 'natural frontiers' – the Atlantic, the Rhine, the Alps and
the Pyrenees – was unknown. What mattered was legality. Charles VIII
had inherited a claim to the kingdom of Naples and viewed its conquest
as a legitimate aim and as a first step to leading a crusade to the Holy
Land. His successors, Louis XII and Francis I, coveted the duchy of
Milan. Claiming it as their own, they provoked a series of wars which
served to satisfy the French nobility's warlike proclivities. As long as
the nobles let off steam in Italy, they remained docile at home. Only the
treason of the constable of Bourbon in 1523 threatened to disturb the
domestic peace, but he failed to get the support of his peers. The defeat
of Francis I at Pavia in 1525 was a disaster on a par with that of King
John at Poitiers in 1356. The king was not only defeated, but captured
and imprisoned in Spain. Yet the monarchy survived. Francis obtained
his freedom by falsely promising to surrender Burgundy to the emperor.
On returning home in 1526, he reasserted his authority, which his
mother had skilfully sustained during his captivity.

As the French became familiar with Renaissance Italy, so they
absorbed some of its culture. The French court, in particular, achieved
a new sophistication of manners and became noted for its sponsorship
of the arts. The châteaux built by Francis I bear witness to his concern
for the projection of monarchy. He combined an interest in the arts
with a strong authoritarianism which has sometimes been mistaken for
absolutism. He was 'absolute' in the sense of having no superior except
the Almighty, but he could not do all that he wanted. He depended on
the support of his nobility and had to operate within narrow financial
constraints. The king's traditional sources of income – his domainial
revenues and taxation, both direct and indirect – failed to keep abreast
of the rapidly rising costs of war. Artillery, fortifications and the hiring
of ever-larger numbers of Swiss and German mercenaries were

extremely expensive. In order to make ends meet, the king was driven to rely on loans, confiscations and expedients, such as the sale of offices, which served to undermine royal authority in the long term.

The year 1559 marked the beginning of another period of crisis for the Valois monarchy. The sudden death of King Henry II as a result of an accident in a tournament held to celebrate the peace of Cateau-Cambrésis plunged France into a political upheaval which revealed all too clearly the basic weaknesses of the crown. Henry II, who had been a strong king, left only children to succeed him. His widow, Catherine de' Medici did her best to defend their inheritance, but she was faced by two major problems: the rapid rise of the Protestant faith, which could not be accommodated within a kingdom traditionally committed to the Roman Catholic church; and a still powerful nobility which the peace of Cateau-Cambrésis had deprived of its battleground in Italy. The combination of Protestant dissent and aristocratic frustration was to prove explosive as Henry II's three sons, Francis II, Charles IX and Henry III, succeeded each other on the throne.

By seeking to impose uniformity by persecuting religious dissenters, Henry II and his successors unleashed serious domestic unrest which culminated in a long series of increasingly bloody civil wars and massacres. The bitter struggle for power between the aristocratic houses of Guise, Bourbon and Montmorency, coupled with the military potential at their disposal, is evidence enough that the Valois monarchy had not yet succeeded in eliminating all threats to its authority. As the crown tried to maintain its independence in the midst of a welter of aristocratic factionalism, so it distanced itself more from its subjects. The easy accessibility which it had cultivated in the past was abandoned. Henry III, the last of the Valois kings, incurred unpopularity by withdrawing as much as possible from public view and consorting with favourites whose extravagant ways brought him and his court into popular disrepute. Intelligent as he was, Henry III committed the blunder of presiding over the assassination of Henri, the third duke of Guise and of his brother, the cardinal of Guise. This action unleashed a wave of Catholic extremism which culminated in the king's own assassination by a fanatical Jacobin friar.

And so to the third dynasty, the Bourbons. As Henry III had no son to succeed him, the Valois died out, and the crown passed to Henri of

Bourbon, king of Navarre, the leader of the Protestant party. His succession was fiercely opposed by a majority of the French people, so that in the end he had to become a Catholic in order to win acceptance. 'Paris', as he allegedly said, 'is worth a mass'. Henry IV is credited with bringing the Wars of Religion to an end by signing the Edict of Nantes, which conceded a large measure of religious and political freedom to his former co-religionists. But religious fanaticism was not extinguished, and in 1610 Henry IV was also stabbed to death by a Catholic hothead. Yet the monarchy held firm. Even at the height of the religious troubles, the Protestant rebels never toyed with the idea of setting up a Dutch-style republic, as has sometimes been alleged. They knew that sooner or later, their leader, the first prince of the blood royal, would succeed to the throne. Yet if the Bourbon monarchy was secure, it still had problems to overcome whose roots lay in the past. Religion was one and an overpowerful nobility another. In 1629 Cardinal Richelieu succeeded in reducing the Protestants to the status of an ineffective minority by cancelling the political concessions given to them in the Edict of Nantes. The nobility, however, remained a potential nuisance, but the Fronde of the Princes proved to be its last fling before the reign of Louis XIV completed the monumental task initiated by the Capetians and so courageously continued by the Valois against all the odds.

Notes

Notes to Introduction

1. The miniature belongs to the National Trust and is no. 184 of the collection at Upton House, Warwickshire.
2. Colette Beaune, *Naissance de la nation France* (Paris, 1985), pp. 188–206.

Notes to Chapter 1: A New Dynasty

1. Craig Taylor, 'The Salic Law and the Valois Succession to the French Crown', *French History*, 15 (2001), pp. 358–77; Fanny Cosandey, *La reine de France: symbole et pouvoir* (Paris, 2000), pp. 19–54.
2. F. Autrand, *Charles V le Sage* (Paris, 1994), pp. 53–54.
3. Ibid., pp. 54–58.
4. Ibid.
5. A. Demurger, *Temps de crises, temps d'espoirs, XIVe-XVe siècle* (Paris, 1990), pp. 11–12; Autrand, *Charles V*, p. 31.
6. Demurger, *Temps de crises*, p. 19.
7. Autrand, *Charles V*, pp. 42–47.
8. Demurger, *Temps de crises*, pp. 13–20.
9. Contamine, P., *Le Moyen Âge* (Paris, 2002), pp. 306–7.
10. B. Guénée, *Un meurtre, une société: l'assassinat du duc d'Orléans, 23 novembre 1407* (Paris, 1992), pp. 25–28.
11. B. Guénée, *Un meurtre, une société*, pp. 28–35.
12. Autrand, *Charles V*, pp. 20–22; P. S. Lewis, *Later Medieval France: The Polity* (London, 1968), p. 110.
13. Autrand, *Charles V*, pp. 77–81.
14. Demurger, *Temps de crises*, pp. 37–39.
15. Autrand, *Charles V*, pp. 751–78.
16. Demurger, *Temps de crises*, pp. 138–47; Martin Wolfe, *The Fiscal System of Renaissance France* (New Haven, Connecticut, 1972), pp. 38–40.

Notes to Chapter 2: The Hundred Years War

1. Nigel Saul, *Richard II* (London, 1997), p. 210.

2. Saul, *Richard II*, p. 217.

3. J. Favier, *La Guerre de Cent Ans* (Paris, 1980), pp. 94–100.

4. Ibid., pp. 130–36.

5. Ibid., pp. 105–14, 117–36. For a full discussion, see J. Sumption, *The Hundred Years War: Trial by Battle* (London, 1990), chapters 14 and 15.

6. Philippe Contamine, 'Les fortifications urbaines en France à la fin du Moyen Âge: aspects financiers et économiques', *Revue historique*, 260 (1978), pp. 23–47.

7. J. B. Henneman, *Olivier de Clisson and Political Society in France under Charles V and Charles VI* (Philadelphia, 1996).

8. Froissart, *Chronicles*, trans. G. Brereton (London, 1978), p. 153. For a full discussion of these events, see J. Sumption, *The Hundred Years War*, ii, *Trial by Fire* (London, 1999), chapters 6 and 7.

9. Favier, *La Guerre de Cent Ans*, pp. 256–62.

10. C. Allmand, *The Hundred Years War* (Cambridge, 1988), pp. 73–76.

11. Philippe Contamine, 'Les compagnies d'aventure en France pendant la guerre de cent ans', in *Mélanges de l'école française de Rome, Moyen Âge, Temps modernes*, 87 (Rome, 1975), pp. 365–96.

12. Perroy, *La Guerre de Cent Ans*, pp. 133–35.

13. Philippe Contamine (ed.), *Histoire militaire de la France*, I, *Des origines à 1715* (Paris, 1992), pp. 145–50.

14. P. Contamine, *Guerre, état et société à la fin du Moyen Âge* (Paris, 1972), pp. 135–50.

15. Eamon Duffy, *Saints and Sinners: A History of the Popes* (London, 1997), pp. 125–27.

16. P. S. Lewis, *Later Medieval France* (London, 1968), pp. 313–19.

Notes to Chapter 3: The Marmousets

1. Françoise Autrand, *Charles VI* (Paris, 1986), pp. 120–36.

2. M. Rey, *Le domaine du roi et les finances extraordinaires sous Charles VI, 1388–1413* (Paris, 1965), pp. 166–67.

3. J. B. Henneman, *Olivier de Clisson and Political Society in France under Charles V and Charles VI* (Philadelphia, 1996), pp. 129–32.

4. Ibid., pp. 134–35.

5. Ibid., pp. 135–37.

6. F. Autrand, *Charles VI*, pp. 198–202.

7. Ibid., pp. 202–13.

8. Ibid., pp. 241 55.

9. Ibid., pp. 179–88.

10. Ibid., pp. 256–65; Henneman, *Olivier de Clisson*, pp. 142–44.

11. R. C. Famiglietti, *Royal Intrigue: Crisis at the Court of Charles VI, 1392–1420* (New York, 1986), pp. 1–21.

12. Henneman, *Olivier de Clisson*, pp. 157–60.

13. Autrand, *Charles VI*, pp. 340–42.

14. Jean Favier, *La Guerre de Cent Ans* (Paris, 1980), p. 409.

15. Ibid., pp. 337–38, 343–44, 409–13.

16. Ibid., pp. 342–43; R. Vaughan, *John the Fearless* (New York, 1966), p. 4.

Notes to Chapter 4: Armagnacs versus Burgundians

1. R. Vaughan, *John the Fearless* (London, 1966), p. 30.

2. Ibid., p. 34.

3. Ibid., p. 37.

4. Ibid., pp. 38–44.

5. Ibid., p. 45; Jean Favier, *La Guerre de Cent Ans* (Paris, 1980), pp. 419–22.

6. B. Guénée, *Un meurtre, une société: l'assassinat du duc d'Orléans, 23 novembre 1407* (Paris, 1992), pp. 7–16.

7. Vaughan, *John the Fearless*, p. 70.

8. Ibid., p. 74.

9. Ibid., p. 82.

10. The Tour Jean-sans-Peur (20, rue Étienne Marcel) is all that remains of the Hôtel de Bourgogne. It was built between 9 February 1409 and 15 May 1411.

11. Vaughan, *John the Fearless*, p. 89.

12. F. Autrand, *Charles VI* (Paris, 1986), pp. 470–500; Favier, *La Guerre de Cent Ans*, pp. 427–33.

13. Autrand, *Charlers VI*, pp. 470–71.

14. Vaughan, *John the Fearless*, pp. 197–202.

15. Ibid., p. 90.

16. Contamine, *Histoire militaire*, pp. 176–80; C. Allmand, *Henry V* (London, 1992), pp. 83–101; Curry, Anne (ed.), *Agincourt, 1415* (Stroud, 2000), pp. 21–36.

17. Allmand, *Henry V*, pp. 102–3.

18. Ibid., pp. 113–35.

19. M. G. A. Vale, *Charles VII* (London, 1974), p. 30.

20. Ibid., p. 14.

21. Ibid., p. 34.

22. Ibid.

23. Allmand, *Henry V*, pp. 171–76.

Notes to Chapter 5: From Bourges to Paris

1. P. S. Lewis, *Later Medieval France: The Polity* (London, 1964), pp. 114–16; M. G. A. Vale, *Charles VII* (London, 1974), pp. 1–12.

2. Ibid., pp. 39–40.

3. Ibid., p. 41.

4. C. Petit-Dutaillis, *Charles VII, Louis XI et les premières années de Charles VIII*, in E. Lavisse, *Histoire de France*, iv, pt 2 (Paris, 1902), pp. 26–28.

5. J. Favier, *La Guerre de Cent Ans* (Paris, 1980), pp. 482–84.

6. E. Perroy, *La Guerre de Cent Ans* (Paris, 1945), p. 240.

7. A. Corvisier (ed.), *Histoire militaire de la France*, i, *Des origines à 1715* (ed. P. Contamine), pp. 185–87, 194–95.

8. Perroy, *La Guerre de Cent Ans*, pp. 246–48; Favier, *La Guerre de Cent Ans*, pp. 493–96.

9. Petit-Dutaillis, *Charles VII, Louis XI*, p. 56; Favier, *La Guerre de Cent Ans*, p. 501.

10. R. A. Jackson, *Vive le Roi! A History of the French Coronation from Charles V to Charles X* (Chapel Hill, North Carolina, 1984), pp. 34–36.

11. M. Bloch, *Les rois thaumaturges* (Paris, 1961), pp. 140–41.

12. Favier, *La Guerre de Cent Ans*, pp. 517–28.

13. M. G. A. Vale, *Charles VII* (London, 1974), pp. 58–59.

14. Perroy, *La Guerre de Cent Ans*, pp. 255–62.

15. J. C. Dickinson, *The Congress of Arras 1435: A Study in Medieval Diplomacy* (Oxford, 1955); Petit-Dutaillis, *Charles VII, Louis XI*, pp. 74–79; Perroy, *La Guerre de Cent Ans*, pp. 260–61.

16. R. Vaughan, *Philip the Good* (London, 1970), pp. 98–107.

17. Perroy, *La Guerre de Cent Ans*, p. 261.

18. Vale, *Charles VII*, p. 104; Favier, *La Guerre de Cent Ans*, pp. 573–75.

19. Petit-Dutaillis, *Charles VII, Louis XI*, pp. 228–29.

20. Ibid., pp. 230–33, 273–75.

21. Ibid., pp. 352–60.

22. N. Valois, *La Pragmatique Sanction de Bourges sous Charles VII* (Paris, 1906); Vale, *Charles VII*, pp. 61–63, 65–66; G. du Fresne de Beaucourt, *Histoire de Charles VII* (Paris, 1881–91), iii, pp. 332–61.

23. P. Imbart de la Tour, *Les origines de la Réforme* (2nd edn, Melun, 1946), ii, p. 211.

24. P. S. Lewis, *Later Medieval France*, p. 318.

25. C. Poulain, *Jacques Coeur* (Paris, 1982).

26. A. Demurger, *Temps de crises, temps d'espoirs* (Paris, 1990), pp. 218–21.

27. Vale, *Charles VII*, pp. 129–31.

28. P. Champion, *Louis XI* (Paris, 1927), i, pp. 127–36.

29. Vale, *Charles VII*, p. 80.

30. P. Contamine, *Guerre, état et société à la fin du Moyen Âge* (Paris, 1972), pp. 277–312.

31. Ibid., pp. 198–200; Perroy, *La Guerre de Cent Ans*, pp. 280–85.

32. Vale, *Charles VII*, pp. 116–19.

33. Contamine, *Guerre, état et société*, p. 200.

34. A. Demurger, *Temps de crises*, pp. 186–87.

35. Vale, *Charles VII*, pp. 151, 158.

36. Ibid., p. 157.

37. Ibid., p. 162; G. Chastellain, *Oeuvres*, ed. Kervyn de Lettenhove (Brussels, 1863–65), iii, pp. 422–43.

38. Vale, *Charles VII*, pp. 154–62.

39. F. Avril (ed.), *Jean Fouquet, peintre et enlumineur du XVe siècle* (Paris, 2003), pp. 29–37, 69–75, 101–9, 272–79.

40. P. M. Kendall, *Louis XI* (London, 1971), pp. 74–75.

41. Ibid., p. 96.

42. Vale, *Charles VII*, pp. 189–91.

Notes to Chapter 6: The 'Universal Spider'

1. Pierre Champion, *Louis XI* (Paris, 1927), i, pp. 183–218; Paul Murray Kendall, *Louis XI* (London, 1971), pp. 62–107; Jean Favier, *Louis XI* (Paris, 2001), pp. 109–85.

2. Champion, *Louis XI*, ii, pp. 1–18; Kendall, *Louis XI*, pp. 111–15; Favier, *Louis XI*, pp. 194–208; Richard Vaughan, *Philip the Good* (London, 1970), p. 354.

3. Favier, *Louis XI*, pp. 213–25.

4. Vaughan, *Philip the Good*, pp. 391–95.

5. Favier, *Louis XI*, pp. 447–65.

6. Champion, *Louis XI*, ii, pp. 61–82; Favier, *Louis XI*, pp. 465.

7. Champion, *Louis XI*, ii, pp. 91–103; Philippe de Commynes, *Mémoires*, ed. Joseph Calmette (Paris, 1924), pp. 125–34; Favier, *Louis XI*, pp. 553–79; Richard Vaughan, *Charles the Bold* (London, 1973), pp. 54–56.

8. Favier, *Louis XI*, p. 325.

9. Ibid., pp. 427–34, 665–70.

10. Ibid., pp. 668–70.

11. Ibid., pp. 425–29, 457, 670.

12. Ibid., pp. 620–29.

13. Ibid., pp. 636–42.

14. Champion, *Louis XI*, ii, pp. 131–35.

15. G. Picot, *Histoire des États-Généraux* (Paris, 1888), i, p. 342.

16. M. Wolfe, *The Fiscal System of Renaissance France* (New Haven, Connecticut, 1972), p. 58.

17. Favier, *Louis XI*, p. 378.

18. Favier, *Louis XI*, pp. 827–35, 839–50.

19. Wolfe, *The Fiscal System of Renaissance France*, p. 58.

20. H. Sée, *Louis XI et les villes* (Paris, 1890), pp. 126–29.

21. A. Demurger, *Temps de crises, temps d'espoirs* (Paris, 1990), p. 146.

22. Champion, *Louis XI*, i, pp. 31–56; Favier, *Louis XI*, pp. 909–17.

23. Philippe de Commynes, *Mémoires*, ed. J. Calmette, 3 vols (Paris, 1924–25).

24. Thomas Basin, *Histoire de Louis XI*, ed. C. Samaran and M. C. Garand, 3 vols (Paris, 1963–72).

25. Jean de Roye, *Chronique scandaleuse (1460–1483)*, ed. B. de Mandrot, 2 vols (Paris, 1894–96); Favier, *Louis XI*, pp. 919–40.

26. Georges Chastellain, *Oeuvres*, ed. Kervyn de Lettenhove, 8 vols (Brussels, 1863–66)

27. Favier, *Louis XI*, pp. 910–12.

28. Ibid., pp. 45–74; P. S. Lewis, *Later Medieval France* (London, 1968), pp. 116–19.

29. J.-M. Cauchies, *Louis XI et Charles le Hardi: De Péronne à Nancy (1468–1477). Le conflit* (Brussels, 1996).

30. Vaughan, *Valois Burgundy* (London, 1975), pp. 23–31.

31. R. Vaughan, *Charles the Bold*, pp. 185–87.

32. Ibid., pp. 84–86, 95–97.

33. Ibid., pp. 140–54.

34. Ibid., pp. 261–84.

35. Ibid., p. 140.

36. On Louis XI's army, see Favier, *Louis XI*, pp. 339–51.

37. Vaughan, *Charles the Bold*, pp. 278–310.

38. Commynes, *Mémoires*, ii, p. 27; J. Calmette and G. Périnelle, *Louis XI et l'Angleterre* (Paris, 1930), pp. 164–68; C. Ross, *Edward IV* (London, 1974), pp. 210–26.

39. Ibid., pp. 229–31.

40. P. de Commynes, *Memoirs*, trans. M. Jones (Harmondsworth, 1972), p. 258; Ross, *Edward IV*, p. 232.

41. Commynes, *Memoirs*, trans. Jones, pp. 258–59.

42. Ibid., p. 233; Calmette and Périnelle, *Louis XI et l'Angleterre*, pp. 202–5; Favier, *Louis XI*, pp. 682–87.

43. Ross, *Edward IV*, p. 236.

44. Kendall, *Louis XI*, pp. 293–96; Favier, *Louis XI*, pp. 687–88.

45. Commynes, *Memoirs*, trans. M. Jones, pp. 249–50.

46. Favier, *Louis XI*, pp. 787–89; Kendall, *Louis XI*, pp. 303–4.

47. Ibid., pp. 343–44.

48. Vaughan, *Charles the Bold*, pp. 365–79.

49. Vaughan, *Valois Burgundy*, p. 216.

50. Ibid., p. 219.

51. Ibid., pp. 223–24; Favier, *Louis XI*, pp. 717–22.

52. Commynes, *Memoirs*, trans. Jones, p. 311.

53. Kendall, *Louis XI*, pp. 312–14; Favier, *Louis XI*, pp. 722–23.

54. Kendall, *Louis XI*, p. 315.

55. Favier, *Louis XI*, pp. 744–46.

56. Kendall, *Louis XI*, pp. 318–19.

57. Favier, *Louis XI*, p. 737.

58. Ibid., pp. 749–51; Demurger, *Temps de crises*, p. 281.

59. Kendall, *Louis XI*, pp. 318–19; Favier, *Louis XI*, pp. 732–35.

60. Kendall, *Louis XI*, pp. 326–27.

61. Ibid., pp. 359–60.

Notes to Chapter 7: The End of Breton Independence

1. Yvonne Labande-Mailfert, *Charles VIII et son milieu (1470–1498). La jeunesse au pouvoir* (Paris, 1975), pp. 31–54.

2. The Sanction had been replaced by a Concordat in 1472.

3. Labande-Mailfert, *Charles VIII et son milieu*, pp. 55–57.

4. Ibid., pp. 58–60.

5. Ibid., p. 62.

6. Ibid., p. 66.

7. Ibid., pp. 67–71.

8. Ibid., pp. 71–78.

9. Ibid., pp. 78–80.

10. Ibid., pp. 81–100.

11. Ibid., p. 85.

12. Ibid., pp. 87–90.

13. Ibid., pp. 91–95.

14. Ibid., pp. 99–100.

15. Ibid., pp. 105–7.

16. Ibid., pp. 110–12.

17. Ibid., p. 120.

18. B. Quilliet, *Louis XII, Père du Peuple* (Paris, 1986), p. 219.

19. Ibid., pp. 221–27.

20. Ibid., pp. 227–29.

21. R. J. Knecht, *Renaissance Warrior and Patron: The Reign of Francis I* (Cambridge, 1994), pp. 9–10.

22. Ibid., p. 11.

23. Ibid., pp. 11–15.

24. Ibid., pp. 349–50.

Notes to Chapter 8: *The Lure of Italy*

1. Yvonne Labande-Mailfert, *Charles VIII et son milieu (1470–1498). La jeunesse au pouvoir* (Paris, 1975), pp. 169–76.

2. M. Vale, *Charles VII* (London, 1974), p. 105.

3. P. M. Kendall, *Louis XI* (London, 1971), pp. 333–42.

4. G. R. Potter (ed.), *The Renaissance, 1493–1520* (Cambridge, 1957), pp. 343–49.

5. Labande-Mailfert, *Charles VIII et son milieu*, pp. 176–96.

6. Ibid., pp. 185–89.

7. Ibid., pp. 196–99.

8. H. F. Delaborde, *L'expédition de Charles VIII en Italie: histoire diplomatique et militaire* (Paris 1888), p. 312.

9. Labande-Mailfert, *Charles VIII et son milieu*, pp. 219–26.

10. D. Weinstein, *Savonarola and Florence* (Princeton, 1970).

11. F. Lot, *Recherches sur les effectifs des armées françaises des Guerres d'Italie aux Guerres de Religion (1494–1562)* (Paris, 1962), pp. 15–21.

12. Bonner Mitchell, *Italian Civic Pageantry in the High Renaissance* (Florence, 1979), pp. 35, 64, 96, 105, 108–9, 111, 135, 141, 143.

13. Philippe de Commynes, *Mémoires*, ed. J. Calmette (Paris, 1924–25), iii, pp. 86–90; Labande-Mailfert, *Charles VIII et son milieu*, pp. 305–25.

14. Ibid., pp. 327–77.

15. Commynes, *Mémoires*, iii, pp. 160–96; Labande-Mailfert, *Charles VIII et son milieu*, pp. 394–406; Piero Pieri, *La crisi militare italiana nel Rinascimento* (2nd edn, Milan, 1952), pp. 303–12.

16. Labande-Mailfert, *Charles VIII et son milieu*, pp. 475–88.

17. Claude Quétel, *History of Syphilis* (Oxford, 1990), pp. 9–11.

18. B. Quilliet, *Louis XII, Père du Peuple* (Paris, 1986), pp. 240–43; F. J. Baumgartner, *Louis XII* (London, 1996), pp. 105–18.

19. L.-G. Pélissier, *Louis XII et Ludovic Sforza: 8 avril 1508–23 juillet 1500* (Paris 1896), i, p. 399.

20. Lot, *Recherches sur les effectifs*, pp. 23–30.

21. Luisa Giordano 'Les entrées de Louis XII en Milanais', in *Passer les monts: Français en Italie – l'Italie en France (1494–1525)*, ed. J. Balsamo, pp. 139–48; Mitchell, *Italian Civic Pageantry*, pp. 2, 56, 58, 80–84, 106, 133.

22. P. Contamine and J. Guillaume (eds), *Louis XII en Milanais* (Paris, 2003).

23. Quilliet, *Louis XII*, pp. 267–94.

24. F. Lot, *Recherches sur les effectifs*, pp. 30–31

25. Baumgartner, *Louis XII*, p. 143.

26. Quilliet, *Louis XII*, pp. 376–83; Lot, *Recherches sur les effectifs*, p. 31.

27. C. Shaw, *Julius II* (Oxford, 1993), pp. 229–34.

28. Ibid., pp. 383–93; F. Lot, *Recherches sur les effectifs*, pp. 31–33.

29. Shaw, *Julius II*, pp. 271, 290–96.

30. Quilliet, *Louis XII*, pp. 411–12.

31. Ibid., p. 420.

32. Ibid., pp. 421–23; J. J. Scarisbrick, *Henry VIII* (London, 1968), pp. 36–37.

33. Quilliet, *Louis XII*, pp. 424–26.

Notes to Chapter 9: Valois versus Habsburg

1. J. R. Hale (ed.), *The Travel Journal of Antonio de Beatis* (London, 1979), p. 108.

2. P. Morgan, 'Un chroniqueur gallois à Calais', in *Revue du Nord*, 47 (1965), p. 199.

3. F. Mignet, *La rivalité de François Ier et de Charles-Quint* (Paris, 1875), I, pp. 77–78.

4. P. Pieri, *Il Rinascimento e la crisi militare italiana* (Turin, 1952), pp. 516–24

5. R. J. Knecht, 'The Concordat of 1516: A Re-Assessment', *University of Birmingham Historical Journal*, 9 (1963), pp. 1–32.

6. Anne-Marie Lecoq, *François Ier imaginaire* (Paris, 1987), pp. 215–57.

7. L. Schick, *Un grand homme d'affaires au début du XVIè siècle, Jacob Fugger* (Paris, 1957), p. 163.

8. Joycelyne G. Russell, *The Field of Cloth of Gold* (London, 1969); S. Anglo, *Spectacle, Pageantry and Early Tudor Policy* (Oxford, 1969), pp. 137–69.

9. J-P. Mayer, *Pavie 1525. L'Italie joue son destin pour deux siècles* (Le Mans, 1998); R. Thom, *Die Schlacht bei Pavia* (Berlin, 1907); C. Oman, *A History of the Art of War in the XVIth Century* (New York, 1937), pp. 186–207.

10. *Captivité du roi François Ier*, ed. A. Champollion-Figeac (Paris, 1847), p. 129.

11. R. J. Knecht, *Renaissance Warrior and Patron: The Reign of Francis I*

(Cambridge, 1994), pp. 227–31; G. Jacqueton, *La politique extérieure de Louise de Savoie* (Paris, 1892), pp. 64–83.

12. H. Hauser, 'Le traité de Madrid et la cession de la Bourgogne à Charles-Quint', *Revue bourguignonne*, 22 (1912).

13. J. Ursu, *La politique orientale de François Ier* (Paris, 1908), pp. 58, 60–61, 66–72; V.-L. Bourrilly, 'Antonio Rincon et la politique orientale de François Ier', *Revue historique*, 113 (1913), pp. 76–83.

14. *Calendar of State Papers, Spanish*, v, 157, p. 455.

15. *Relations des ambassadeurs vénitiens sur les affaires de France*, ed. N. Tommaseo (Paris, 1838), i, p. 67.

16. R. J. Knecht, *Catherine de' Medici* (London, 1998), pp. 12–17.

17. G. Procacci, 'La Provence à la veille des Guerres de Religion: une periode décisive, 1535–45', *Revue d'histoire moderne et contemporaine*, 5 (1958), pp. 249–50.

18. Knecht, *Renaissance Warrior and Patron*, pp. 385–97.

19. C. Terrasse, *François Ier: le roi et son règne* (Paris, 1945–70), ii, p. 293.

20. R. J. Knecht, 'Charles V's Journey through France, 1539–40', in *Court Festivals of the European Renaissance*, ed. J. R. Mulryne and Elizabeth Goldring (Aldershot, 2002), pp. 153–70.

21. The château of Boulogne near Paris was popularly called 'Madrid'. See below p. 204.

22. M. François, *Le cardinal François de Tournon* (Paris, 1951), p. 179n.

23. *Calendar of State Papers, Spanish*, ix, pp. 62–64.

24. Knecht, *Renaissance Warrior and Patron*, pp. 541–49.

25. I. Cloulas, *Henri II* (Paris, 1985), pp. 317–22.

26. L. Romier, *Les origines politiques des Guerres de Religion* (Paris, 1914), ii, pp. 108–87.

27. Ibid., ii, pp. 331–47.

28. Cloulas, *Henri II*, pp. 589–94.

Notes to Chapter 10: A Renaissance Court

1. R. J. Knecht, *Renaissance Warrior and Patron: The Reign of Francis I* (Cambridge, 1994), pp. 128, 318; *Ordonnances des rois de France: règne de François Ier* (Paris, 1902–75), vi, pp. 122–23.

2. Monique Chatenet, *La cour de France au XVIe siècle: vie sociale et architecture* (Paris, 2002), pp. 15–32; R. J. Knecht, 'The Court of Francis I', *European Studies Review*, 8 (1978), pp. 1–22.

3. D. Starkey, *The English Court from the Wars of the Roses to the Civil War* (London, 1987), pp. 81–82.

4. Knecht, *Renaissance Warrior and Patron*, pp. 121–22; *Letters and Papers of Henry VIII*, iv, nos 2087, 2092.

5. Ibid., iv, pt 1, no. 1938.

6. Knecht, *Renaissance Warrior and Patron*, pp. 130–31; J. Chartrou, *Les entrées sollennelles et triomphales à la Renaissance (1484–1551)* (Paris, 1928), pp. 26–27, 32–33, 37; L. M. Bryant, *The King and the City in the Parisian Royal Entry Ceremony: Politics, Ritual and Art in the Renaissance* (Geneva, 1986), pp. 99–124.

7. N. Tommaseo (ed.), *Relations des ambassadeurs vénitiens sur les affaires de France* (Paris, 1838), I, pp. 107–11.

8. Monique Chatenet, 'Une demeure royale au milieu du XVIe siècle: la distribution des espaces au château de Saint-Germain-en-Laye', *Revue de l'Art*, 81 (1988), pp. 20–30.

9. J. Pope-Hennessy (ed.), *The Life of Benvenuto Cellini Written by Himself* (London, 1949), p. 264.

10. Chatenet, *La cour de France*, p. 300.

11. A. Blunt, *Art and Architecture in France, 1500–1700* (Harmondsworth, 1957), pp. 3–13, 23–30.

12. Monique Chatenet, *Chambord* (Paris, 2002), pp. 37–66.

13. Chatenet, *Le château de Madrid au Bois de Boulogne* (Paris, 1987), pp. 13–27.

14. Françoise Boudon and J. Blécon, *Le château de Fontainebleau de François Ier à Henri IV: les bâtiments et leurs fonctions* (Paris, 1998), pp. 16–53.

15. *State Papers of Henry VIII* (London, 1830–52), viii, pt 5, pp. 482–84.

16. Cécile Scailliérez, *François Ier et ses artistes* (Paris, 1992); Janet Cox-Rearick, *The Collection of Francis I: Royal Treasures* (Antwerp 1995).

17. Alexandra Zvereva, *Les Clouet de Catherine de Mèdicis* (Paris, 2002); P. Mellen, *Jean Clouet* (London, 1971).

18. Pope-Hennessy, *Cellini*; B. Jestaz, 'Benvenuto Cellini et la cour de France (1540–1545)', *Bibliothèque de l'Ecole des Chartes*, 161 (2003), pp. 71–132; Knecht, *Renaissance Warrior and Patron*, pp. 449–57.

19. Pope-Hennessy, *Cellini*, p. 115. Recently stolen from the Kunsthistorischesmuseum in Vienna, and still not recovered!

20. Knecht, *Renaissance Warrior and Patron*, pp. 439–47; Caroline Elam, 'Art in the Service of Liberty: Battista della Palla, Art Agent for Francis I', in *I Tatti Studies: Essays in the Renaissance*, 5 (Florence, 1993).

21. Anne-Marie Lecoq, 'La fondation du Collège Royal et *L'Ignorance chassée* de Fontainebleau', in *Les Origines du Collège de France (1500–1560)*, ed. M. Fumaroli (Paris, 1998), pp. 185–206.

22. J. K. Farge, *Le parti conservateur au XVIe siècle: Université et Parlement de Paris à l'époque de la Renaissance et de la Réforme* (Paris, 1992), pp. 37–44.

23. A. Coron, 'Collège Royal et *Bibliotheca regia*: la bibliothèque savante de François Ier' in *Les origines du Collège de France*, pp. 143–83.

24. Blunt, *Art and Architecture*, p. 48; A. Blunt, *Philibert de l'Orme* (London, 1958).

25. Sylvie Béguin, *L'Ecole de Fontainebleau: le Maniérisme à la cour de France* (Paris, 1960), pp. 37–79; H. Zerner, *L'art de la Renaissance en France: l'invention du classicisme* (Paris, 1996), pp. 98–111.

26. Sylvie Béguin, J. Guillaume and A. Roy, *La Galerie d'Ulysse à Fontainebleau* (Paris, 1985), pp. 81–105.

27. Margaret M. McGowan, *Ideal Forms in the Age of Ronsard* (Berkeley, California, 1985), pp. 143–48.

Notes to Chapter 11: Royal Authority

1. Monique Chatenet, *La cour de France au XVIe siècle: vie sociale et architecture* (Paris, 2002), p. 109.

2. R. Doucet, *Etude sur le gouvernement de François Ier dans ses rapports avec le Parlement de Paris* (Paris, 1921), i, p. 49.

3. R. J. Knecht, *Renaissance Warrior and Patron: The Reign of Francis I* (Cambridge, 1994), pp. 90–103.

4. Ibid., p. 232; Archives Nationales, Paris, Xla 1528, fol. 411.

5. R. J. Knecht, 'Francis I and the *Lit de Justice*: A "Legend" Defended', in *French History*, 7 (1993), pp. 53–83.

6. Knecht, *Renaissance Warrior and Patron*, pp. 264–68.

7. Ibid., pp. 528–30; A. Floquet, *Histoire du parlement de Normandie* (Rouen, 1840), I, pp. 505–35; ii, pp. 1–15.

8. J. Russell Major, *Representative Institutions in Renaissance France, 1421–1559* (Madison, Wisconsin, 1960), p. 126.

9. H. Hauser, 'Le traité de Madrid et la cession de la Bourgogne à Charles-Quint', *Revue bourguignonne*, 22 (1912).

10. Knecht, 'Francis I and the *Lit de Justice*', pp. 70–72.

11. P. Dognon, *Les institutions politiques et administratives du Pays de Languedoc du XIIe siècle aux Guerres de Religion* (Toulouse, 1895), pp. 576–77.

12. J. Jacquart, *François Ier* (Paris, 1981), p. 282–83.

13. P. Hamon, *L'argent du roi. Les finances sous François Ier* (Paris, 1994), pp. 3–64.

14. S.-C. Gigon, *La révolte de la gabelle en Guyenne, 1548–1549* (1906), p. 18.

15. Knecht, *Renaissance Warrior and Patron*, pp. 480–83; I. Cloulas, *Henri II* (Paris, 1985), pp. 190–96.

16. Archives Nationales, Paris, Xla 1556, fol. 84 a-b.

17. Hamon, *L'argent du roi*, pp. 200–1.

18. Ibid., pp. 104–10.

19. Ibid., pp. 252–57.

20. Ibid., pp. 293–95.

21. Ibid., pp. 295–301.

22. R. R. Harding, *Anatomy of a Power Elite: The Provincial Governors of Early Modern France* (New Haven, Connecticut and London, 1978).

23. G. Pagès, *La monarchie d'ancien régime en France* (Paris, 1946), p. 3.

24. Arlette Jouanna, *Le devoir de révolte: la noblesse française et la gestation de l'état moderne, 1559–1661* (Paris, 1989), pp. 92–98.

Notes to Chapter 12: The Challenge of Heresy

1. The word 'Sorbonne' is less cumbersome than 'the Faculty of Theology of the University of Paris'. The two institutions were bastions of scholasticism, but they were distinct. The Sorbonne was one of many colleges in the university.

2. R. J. Knecht, *Renaissance Warrior and Patron: The Reign of Francis I* (Cambridge, 1994), pp. 142–49.

3. A. Renaudet, *Préréforme et humanisme à Paris pendant les premières guerres d'Italie* (Paris, 1953); Margaret Mann, *Erasme et les débuts de la Réforme française, 1517–1536* (Paris, 1934), pp. 24–46.

4. Anne-Marie Lecoq, *François Ier imaginaire* (Paris, 1987), pp. 301–8.

5. D. O. McNeil, *Guillaume Budé and Humanism in the Reign of Francis I* (Geneva, 1975), pp. 3–36.

6. A. Lefranc, *Histoire du Collège de France* (Paris, 1893), pp. 45, 48–49, 53–56, 63–82.

7. P. E. Hughes, *Lefèvre: Pioneer of Ecclesiastical Renewal in France* (Grand Rapids, Michigan, 1984).

8. J. K. Farge, *Orthodoxy and Reform in Early Reformation France* (Leiden, 1985), pp. 124, 171, 237–40; M. Veissière, *L'évêque Guillaume Briçonnet (1470–1534)* (Provins, 1986), pp. 197–220, 233–37.

9. L. Febvre, *Autour de l'Heptaméron: amour sacré, amour profane* (Paris, 1944), pp. 189–94.

10. Farge, *Orthodoxy and Reform*, pp. 168–70, 253–54.

11. R. Doucet, *Etude sur le gouvernement de François Ier dans ses rapports avec le Parlement de Paris* (Paris, 1921), i, pp. 336–40; Farge, *Orthodoxy and Reform*, pp. 173–74, 255–56.

12. Ibid., p. 132.

13. A. Herminjard (ed.), *Correspondance des réformateurs dans les pays de langue française* (Geneva, 1886–87), I, pp. 401–3.

14. Knecht, *Renaissance Warrior and Patron*, pp. 236–39; Farge, *Orthodoxy and Reform*, pp. 259–60.

15. Ibid., pp. 192–93, 260–63.

16. Herminjard, *Correspondance des réformateurs*, ii, p. 4.

17. Farge, *Orthodoxy and Reform*, pp. 259–60, 264.

18. Knecht, *Renaissance Warrior and Patron*, p. 282.

19. Herminjard, *Correspondance des réformateurs*, ii. p. 179.

20. Ibid., ii. p. 249.

21. Farge, *Orthodoxy and Reform*, pp. 203–4, Herminjard, *Correspondance des réformateurs*, iii. pp. 93–5, 107.

22. Knecht, *Renaissance Warrior and Patron*, pp. 313–21.

23. Ibid., pp. 321–23.

24. Herminjard, *Correspondance des réformateurs*, iv. pp. 3–23.

25. Knecht, *Renaissance Warrior and Patron*, pp. 326–28.

26. H. Heller, *The Conquest of Poverty* (Leiden, 1986), p. 66.

27. Ibid., pp. 323–25; G. Audisio, *The Waldensian Dissent: Persecution and Survival, c. 1170–c. 1570* (Cambridge, 1999), pp. 90–94.

28. D. Crouzet, *La genèse de la Réforme française* (Paris, 1996), pp. 412–15; D. Nicholls, 'The Theatre of Martyrdom in the French Reformation', *Past and Present*, 121, pp. 49–73; N. Weiss, *La Chambre Ardente* (Paris, 1889), pp. 419–22.

29. N. M. Sutherland, *The Huguenot Struggle for Recognition* (New Haven, Connecticut, 1980), pp. 44–47, 342–43.

30. R. M. Kingdon, *Geneva and the Coming of the Wars of Religion in France, 1555–1563* (Geneva, 1956), p. 59.

31. Sutherland, *The Huguenot Struggle*, pp. 55–56, 344–45.

32. Kingdon, *Geneva and the Coming of the Wars of Religion*, pp. 31–40.

33. Ibid., pp. 62–63.

34. I. Cloulas, *Henri II* (Paris, 1985), p. 561.

35. Ibid., pp. 559–60.

36. Kingdon, *Geneva and the Coming of the Wars of Religion*, p. 46.

Notes to Chapter 13: Mother and Sons

1. A. de Reumont and A. Baschet, *La jeunesse de Catherine de Médicis* (Paris, 1866), p. 251.

2. R. J. Knecht, *Catherine de' Medici* (London, 1998), pp. 1–17.

3. Ibid., pp. 16–17.

4. A. Desjardins (ed.) *Négotiations diplomatiques de la France avec la Toscane* (Paris, 1859–86), iii, p. 140; P. Blanchemain (ed.), *Oeuvres complètes de Ronsard* (Paris, 1857–67), ii, p. 182.

5. E. Albèri, *Relazioni degli ambasciatori veneti al Senato* (Florence, 1839–63), series 1a, iv, p. 73.

6. J.-M. Constant, *Les Guise* (Paris, 1984), pp. 20–22.

7. N. M. Sutherland, *Princes, Politics and Religion, 1547–1589* (London, 1984), pp. 55–64.

8. R. R. Harding, *Anatomy of a Power Elite: The Provincial Governors of Early Modern France* (New Haven, Connecticut, 1978), pp. 34–35.

9. N. M. Sutherland, *The Huguenot Struggle for Recognition* (New Haven, Connecticut, 1980), pp. 346–47.

10. Knecht, *Catherine de' Medici*, p. 63.

11. L. Romier, *La conjuration d'Amboise* (Paris, 1923), pp. 80–125.

12. Sutherland, *The Huguenot Struggle*, pp. 113–14, 349–51.

13. *Lettres de Catherine de Médicis*, ed. H. de la Ferrière and Baguenault de Puchesse (1880–1909), I, p. 158.

14. L. Romier, *Catholiques et Huguenots à la cour de Charles IX* (Paris, 1924), pp. 99–109.

15. D. Nugent, *Ecumenism in the Age of the Reformation: The Colloquy of Poissy* (Cambridge, Massachusetts, 1974), passim; Knecht, *Catherine de' Medici*, pp. 77–82.

16. Sutherland, *The Huguenot Struggle*, pp. 133–35, 354–56.

17. Knecht, *Catherine de' Medici*, pp. 87–88.

18. F. de La Noue, *Discours politiques et militaires*, ed. F. E. Sutcliffe (Geneva, 1967), p. 661.

19. The best accounts of the Grand Tour are P. Champion, *Catherine de Médicis présente à Charles IX son royaume (1564–1566)* (Paris 1937), and J. Boutier, A. Dewerpe and D. Nordman, *Un tour de France royal: le voyage de Charles IX (1564–1566)* (Paris, 1984).

20. Boutier, Dewerpe and Nordman, *Un tour de France*, p. 245.

21. Ibid., pp. 87–104; Champion, *Catherine de Médicis*, pp. 262–93.

22. I. Cloulas, *Catherine de Médicis* (Paris, 1979), p. 214.

23. *Lettres de Catherine de Médicis*, iii, p. 59.

24. Ibid., iii, p. 62.

25. R. J. Knecht, *The French Civil Wars* (London, 2000), pp. 137–38.

26. La Noue, *Discours*, pp. 708–10.

27. Knecht, *The French Civil Wars*, pp. 150–51.

28. Ibid., p. 152.

29. Sutherland, *The Huguenot Struggle*, pp. 358–60.

30. F. Yates, *Astraea. The Imperial Theme in the Sixteenth Century* (London, 1975), pp. 127–48.

31. Cloulas, *Catherine de Médicis*, p. 269.

32. M. P. Holt, *The Duke of Anjou and the Politique Struggle during the Wars of Religion* (Cambridge, 1986), pp. 22, 24.

33. D. Crouzet, *La nuit de la Saint-Barthélemy: un rêve perdu de la Renaissance* (Paris, 1994), pp. 378–79.

34. J.-L. Bourgeon, *L'assassinat de Coligny* (Geneva, 1992), p. 117; P. Benedict, 'The St Bartholomew's Massacres in the Provinces', *Historical Journal*, 21 (1978), pp. 201–25.

35. J. Wood, *The King's Army: Warfare, Soldiers and Society during the Wars of Religion in France, 1562–1576* (Cambridge, 1996), pp. 246–74.

36. P. Chevallier, *Henri III* (Paris, 1985), pp. 181–207.

37. Holt, *The Duke of Anjou*, pp. 36–43.

Notes to Chapter 14: The Last Valois

1. P. Chevallier, *Henri III* (Paris, 1985), pp. 228–31.

2. Ibid., pp. 233–44.

3. M. P. Holt, *The Duke of Anjou and the Politique Struggle during the Wars of Religion* (Cambridge, 1986), p. 52.

4. R. J. Knecht, *Catherine de' Medici* (London, 1998), p. 182.

5. Holt, *The Duke of Anjou*, p. 65.

6. N. M. Sutherland, *The Huguenot Struggle for Recognition* (New Haven, Connecticut, 1985), pp. 228–39, 244–49, 260–74.

7. J.-M. Constant, *La Ligue* (Paris, 1996), pp. 71–75.

8. J.-M. Constant, *Les Guise* (Paris, 1984), pp. 193–96.

9. Chevallier, *Henri III*, pp. 342–56.

10. Ibid., p. 353.

11. Holt, *The Duke of Anjou*, pp. 88–89; Chevallier, *Henri III*, pp. 357–58.

12. J.-A. De Thou, *Histoire universelle* (Basel, 1742), v, p. 373.

13. Sutherland, *The Huguenot Struggle*, pp. 362–63.

14. R. J. Sealy, *The Palace Academy of Henry III* (Geneva, 1981); Frances A. Yates, *The French Academies of the Sixteenth Century* (2nd edn, London, 1988), pp. 31–35, 105–30.

15. Jacqueline Boucher, *La cour de Henri III* (Rennes, 1986), pp. 9–23.

16. D. Potter and P. R. Roberts, 'An Englishman's View of the Court of Henri III, 1584–1585: Richard Cook's "Description of the Court of France"', *French History*, 2 (1988), pp. 312–44.

17. Monique Chatenet, *La Cour de France au XVIe siècle: vie sociale et architecture* (Paris, 2002), pp. 179–84.

18. N. Le Roux, 'Henri III and the Rites of Monarchy', *Europa Triumphans* (forthcoming).

19. *Les triumphes et magnificences faictes à l'entrée du roy et de la royne en la ville d'Orléans le quinziesme iour de Nouembre, 1576* (Paris, Jean de Lastre, 1576).

20. Yates, *The French Academies*, pp. 152–76. Boucher, *La cour de Henri III*, pp. 175–93.

21. N. Le Roux, *La Faveur du roi* (Seyssel, 2000); Boucher, *La cour de Henri III*, p. 23.

22. Frances A. Yates, *Astrea. The Imperial Theme in the Sixteenth Century* (London, 1975), pp. 149–72; Le Roux, *La faveur du roi*, pp. 486–92.

23. Boucher, *La cour de Henri III*, pp. 13–16.

24. Constant, *La Ligue*, pp. 112–16.

25. Knecht, *Catherine de Medici*, pp. 248–52.

26. R. Descimon, *Qui étaient les Seize? Mythes et réalités de la Ligue parisienne (1585–1594)* (Paris, 1983).

27. Chevallier, *Henri III*, pp. 587–91.

28. Ibid., p. 600.

29. D. Buisseret, *Henry IV* (London, 1984), pp. 21–25.

30. Le Roux, *La faveur du roi*, p. 660.

31. *Journal de l'Estoile pour le règne de Henri III (1574–1589)*, ed. L.-R. Lefèvre (Paris, 1943), p. 544.

32. Chevallier, *Henri III*, pp. 628–38.

33. Ibid., pp. 676–81.

34. Ibid., pp. 662–70; Constant, *La Ligue*, pp. 201–12.

35. Chevallier, *Henri III*, pp. 671–72; Desjardins, *Négociations diplomatiques de la France avec la Toscane*, iv, pp. 842–43.

36. Chevallier, *Henri III*, p. 672.

37. R. Cooper, 'The Blois Assassinations: Sources in the Vatican', *From Valois to Bourbon: Dynasty, State and Society in Early Modern France*, ed. K. Cameron (Exeter, 1989), pp. 51–72.

38. Knecht, *Catherine de' Medici*, p. 267.

39. M. Greengrass, *France in the Age of Henry IV* (2nd edn, London, 1995), p. 60.

40. D. Crouzet, 'Henri IV, King of Reason?' *From Valois to Bourbon*, pp. 73–106.

41. Greengrass, *France in the Age of Henry IV*, p. 60.

Note to Chapter 15: Assessment

1. Elizabeth M. Hallam, *Capetian France, 987–1328* (London, 1980).

Bibliography

Allmand, Christopher, *Henry V* (New Haven and London, 1992).

Allmand, Christopher, *The Hundred Years War. England and France at War, c. 1300–c. 1450* (Cambridge, 1988).

Anglo, S., *Spectacle, Pageantry and Early Tudor Policy* (Oxford, 1969).

Autrand, Françoise, *Charles V* (Paris, 1994).

Autrand, Françoise, *Charles VI* (Paris, 1986).

Avril, François (ed.), *Jean Fouquet, peintre et enlumineur du XVe siècle* (Paris, 2003).

Barbiche, Bernard, *Les institutions de la monarchie française à l'époque moderne* (Paris, 2nd edn, 2001).

Baumgartner, Frederic, *France in the Sixteenth Century* (London, 1995).

Baumgartner, Frederic, *Henry II King of France, 1547–1559* (Durham, North Carolina, 1988).

Baumgartner, Frederic, *Louis XII* (London, 1996).

Beaune, Colette, *Naissance de la nation France* (Paris: Gallimard, 1985). Translated as *The Birth of an Ideology: Myths and Symbols of Nation in Late-Medieval France* (Berkeley, California, 1991).

Bloch, Marc, *Les rois thaumaturges* (Paris, 1961).

Blunt, A., *Art and Architecture in France, 1500–1700* (Harmondsworth, 1953).

Bonney, Richard (ed.), *The Rise of the Fiscal State in Europe, c. 1200–1815* (Oxford, 1999).

Boucher, Jacqueline, *La cour de Henri III* (Rennes, 1986).

Bourgeon, J.-L., *L'assassinat de Coligny* (Geneva, 1992).

Boutier, Jean, Alain Dewerpe, Daniel Nordman, *Un tour de France royal: le voyage de Charles IX (1564–1566)* (Paris, 1984).

Calmette, Joseph, *Les Grands Ducs de Bourgogne* (Paris, 1949).

Calmette, J. et G. Périnelle, *Louis XI et l'Angleterre* (Paris, 1930).

Cameron, Keith (ed.), *From Valois to Bourbon: Dynasty, State and Society in Early Modern France* (Exeter, 1989).

Cassagnes-Brouquet, Sophie, *Culture, artistes et société dans la France médiévale* (Paris, 1998).

Cauchies, Jean-Marie, *Louis XI et Charles le Hardi: De Péronne à Nancy (1468–1477). Le conflit* (Brussels, 1996).

Cazelles, Raymond, *Société politique, noblesse et couronne sous Jean le Bon et Charles V* (Geneva, 1982).

Champion, Pierre, *Catherine de Médicis présente à Charles IX son royaume (1564–1566)* (Paris, 1937).

Champion, Pierre, *Louis XI*, 2 vols (Paris, 1927).

Chatenet, Monique, *La cour de France au XVIe siècle: vie sociale et architecture* (Paris, 2002).

Chaunu, Pierre, and Richard Gascon, *Histoire économique et sociale de la France*, i, *1450–1660: l'état et la Ville* (Paris, 1977).

Chevalier, Bernard, *Les bonnes villes de France du XIVe au XVIe siècle* (Paris, 1982).

Chevallier, Pierre, *Henri III* (Paris, 1985).

Cloulas, Ivan, *Henri II* (Paris, 1985).

Commynes, Philippe de, *Mémoires*, ed. J. Calmette and G. Durville, 3 vols (Paris, 1924–25).

Commynes, Philippe de, *Memoirs*, trans. M. Jones (Harmondsworth, 1972).

Constant, J.-M., *Les Guise* (Paris, 1984).

Contamine, Philippe (ed.), *Histoire militaire de la France*, i, *Des origines à 1715* (Paris, 1992).

Contamine, Philippe, *La France au XIVe et XVe siècles: hommes, mentalités, guerre et paix* (London, 1981).

Contamine, Philippe, *La Guerre de Cent Ans: France et Angleterre* (Paris, 1976).

Contamine, Philippe, *Le Moyen Âge: Le roi, l'église, les grands, le peuple, 481–1514* (Paris, 2002).

Contamine, Philippe, *War in the Middle Ages* (first published in French, 1980; English edn, Oxford, 1984).

Cosandey, Fanny, *La reine de France: symbole et pouvoir, XVe–XVIIIe siècle* (Paris, 2000).

Croix, Alain, *L'âge d'or de la Bretagne, 1532–1675* (Rennes, 1993).

Crouzet, D., *La nuit de la Saint-Barthélemy: un rêve perdu de la Renaissance* (Paris, 1994).

Curry, Anne (ed.), *Agincourt, 1415: Henry V, Sir Thomas Erpingham and the triumph of the English archers* the (Stroud, 2000).

Curry, Anne, *The Hundred Years War* (London, 1993).

Delaruelle, E., E.-R. Labande and Paul Ourliac, *L'Église au temps du Grand Schisme et de la crise conciliaire (1378–1449)* (Paris, 1962).

Demurger, Alain, *Temps de crises, temps d'espoirs, XIVe–XVe siècle* (Paris, 1990).

Derville, Alain, *La société française au Moyen Âge* (Villeneuve d'Ascq, 2000).

Doucet, Roger, *Les institutions de la France au XVIe siècle*, 2 vols (Paris, 1948).

Duby, Georges (ed.), *Histoire de la France urbaine*, ii, *La ville médiévale des Carolingiens à la Renaissance* (Paris, 1980).

Duby, Georges. and Armand Wallon (eds), *Histoire de la France rurale*, ii, *1340–1789* (Paris, 1973).

Duffy, Eamon, *Saints and Sinners. A History of the Popes* (London, 1997).

Famiglietti, R. C., *Royal Intrigue: Crisis at the Court of Charles VI* (New York, 1986).

Farge, J. K., *Orthodoxy and Reform in Early Reformation France* (Leiden, 1985).

Favier, Jean, *La Guerre de Cent Ans* (Paris, 1980).

Favier, Jean, *Louis XI* (Paris, 2001).

Gauvard, Claude, *La France au Moyen Âge du Ve au XVe siècle* (Paris, 1996).

Greengrass, Mark, *France in the Age of Henri IV* (London, 2nd edn, 1995).

Guénée, Bernard, *States and Rulers in Later Medieval Europe* (Oxford, 1985).

Guénée, Bernard, *Un meurtre, une société: l'assassinat du duc d'Orléans 23 novembre 1407* (Paris, 1992).

Guénée, Bernard, and F. Lehoux, *Les entrées royales françaises de 1328 à 1515* (Paris, 1968).

Hamon Philippe, *L'argent du roi: les finances sous François Ier* (Paris, 1994).

Harding, R. R., *Anatomy of a Power Elite: The Provincial Governors of Early Modern France* (New Haven, Connecticut, 1978).

Henneman, John Bell, *Olivier de Clisson and Political Society in France under Charles V and Charles VI* (Philadelphia, Pennsylvania, 1996).

Holt, M. P., *Renaissance and Reformation France* (Oxford, 2002).

Holt, M. P., *The Duke of Anjou and the Politique Struggle during the Wars of Religion* (Cambridge, 1986).

Holt, M. P., *The French Wars of Religion, 1562–1629* (Cambridge, 1995).

Jackson, Richard A., *Vive le Roi! A History of the French Coronation from Charles V to Charles X* (Chapel Hill, North Carolina, 1984).

Jacquart, Jean, *François Ier* (Paris, 1981).

Jouanna, Arlette, *La France du XVIe siècle, 1483–1598* (Paris, 1996).

Kantorowicz, Ernst H., *The King's Two Bodies. A Study in Medieval Political Theology* (Princeton, New Jersey, 1957).

Kendall, Paul Murray, *Louis XI* (London, 1971).

Krynen, Jacques, *L'empire du roi: idées et croyances politiques en France XIIIe–XVe siècle* (Paris, 1993).

Knecht, R. J., *Catherine de' Medici* (London, 1998).

Knecht, R. J., *Renaissance Warrior and Patron: The Reign of Francis I* (Cambridge, 1994).

Knecht, R. J., 'The Concordat of 1516: A Re-Assessment', in *Government in Reformation Europe, 1520–1560*, ed. H. J. Cohn (London, 1971).

Knecht, R. J., *The French Civil Wars* (Harlow, 2000).

Knecht, R. J., *The Rise and Fall of Renaissance France* (2nd edn, Oxford, 2001).

Labande-Mailfert, Yvonne, *Charles VIII* (Paris, 1986).

Lavisse, Ernest, *Histoire de France*, iv (Paris, 1902).

Lecoq, Anne-Marie, *François Ier imaginaire: symbolique et politique à l'aube de la Renaissance française* (Paris, 1987).

Le Goff, Jacques and René Rémond (eds), *Histoire de la France religieuse*, ii, *Du Christianisme flamboyant à l'aube des Lumières* (XIVe–XVIIIe siècle) (Paris, 1988).

Le Roy Ladurie, Emmanuel, *L'état royal, 1460–1610* (Paris, 1987).

Lewis, P. S., *Essays in Later Medieval French History* (London, 1985).

Lewis, P. S., *Later Medieval France* (London, 1968).

Lewis, P. S. (ed.), *The Recovery of France in the Fifteenth Century* (London, 1971).

Mignet, F., *La rivalité de François Ier et de Charles-Quint*, 2 vols (Paris, 1875).

Oman, C., *A History of the Art of War in the XVIth Century* (New York, 1937).

Perroy, Edouard, *La Guerre de Cent Ans* (Paris, 1945; English trans. New York, 1965).

Pettegree, A., *The Early Reformation in Europe* (Cambridge, 1992).

Pieri, P., *Il Rinascimento e la crisi militare italiana* (Turin, 1952).

Potter, David, *A History of France, 1460–1560* (London, 1995).

Quilliet, Bernard, *Louis XII, Père du Peuple* (Paris, 1986).

Renaudet, A., *Préréforme et humanisme à Paris pendant les premières guerres d'Italie* (Paris, 1953).

Romier, L., *Catholiques et Huguenots à la cour de Charles IX* (Paris, 1924).

Romier, L., *La Conjuration d'Amboise* (Paris, 1923).

Romier, L., *Les origines politiques des guerres de religion*, 2 vols (Paris, 1914).

Russell, Joycelyne G., *The Field of Cloth of Gold* (London, 1969).

Salmon, J. H. M., *Society in Crisis: France in the Sixteenth Century* (London, 1975).

Saul, Nigel, *Richard II* (New Haven and London, 1997).

Shennan, J. H., *The Parlement of Paris* (2nd edn, Stroud, 1998).

Simonin, Michel, *Charles IX* (Paris, 1995).

Sumption, Jonathan, *The Hundred Years War*, i, *Trial by Battle* (London, 1990).

Sumption, Jonathan, *The Hundred Years War*, ii, *Trial by Fire* (London, 1999).

Sutherland, N. M., *Princes, Politics and Religion, 1547–1589* (London, 1984).

Sutherland, N. M., *The Huguenot Struggle for Recognition* (New Haven, Connecticut, 1980).

Vale, M. G. A., *Charles VII* (London, 1974).

Vale, M. G. A., *English Gascony, 1399–1453* (Oxford, 1970).

Vaughan, Richard, *Charles the Bold* (London, 1973).

Vaughan, Richard, *John the Fearless* (London, 1966).

Vaughan, Richard, *Philip the Bold* (Cambridge, Massachusetts, 1962).

Vaughan, Richard, *Philip the Good* (London, 1970).

Vaughan, Richard, *Valois Burgundy* (London, 1975).

Wood, J., *The King's Army: Warfare, Soldiers and Society during the Wars of Religion in France, 1562–1576* (Cambridge, 1996).

Wolfe, M., *The Fiscal System of Renaissance France* (New Haven, Connecticut, 1972).

Yates, Frances A., *The French Academies of the Sixteenth Century* (London, 2nd edn, 1988).

Yates, Frances A., *The Valois Tapestries* (2nd edn, London, 1975).

Zerner, H., *L'art de la Renaissance en France: l'invention du classicisme* (Paris, 1996).

Index